A SOURCEBOOK OF FEMINIST
PERFORMANCE

A Sourcebook of Feminist Theatre and Performance brings together key articles first published in *The Drama Review* (*TDR*), to provide an intriguing overview of the development of feminist theatre and performance.

Divided into the categories of "history," "theory," "interviews," and "texts," the materials in this collection allow the reader to consider the developments of feminist theatre through a variety of perspectives. This book contains the seminal texts of theorists such as Elin Diamond, Peggy Phelan, and Lynda Hart, interviews with performance artists including Anna Deveare Smith and Robbie McCauley, and the full performance texts of Holly Hughes' *Dress Suits to Hire* and Karen Finley's *The Constant State of Desire*. The outstanding diversity of this collection makes for an invaluable sourcebook.

A Sourcebook of Feminist Theatre and Performance will be read by students and practitioners of theatre and performance, as well as those interested in the performance of sexualities and genders.

Carol Martin is Assistant Professor of Drama at Tisch School of the Arts, New York University.

WORLDS OF PERFORMANCE

What is a "performance"? Where does it take place? Who are the participants? Not so long ago these were settled questions, but today such orthodox answers are unsatisfactory, misleading, and limiting. "Performance" as a theoretical category and as a practice has expanded explosively. It now comprises a panoply of genres ranging from play, to popular entertainments, to theatre, dance, and music, to secular and religious rituals, to "performance in everyday life," to intercultural experiments, and more.

For nearly forty years, *The Drama Review* (*TDR*), the journal of performance studies, has been at the cutting edge of exploring these questions. The Worlds of Performance Series is designed to mine the extraordinary riches and diversity of *TDR*'s decades of excellence, bringing back into print important essays, interviews, artists' notes, and photographs. New materials and introductions bring the volumes up to date. Each Worlds of Performance book is a complete anthology, arranged around a specific theme or topic. Each Worlds of Performance book is an indispensable resource for the scholar, a textbook for the student, and an exciting eye-opener for the general reader.

Richard Schechner
Editor, *TDR*
Series Editor

Other titles in the series:

Acting (Re)Considered edited by Phillip B. Zarrilli
Happenings and other Acts edited by Mariellen R. Sandford
The Grotowski Sourcebook edited by Richard Schechner and Lisa Wolford

A SOURCEBOOK OF FEMINIST THEATRE AND PERFORMANCE

On and Beyond the Stage

Edited by Carol Martin

London and New York

First published 1996
by Routledge
11 New Fetter Lane, London EC4P 4EE

Simultaneously published in the USA and Canada
by Routledge
29 West 35th Street, New York, NY 10001

Typeset in Times by Solidus (Bristol) Limited
Printed and bound in Great Britain by
Biddles Ltd, Guildford and King's Lynn

British Library Cataloguing in Publication Data
A catalogue record for this book is available from the British Library

Library of Congress Cataloging in Publication Data
A sourcebook on feminist theatre and performance: on and beyond the
    stage/edited by Carol Martin; with an introduction by Jill Dolan.
        p.   cm. – (Worlds of performance)
    Includes bibliographical references and index.
    ISBN 0–415–10644–3 (alk. paper). – ISBN 0–415–10645–1 (pbk.:
    alk. paper)
        1. Feminist theatre–United States–History.   2. Feminism and
    theater.   3. Women in the theater.   I. Martin, Carol, 1952–   .
    II. Series.
    PN2270.F45S68   1996   96–17794
    792'.082-dc20   CIP

To R.S.

CONTENTS

ILLUSTRATIONS

CONTRIBUTORS

Misha Berson is the head theatre critic of the *Seattle Times* and a part-time instructor in the Drama Department of the University of Washington, Seattle. She edited the 1990 anthology, *Between Worlds: Contemporary Asian American Plays* (New York: Theatre Communications Group).

Helen Krich Chinoy, Professor Emeritus, Theatre Department, Smith College, edited *Women in American Theatre* with Linda W. Jenkins; this article is an abridged version of her introduction to the first edition, 1981 (New York: Crown Publishers); an expanded, paperback edition appeared in 1987 (New York: Theatre Communications Group).

Kate Davy is Professor of Theatre and Dean of the School of Fine Arts at the University of Wisconsin-Milwaukee. She's working on a book entitled *The WOW Cafe: Genealogy of the Women's Theatre*.

Elin Diamond is an Associate Professor of English at Rutgers University. She is completing her book, *Unmaking Mimesis*, and is the editor of *Performance and Cultural Politics* (Routledge, 1995).

Jill Dolan is the author of *The Feminist Spectator as Critic* (UMI, 1988; University of Michigan Press, 1991) and *Presence and Desire: Essays on Gender, Sexuality, and Performance* (University of Michigan Press, 1993). She is Professor of Theatre and Executive Officer of the Theatre Program at the CUNY Graduate Center and the President-Elect of the Association for Theatre in Higher Education. She is a past president of the Women and Theatre Program of ATHE.

Karen Finley's *The Constant State of Desire* premiered at The Kitchen in New York City in December 1986. Karen Finley has performed it in San Francisco, Chicago, New Orleans, Boston, Washington DC, Milwaukee, Berlin, Helsinki, and other American and European cities.

Lynda Hart is Associate Professor of English/Theatre Arts at the University of Pennsylvania. She is the author of *Fatal Women: Lesbian Sexuality and the Mark of Aggression* (Princeton and Routledge, 1994), co-editor with Peggy Phelan of *Acting Out: Feminist Performances* (University of Michigan, 1993), and editor of *Making a Spectacle: Feminist Essays on Contemporary Women's Theater* (University of Michigan, 1989).

Holly Hughes' other plays include: *The Well of Horniness*, *The Lady*

Dick, Into Temptation, World Without End, No Trace of the Blonde, and *Clit Notes.* Her writing has been published in *The Drama Review, City Pages, High Performance,* the *New York Times,* and the *Village Voice,* in addition to being included in *Angry Women* (ReSearch Publications), *Out from Under* (Theatre Communications Group), and *Out Front: Gay and Lesbian Plays* (Grove Press).

Dona Ann McAdams' photographs have been published in many newspapers and periodicals including the *Village Voice,* the *New York Times,* the *Los Angeles Times, Art in America, Time, People* and *Stern.* Her photographs are in the collections of the Museum of Modern Art, the Metropolitan Museum of Art, the San Francisco Art Institute, the Bibliothèque Nationale and The Print Club, Philadelphia.

Carol Martin is an Assistant Professor of Drama at Tisch School of the Arts, New York University. She is the author of *Dance Marathons: Performing American Culture in the 1920s and 1930s* (University of Mississippi Press, 1994) which was awarded the De La Torre Bueno Honorable Citation, and co-editor, with Ann Daly, of the book review section of *The Drama Review.*

Vivian Patraka, Professor of English at Bowling Green State University, teaches drama, performance, and feminist studies. Her work has appeared in numerous journals and edited collections and she is completing a book entitled *Spectacular Suffering: Theatre, Fascism and the Holocaust* for Indiana University Press.

Peggy Phelan is the Chair of the Department of Performance Studies, Tisch School of the Arts, New York University. She is the author of *Unmarked: The Politics of Performance* (Routledge, 1993). With Lynda Hart, she is the co-editor of *Acting Out: Feminist Performances* (University of Michigan, 1993). She is currently writing a book called *Mourning Sex.*

Charlotte Rea has taught and administered in independent schools in New York City, in Los Angeles, and in Northfield, Massachusetts. She was the Assistant Head of School for The Westlake School for Girls in Los Angeles from 1985–1989 and is currently the Head of the Upper School at the Brearley School, an independent school for girls in New York City.

Richard Schechner is the editor of *The Drama Review* and the author of *The Future of Ritual* (Routledge, 1993), *Performance Theory* (Routledge, 1988), *Environmental Theatre* (Applause, 1994), *Between Theatre and Anthropology* (University of Pennsylvania Press, 1985), among others. Schechner is a University Professor at New York

University where he teaches in the Department of Performance Studies, Tisch School of the Arts.

Rebecca Schneider is a contributing editor to *The Drama Review*. She is a visiting Assistant Professor at Dartmouth College and Lecturer at Yale University. She is working on a book on cultural theory and feminist performance art entitled *The Explicit Body* (Routledge, forthcoming).

Emily L. Sisley, co-author of *The Joy of Lesbian Sex*, has also published fiction, criticism, poetry, and essays. Her comedy, *The Freddie Corvo Show*, was produced by *The Games*.

Alisa Solomon is an Associate Professor of English/Journalism at Baruch College-CUNY and a staff writer at the *Village Voice*. Her writing has appeared in the *New York Times*, *New York Newsday*, *Ms Magazine*, *Glamour*, *Mirabella*, *Theater*, *American Theater*, and other publications.

EDITOR'S INTRODUCTION

During the last 30 years or so a new body of literature has emerged in conjunction with the wave of feminism that began in the 1960s. Feminist historians, theorists, and practitioners have been united in their examination of the impact of gender, race, and class on women's lives. Happily, despite this unity of concern, strikingly diverse points of view in the form of different kinds of scholarship and stage practices have emerged. It is my hope that the articles, interviews, and scripts collected in this book reflect and express complex perspectives on the theatre practices, productions, and scholarship of women. Most of the contents of this book were originally published in *TDR: The Journal of Performance Studies* over a period of nearly 20 years (1975–1993). These writings show the journal's long-standing commitment not only to women in theatre but to the avant-garde, interculturalism, and more recently to the feminist analysis that emerged in theatre scholarship in the 1980s and continues into the 1990s. Moreover, the collection also reflects *TDR*'s consistent inclusion of the voices of critics, practitioners, and scholars.

This array of viewpoints is recuperative in that it gives continuity to what is, in fact, a continuum of concerns which nevertheless has sometimes broken into different factions. In the collection before you, the historical work of Helen Krich Chinoy has a proper place next to the theoretical work of Peggy Phelan and next to the performance text of Holly Hughes. The juxtaposition of the historian, the theorist, and the artist reflects more than a contrast in methodologies and writing styles. It demonstrates the potential for the mutual dependence of the endeavors: history informed by theory and theory cognizant of history, and both relating to an artistic practice that is aware of history and theory.

The content of this *Sourcebook* seems to fall easily into four categories: History, Theory, Interviews, Texts. It is my desire that each section reflect upon the others. While the same artists and theoretical considerations tend to re-emerge, the overall focus of the book shifts with each section. Thus the reader has the opportunity to inhabit subjects from a variety of perspectives. For example, with both Holly Hughes and Karen Finley, the presence of theoretical articles, interviews, and texts in one collection allows the reader to contemplate the discourse their work generates, the artists' view of their works, and the works themselves.

Even though some of the articles are much older than others, I have not intended to demonstrate a progression of scholarship as much as

I have wanted to document discussions and changing points of view. For some, the work of liberal feminists such as that in the History section has been disquieting because it does not critique the debatable conventions of mainstream theatre. Yet the academy is as much a part of this mainstream as commercial theatrical venues, and its work as open to criticism. For example, for some, the ideas and language in the Theory section are ivory tower academic formulations. Furthermore, feminist scholars of all persuasions striving for tenure or wanting to enhance their reputations can be as duplicitous (driven by the desire for job security and success) as any artist seeking mainstream recognition and the money that comes with it. While the debates between liberal, cultural, and materialist feminists inform the texts collected in this book, each position is necessarily flawed. Examination of these flaws will help eradicate the binary way of thinking that has compartmentalized these positions into seemingly discrete perspectives and practices.

This work has already begun. And, as many postmodern theorists have pointed out, the production of new meanings may necessarily be doubly coded. However alienating the debate within the field has sometimes been, creatively speaking, it has also served to help erode entrenched practices and formulate new ideas – in theatre, in scholarship, and in the impact of feminists in the academy. The endeavor now is, beyond the formulations of postmodernism, to more fully engage the processes of critical debate and artistic production that are not based on binary formulations. To this end, feminist studies has most recently been deeply provoked by queer theory and race theory, both of which have aided in the reconsideration of problems of identity and overly determined theoretical positions.

Still, there are recurring themes that bind the essays in this collection: what was a concern about all female audiences re-emerges as an examination of the impact of change in venues on the production of meaning and a compelling reconceptualization of the gaze in live performance; the history of women in theatre has been recast as an examination of the politics of power; the problems of female identity in performance reconfigured in the light of new work that overpowers any desire for correct representations, whatever they may be.

To augment these articles, I invited Jill Dolan – long associated with *TDR* – to introduce the collection. Dolan served as *TDR*'s managing editor from 1982 to 1985 and has since published several essays in *TDR*. With Brooks McNamara, Dolan co-edited a collection of articles from *TDR* entitled *The Drama Review: Thirty Years of Commentary on the Avant Garde*. I have also included an article about women in regional theatre by Misha Berson originally published in *American Theatre*, and my own article about the work of Anna Deavere Smith.

Scholarship and artistic ideas are informed by an archeological record which is often difficult to unearth. Hopefully this collection of texts will uncover one of the paths feminist theatre took in the pages of one decisive journal.

Carol Martin

ACKNOWLEDGMENTS

This book represents one facet of my long-term engagement with feminism and performance. My first dissertation proposal was to document and analyze the work of Laurie Anderson, Laura Dean, Johanna Boyce, and JoAnne Akalaitis. Even though they worked in the different areas of performance art, dance, and theatre, they were linked, in my mind at the time, by the experimental nature of their work. Interestingly enough, the title of my dissertation was to be "Women in Performance." For a variety of reasons, I eventually changed my subject to the historical dance marathons of the 1920s and 1930s, a subject which engaged my interest in working across the many artificial boundaries of genres. With this collection I feel I have both come full circle and furthered my engagement with feminist scholarship and practices.

A Sourcebook of Feminist Theatre and Performance: On and Beyond the Stage is obviously the result of many different scholars and artists. I want to thank all of them for their contributions. Photographs and other visual material were generously contributed by Angelika Festa, Karen Finlay, Nordisk Teaterlaboratorium, Timothy Greenfield-Sanders, Robbie McCauley, Vivian Selbo, Jay Thompson, and Yvonne Rainer. I am especially grateful to Dona Ann McAdams for her assistance and permission to use so many of her photographs. I also want to thank Jill Dolan for her introductory essay.

Several of the articles included in this collection appeared in *TDR* when Ann Daly and Rebecca Schneider were working on the journal as either managing editor or assistant editor. In those positions they were both dedicated to soliciting and editing articles on feminism and performance. Michael Kirby deserves recognition for first including women's theatre in *TDR*.

Among my theatre department colleagues in the Department of Drama at New York University I want to thank Karen Malpede, Kay Matschullat, Una Chaudhuri and Sharon Mazer, who is now at the University of Canterbury, for their support.

Finally my teaching assistants Bill Doyle, Leah Garland, and Henry Bial all worked on this project. Most of all, thanks to Maria Lomanto for the photograph research.

As usual, Richard Schechner has been his indefatigable, enthusiastic, and supportive self, etc. etc. etc., as well as editor of the Worlds of Performance Series.

"Woman at the Helm" (*American Theatre*, 1994 May/June 14–21, 66) by Misha Berson is reprinted by permission of Theatre Communications Group.

The following essays, cited in the order in which they appear in this book, were previously published in *TDR* and are reprinted by permission of MIT Press and/or the authors:

"Art Versus Business: The Role of Women in American Theatre" by Helen Krich Chinoy 24, no. 2:3–10 (T86, 1980).

"Women for Women" by Charlotte Rea 18, no. 4:77–87 (T64, 1979).

"The WOW Cafe" by Alisa Solomon 29, no. 1:92–101 (T105, 1985).

"Notes on Lesbian Theatre" by Emily L. Sisley 25, no. 1:47–56 (T89, 1981).

"In Defense of the Discourse: Materialist Feminism, Postmodernism, Poststructuralism . . . and Theory" by Jill Dolan 33, no. 3:58–71 (T123, 1989).

"Motherhood According to Finley: *The Theory of Total Blame*" by Lynda Hart 36, no. 1:124–134 (T133, 1992).

"Brechtian Theory/Feminist Theory: Toward a Gestic Feminist Criticism" by Elin Diamond 32, no. 1:82–94 (T117, 1988).

"Reading Past the Heterosexual Imperative: *Dress Suits to Hire*" by Kate Davy 33, no. 1:153–170 (T121, 1989).

"Feminist theory, Poststructuralism, and Performance" by Peggy Phelan 32, no. 1:107–127 (T121, 1988).

"Anna Deavere Smith: The Word Becomes You", an interview by Carol Martin 37, no. 4:45–62 (T140, 1993).

"Robbie McCauley: Obsessing in Public", an interview by Vivian Patraka 37, no. 2:25–55 (T138, 1993).

"Holly Hughes: Polymorphous Perversity and the Lesbian Scientist", an interview by Rebecca Schneider 33, no. 1:171–183 (T121, 1989).

"Karen Finley: A Constant State of Becoming", an interview by Richard Schechner 32, no. 1:152–158 (T117, 1988).

Dress Suits to Hire written by Holly Hughes (co-created with Lois Weaver and Peggy Shaw) 33, no. 1:132–152 (T121, 1989).

The Constant State of Desire, a text by Karen Finley 32, no. 1:140–151 (T117, 1988).

INTRODUCTORY ESSAY

Fathom Languages:
Feminist Performance Theory, Pedagogy,
and Practice

Jill Dolan

Although it's an old saw of theatre studies that our theory always lags behind other fields from which it borrows (film studies, cultural studies, popular culture studies, especially), this collection of articles first published in *TDR* indicates how quickly thinking indigenous to feminist theatre and performance has moved, changed, and grown over a very short (not even 20-year) period. This anthology of writing spans a generation of work in which the critical and creative terrain often changed before people had a chance even to locate their direction, let alone their destination. The performers about whom we write also have a new cachet, perhaps in some small part because of our writing. Their notoriety is now exemplified by the astounding popular success of solo performers like Anna Deavere Smith, the perhaps more prurient – but nonetheless nationally reported – contentions around public funding for Holly Hughes and Karen Finley, and the persistent, no less significant body of work developed by Robbie McCauley, Lois Weaver, and Peggy Shaw. Texts by and about and dialogues with these women take up a number of the pages that follow; that their work represents only a small percentage of the amount of performance now generated under the rubric of "feminism" (in all its contentiousness), and consumed, discussed, and theorized from various feminist ideological perspectives, is no small measure of the distance that this discourse has come.

The contribution these articles have made to the field is significant. Before theatre studies recognized and slowly began to advance the necessity for interdisciplinary work, the critical writers collected here were looking at other disciplines for ways to theorize about performance and theatre. This work represents a number of strategies undertaken by feminists in other fields: the compensatory history of the early essays embraces assumptions made by women's historians that there were stories that had not yet been heard. The gesture of recovery characteristic of most of the articles in the historical section of this book is one shared by many feminist academics across fields. We tried to write into history what had so long been absent – the simple presence and acknowledgment of women's work in the field.

The theoretical articles gathered here participated in an inter-disciplinary discussion with feminist theory when most theatre depart-ments were content to teach positivist history and criticism. Many of these articles were among the first to use psychoanalysis as a critical tool for studying representations of gender, race, and sexuality. By employing the tools of poststructuralism they redirected conversations away from the quagmire of author's intent. That is, rather than focusing on biography to ascertain or secure a feminist perspective on performance, the poststructuralist strategy employed by those in the Theory section of this book opened the critical purview into questions of form, context, history, and representation. Most of the theoretical essays were written during poststructuralism's ascendance as a critical method in the academy. They also reflect the influence of materialism/Marxism, and predict work in cultural studies that has come to provide the next context for debates about gender, race, sexuality, and representation.[1]

The articles on feminist theatre history collected here are useful and important. As a teacher, I realize how easy it is to forget history as academic discourses and the media push us inexorably forward. We need to read and reread Helen Krich Chinoy's article on the role of women in the American theatre to ground our understanding of their historical situation. This will enable us to measure where certain kinds of women have been and where they have gone, and how, and why, and to assess who is left behind on the American road toward "progress." We need to remind ourselves of work in the experimental theatre movement of the 1960s and 1970s – addressed here by Charlotte Rea, Emily Sisley, and Alisa Solomon – that spawned a generation of feminist and lesbian performances, and which remains the legacy (acknowledged or not) for many of the solo performances collected in this anthology and created internationally.[2] The political and artistic history created by early "women's" and "lesbian" theatre and performance needs to be con-tinually retold to keep feminist modes of representation moving forward.

At the Women and Theatre Program conference in Chicago in summer 1994, a keynote panel addressed the ways in which the WTP, once an upstart feminist enclave in theatre and performance studies, has become both an oppositional and an institutional structure.[3] Feminist studies in theatre and performance in the 1990s has lost much of its outlaw status, around which the WTP seemed to cohere in the 1980s, and out of which many of the articles in this anthology were written. Rather than a site of resistance, feminism is now central to the field and to the profession, and vulnerable to the same exclusionary problems of all sites, identities, communities, and methods. But if feminism is closer to the center of theatre and performance studies, being there requires that we *continually* reflect on how the center and the margins can and should shift, on what feminists are doing, what they're forgetting, and who they serve.

My own history of feminism in the academy is about thinking I was going to be the only one; going to theatre conferences about women and worrying I would be the only feminist; going to theatre conferences about feminism and worrying I would be the only lesbian. I can still remember my pleasure and surprise at finding I *was not* the only one, or that I could have conversations and arguments over whatever I perceived as my differences. The institutionalization of feminism has meant a move away from this fearful singularity, a move from frustrating isolation, to the empowerment of community, to the power of *position* in academic systems. I think such an historical sense of what has happened in the last 15 years is the key to understanding the status of feminism, particularly in theatre studies.[4]

I do not think the story of feminism in the academy is one of a fall from grace, a fall from the purity of activism in the social movement into the corrupt panderings of the institution. Especially for cultural critics, the academy provides a site for feminist writing about representations and their relationship to culture. All of the authors of the critical articles in this anthology are academics and all the performers mentioned or interviewed have benefited from the largesse of the academy as a site of production, usually because scholars determined that their students and colleagues should see these performers' work. Because of the dearth of good writing on culture, and because of the ever-shorter list of producing houses that will fund work, especially work by more subversive feminist or lesbian performance artists, colleges and universities in late 20th-century America have become one of the last places in which intellectual feminist cultural critics can earn a living wage and support an occupation.

Such cultural criticism has also left its impact on the academy, as the emphasis on performance art, postmodern forms, the body as text, and new critical methods has reshaped theatre studies as a field. Feminist theoretical work has been an important link between performance studies and theatre studies (and now cultural studies) over the last 10 or 15 years. While some theatre scholars, attached to more modernist paradigms of theory and performance, were reluctant to leave the comfortable structures of dramatic literature as the object of their study, feminists found that some of the most exciting work, aesthetically and politically, was happening outside of conventional theatre genres and architectures. Performance art, for example, seemed to allow women to insert their subjectivities into a representational apparatus scoured with a newly critical poststructuralist, postmodernist eye.

Feminist critical mediation offered the idea of the body as a material and representational site at which ideology might be rewritten. As the palpable material of feminist theatre and performance studies, the body has been theorized (first) here in ways that other disciplines have yet to cite. This collection redresses a critical omission in this politics of citation. Theorizing the live body onstage is our peculiar, vital contribution to discourse in the academy and in performance.

MARKING CONTEXT

As Nancy Miller argues in her book, *Getting Personal*, the occasion of writing is often erased when, for example, a paper given as a lecture for a specific event is printed as an article.[5] That all of these essays but one were originally published in *TDR* is significant. Retaining the original mark of their publication is important, partly because *TDR* itself has a long history as a forum for contentious debates in American and global theatre and performance studies and practice.[6] The articles collected here straddle two very different *TDR* editorships and their style reflects those ideological variations. Michael Kirby, who edited the very first special issue on women and theatre in 1972 for what he insisted be called *The Drama Review*, supervised the publication of four of the articles in the History section of this anthology. Kirby preferred not to engage with performance critically or theoretically, and his dedication to a structuralist documentation of events and trends required writing that often suppressed a more active political perspective.[7] Despite those constraints, the historical work collected here retains a passion for its subject.

Richard Schechner's return as editor in 1985 after a 16-year hiatus meant that *TDR* once again became partisan in its concern with intercultural and interdisciplinary theoretical work collected under the subtitle of *TDR*, "the journal of performance studies." With Schechner's keen eye for a fight, a cause (especially those considered *célèbre*), and/or a polemic, he and his staff actively solicited work from feminist scholars who were, in fact, looking for supportive places to publish. *TDR* provided exposure that often was not forthcoming from differently institutionalized publications.[8]

The articles in this anthology are necessarily defined by *TDR*'s editorial policies. Significant voices in the history, theory, criticism, and practice of the field of feminist theatre and performance are not present because *TDR* under both Schechner and Kirby has focused on avant-garde and contemporary work rather than critical work on dramatic literature. Thus *TDR* is also a specific context, one with an historical link to the American and European avant-garde, one moving toward the popular/mass culture emphasis of theoretical work in cultural studies, as it makes its own theories of performance. In addition to a focus on performance, there's also something New York-specific about the performance artists interviewed and discussed here. This illustrates the pervasive power of the local, and New York City's continued centrality to feminist discourse in the arts.

The performances and performers included here are influenced by a relationship to an avant-garde and feminist theatre tradition – *The Constant State of Desire* and *Dress Suits To Hire* both resonate with Beckett and Pinter, as well as the non-linear, fragmentary textual deconstructions of Foreman and LeCompte.[9] This work is very different from performances like, for instance, the Five Lesbian Brothers' collaborative pieces *The Secretaries* and *Brave Smiles*, both of which rely on audiences' familiarity with popular culture genres like the horror film, among others, for their meanings to become readable and pleasurable. *Dress Suits* and *Constant State* require other reading competencies from readers and spectators, among which an under-standing of avant-garde traditions is helpful.

The performance texts reprinted here circulate as examples of feminist work in the field. Yet they remain insistently incomplete without the bodies of the actors who performed them (Shaw and Weaver and Finley, decidedly). These texts remain partial documentations of past events, which offer the flavor of form and content without the visceral impact of the bodies' seductions and repulsions. The language is to be consumed, studied, experienced, and (especially in Hughes' writing) treasured for its interventions into conventional American dramaturgy. Language in feminist performance, however, is only part of the story. The body writes the largest portion of the text.

Despite necessary gaps and omissions, these essays, interviews, and performance texts offer an invigorating, important precis of work done since the mid-1970s to create and critically engage with feminist performances. What links the historical, theoretical, dialogic, and performance work gathered here is its insistent connection to cultural meanings, the interpretive language of which has been provided by feminism and multicultural studies and queer theory. Performance here is a critical social tool, an embodied moment of theory and practice, not just the commodified trope that "performativity" has become in critical theory.[10] That's the specific, vital contribution of feminist performance studies.

THE ARTICLES: HISTORY AS MEMORY

"Art Versus Business: The Role of Women in American Theatre" demonstrates the persistence of binaries in the history of feminist work in performance. While Chinoy's article documents the struggle to make an aesthetics of work by American women from earlier moments in history – an aesthetics often at odds with the growing industry that mainstream (and avant-garde) American theatre ultimately became – feminist criticism continues to find performance work drawn in binary relations: political vs. aesthetics, avant-garde vs. accessible, popular vs. political, etc. Chinoy's documentary history provides a roll call of the names of (mostly) white women who have worked in the center and at the margins of American theatre, especially in the 20th century but notably since the country's inception. Chinoy documents work by Mercy Otis Warren, Anna Cora Mowatt, Olive Logan, Ada Isaacs Menken, Eva Le Gallienne, Susan Glaspell, Edith Isaacs, Cheryl Crawford, Margaret Webster, Hallie Flanagan Davis, and more. Many of these women worked outside the limits of "good society," or offered their resources to little theatres that formed in opposition to the business of theatre, dedicated to a different notion of art and craft. The need for such role models persists, even while some critics might question the value of installing a linear narrative of progress and/or tradition within the work of women producers, actors, directors, and theorists. Those of us who teach young female students know the importance of role models, of being able to point to and to discuss women who have grappled with the continuing question of how to form oneself as a powerful, purposeful woman in the theatre.[11]

A singular focus on dominant production venues can perpetuate racial exclusions, since women of color working at the intersections of gender and race do not often have access to more powerful, financially secure mainstream theatres. Misha Berson's article, "Women at the Helm," first published in *American Theatre* in May/June 1994, argues that women are breaking through the glass ceiling engineered by a predominantly white and male industry. But Berson was excoriated in subsequent letters in *AT* for disregarding the absence of women of color from top artistic directorships in large regional theatres and from note in her article.

Read beside Chinoy's article, a sense of historical continuity appears in the similarity of questions Berson posed. Do white women change things when they achieve positions of power? What happens when women come to want the same kinds of success that dominant venues historically provide to white men, rather than trying to change the measure of success these venues grant? Because generations of female actors are still being trained for participation in dominant modes of theatre production, feminist critics and theatremakers need to continue to generate and comment on texts written in the more theatrical or literary tradition with which Berson and Chinoy are concerned. While performance art – on which feminist theorists tend to focus – has offered a resistant site of production, it remains culturally marginalized and "avant-garde" in its traditions. Because of the Republican Right's determination to end public funding for the arts, on which most performance artists and the organizations that produce them draw, performance art as a form might also be doomed, while more orthodox theatrical forms might linger a bit longer. Feminists in theatre need to consider the economic structures in which this work takes place.

Charlotte Rea's article, "Women for Women," moves from questions about women's work in dominant culture to those raised by performance inspired by the activist American women's movement – from the politics of theatre to political theatre. Gender becomes a category not just of employment, but of analysis, which saturates performance forms and contexts as well as contents. Theatre in the 1960s and 1970s becomes a site for women's counterculture. Rea's article is marked by its historical moment. She spends a great deal of time worrying about men in the audience for feminist work, and assumes, along with her contemporaries, that *all* men would use the work in a prurient way. Twenty years later, feminism has lost faith in the notion that a safe space is one without men, whether at the theatre, in women's studies classes, or elsewhere. Rea's article assumes commonalities among women that theories by women of color were already discounting in the 1970s. Nonetheless, the importance of developing new audiences for feminist work, and educating them to a new horizon of expectations for their experiences of performance and theatre, is palpable in Rea's writing.

Emily Sisley's "Notes on Lesbian Theatre" describes wonderfully contradictory definitions of "lesbian" that very much concerned those who worked under the rubric of an identity even more marginalized than "woman." Her article represents the inevitable historical slippage between "lesbian" and "feminist" as categories of production, and describes the relatively small amount of theatre or performance work that *called* itself lesbian in the early 1970s. Implicit in the description of much feminist theatre work in the 1960s and 1970s was the specter of "lesbian" as an unnamed but foundational category. Influenced by Adrienne Rich's article, "Compulsory Heterosexuality and Lesbian Existence," "woman-identification" became the category under which much cultural work was produced and received.[12] Alisa Solomon's article on performances at the WOW Cafe a decade later indicates shifting definitions of lesbian identity – at this site and in women's culture at large – from a reliance on gender to understanding lesbian

meanings as insistently grounded in sexual practice. This shift charac-
terized the performances at WOW as much more bawdy in how lesbian
bodies were signified, and appealed to audience communities that often
defined themselves against dominant categories of feminism.[13]

Alisa Solomon's early feature article on the WOW Cafe first appeared
in an issue of *TDR* that Kirby organized around the then-flourishing East
Village performance scene. A group of writers went to see performances
on the same evening (30 November 1984) and recorded their impressions
of the spaces and events happening simultaneously within a few blocks
of each other on the Lower East Side. Many of these spaces proved short-
lived, although they produced significant bodies of work: The Limbo
Lounge offered an initial home for Charles Busch's drag performances,
which have now found places on and off-Broadway; The Pyramid Club
sponsored John Jesurun's weekly pomo soap opera *Chang in a Void
Moon*; Club Chandalier [*sic*] offered the lesbian variety shows that
premiered Alina Troyana's persona, Carmelita Tropicana, who now
performs mostly at P.S. 122; and the WOW Cafe, at the time, was
producing the earliest performances by Split Britches and Holly Hughes,
among other lesbian performers.

There is a history waiting to be written about how spaces like the
WOW Cafe (and later P.S. 122) organized performance around the
particularities of location. That is, the downtown scene developed
audiences for its work that were about community, about local groups of
people using theatre to socialize, entertain themselves, and provoke
themselves. The work at WOW was homegrown in its first incarnations,
and concerned with a social tradition rather than a theatrical one. The
women who created performances there were often drawn by the fun and
the seductions of performing for each other. Their impulse was not the
same as that of the Women's Experimental Theatre, for example, which
wrote a compensatory creative history against the omissions of the male-
dominated American experimental theatre in which many of its members
had worked. As a result, the work at WOW made alliances with gay
culture, sometimes to the exclusion of dominant feminist culture
(especially the women's counterculture formed in the 1970s and early
1980s). Drag and a kind of camp became the prevailing aesthetic, as
sexuality, rather than gender as identity, and sexual practice as an
unstable, pleasurable exchange of meanings, fueled the multiple meanings generated by the work.[14] The common reference at WOW was
popular culture, rather than high art. Performers used a form based on
genre parodies to create different lesbian meanings.

WOW's historical refusal to write grants, or to audition its performers,
writers, or directors, meant that the work retained the markings and the
control of the community that fueled it. WOW was never about quality

art, but was always about experimentation, community, and pleasure. WOW eventually moved from its storefront space on E. 11th Street to a fourth floor in a warehouse building on E. 4th Street – the East Village's theatre row – and still produces work on a regular basis. The audiences are different, more anonymous and gender-mixed than they were in the early 1980s, and not everyone in the audience knows everyone else. The work is reviewed on a fairly regular basis, which brings audiences that might never have found the out-of-the-way location years before. As a result, WOW now has cachet, even if it still does not have money.

THEORIZING ABOUT PERFORMANCE

The postmodernist theory represented in this collection of articles moved feminist critical discourse in the mid-1980s and 1990s away from textual explications, inquiries into feminist collective work, and access to modes of production toward solo performance. The theoretical articles are concerned with the female body's potential interventions into dominant meanings. The shift in emphasis from collective or literary-based performance to solo performance and/or performance art (although these terms have different histories) might be explained in several ways. First, it is often financially more feasible and logistically more practical to work alone than it is to work collectively. But second, performance art tends to reject more modernist (perhaps utopic) notions of community on which the experimental collectives of the 1960s and 1970s were modeled.

The theoretical articles in the anthology insist again and again on the problems and pleasures of representing the female body, as well as the configuration of desire as a motivating force in the exchange of performed meanings. They have made methodological contributions to feminist theatre and performance studies by reading performances intertextually with critical practices in poststructuralism, cinema studies, postmodernism, reception theory, and/or psychoanalysis. Elin Diamond's "Brechtian Theory/Feminist Theory" is perhaps the most theatre- and performance-specific, as she offers an enormously influential intertextual reading of feminism and Brecht, an inquiry into the particular conditions of performance spectatorship, and the politicized creation of meanings between productions and their audiences.[15]

Working through each of Brecht's key topoi, Diamond manipulates notions of Gestus, the "not, but," historicization, and the alienation-effect away from the Marxist emphasis on class that blinds Brecht's theory to gender, and searches out its possibilities for feminism. Diamond extends Laura Mulvey's important early article "Visual Pleasure and Narrative Cinema" (1975) into live performance, where the possibilities for gazing and pleasure open in many more and different directions. She revises Mulvey's notion of the female performer in film as connoting "to-be-looked-at-ness" into the potentially subversive Brechtian-inflected "looking-at-being-looked-at-ness" as the contribution of the live female performer. Diamond's work has been key to materialist feminist work in the field and to experiments with feminist theatre praxis.

Lynda Hart's article, "Motherhood According to Karen Finley: *The Theory of Total Blame*," works with Freudian precepts as its Ur-text, which seems appropriate and necessary in addressing Finley's attack on the American domestic drama that persistently structures social relations. Hart locates Finley's "play," *The Theory of Total Blame*, "squarely within American familial representations, not unlike Sam Shepard's *Buried Child* or Edward Albee's *American Dream*". Echoing another Diamond article, Hart questions "whether mimesis can be played with a difference … it is this question that intrigues me about Finley's *Blame*, an unconventionally conventional play".[16] Hart goes on to argue that the conditions of the speaking female body continue to summon forth the regulations of a power bloc that would prefer to keep it silent. Hart writes, "The female body with an active tongue is still, evidently, a violation".

Hart's strategy follows feminist literary critics, who use Freudian and Lacanian psychoanalytic methods to investigate the unconscious of culture and texts. Although some more materialist feminist critics dispute the efficacy of psychoanalysis, and critique its ahistorical, generalizing tendencies, there is a way in which this method unlocks textual exegesis on a complex and perhaps cultural level. Unlike much of the psychoanalytic feminist work in literary studies, feminists using this method in performance studies – Hart, Diamond, and Phelan, especially – have grounded psychoanalysis in history in ways that inflect their critical strategies with materialist concerns. Once again, the palpability of the live female body keeps insisting on an attention to history and material effects.[17]

Peggy Phelan also engages with psychoanalysis, and with Mulvey's paradigm and the notion of "the gaze" foundational to feminist film theory. In her article, "Feminist Theory, Poststructuralism, and Performance," Phelan reads intertextually with poststructuralist theory in search of a critical method to inform feminist work on representation and performance. She explicates the nexus of gazing, desire, and pleasure in *performance* as a unique event, contending that feminist performance criticism has something singular to offer critical discourse. This piece predicts some of the issues on which she came to focus in her important book, *Unmarked*.[18] Phelan proposes a distinction between "reading" and "seeing" that works across different levels of language and culture. She brackets the register of sight, explicating Yvonne Rainer's film *The Man Who Envied Women*, and studying performances by Angelika Festa, in which seeing and reading are foregrounded and refocused. Phelan points out that "Festa's work is allied with much postmodern performance art in that its primary interest comes from the discourse it promotes after the fact, rather than from the immediacy of the image it creates when it is 'presented'". The female body provides textuality both during and after the performance, a site to be read critically and variously even as it disappears or merely records its own absence. Phelan in later work takes up the status of performance as absence, revising the melancholic humanism of a thinker like Herbert Blau (who worries about similar issues) into a nuanced feminist argument for how performance and performative writing might harness the political power of an aesthetic of disappearance.[19] Phelan's critical associations and allusions offer a rich model for feminist criticism that is adept at theory, but also at the complex pleasures of hermeneutics. This article holds the kernel of Phelan's later critique: that the visible carries with it a limiting stability, and provides the fulcrum of power/knowledge.

Kate Davy's work on the WOW Cafe has contributed significantly to feminist and lesbian theoretical debates about performance and representation. With reception theory as its methodology, "Reading Past the Heterosexual Imperative" remains key to interventions in cultural assumptions of heterosexuality by problematizing the stability of both authorship and spectatorship. Davy couches her critical analysis of *Dress Suits to Hire* in an historicized reading of the WOW Cafe as a production site, and studies how lesbian meanings shift when they are taken out of particular contexts, or when the "common referents" of the work become destabilized by form (the higher art trappings of this particular text) or location. In the process of documenting the belligerent discussion that ensued when the piece was performed at the University of Michigan, in which some feminists felt the work was coopted by its move to a mixed, institutionalized audience site,[20] Davy addresses the historical performativity of butch/femme identities, well before Judith Butler "popularized" this critical notion. In Davy's reading, social identities are strategies of *performance* that can be useful, material sites of subversion and study.

Carol Martin's article on Anna Deavere Smith, "Bearing Witness: Anna Deavere Smith from Community to Theatre to Mass Media," offers to resurrect postmodernism as a resistant cultural form. While she cites Philip Auslander citing an art critic who announced that postmodernism was dead in 1990, Martin's article and Smith's work, along with much of the performance work collected or theorized here, suggests that feminism has not acquiesced to the death of a style that might still have

something to offer political performance work. Martin sees appropriation, quotation, discontinuity, and pastiche as postmodern strategies that
profitably critique modernist notions of art as an origin, as property, by
valuing "theft" over originality.[21] Smith's solo performances walk the
line into the postmodern: she refuses originary narratives by using other
people's speech to weave arguments in which cultural difference is
maintained as a necessary tension. Smith's position in regard to her own
authorship of the *On the Road* series is vexed, as she both is and is not
the final arbiter of her texts' meanings. Yet Smith's sudden fame, after
the New York Shakespeare Festival at the Public Theatre-produced *Fires
in the Mirror* in 1993, writes her work back into a capitalist mode of
production in which she *is* more secured as the author/star/commodity of
the piece, whether or not it originates from *her* words, *her* experience.[22]

Martin reads Smith's work through a tradition of community-based
women's performance art, but also remarks on Smith's mediatization, as
Fires was reproduced for broadcast on PBS, and her subsequent piece,
Twilight: LA, 1992, was produced on Broadway. Broadway retains the
vestiges of live theatre even as it strives to become more like film, but
its commodification makes it more analogous to the objects of media
culture, as Martin points out, moving the work further from the live and
local community from which it sprang. *Twilight* and *Fires* were also
created for larger audiences than other pieces in Smith's *On the Road*
series, which Martin suggests marked both pieces with the residue of "art
work" in their creation and distribution. Despite what might be an
appropriative, popular, mediatized context, Martin argues that the
content of Smith's work disrupts traditional conventions of form and
context by representing racial identity as fluid and negotiable, rather than
fixed and certain, written over the body of the African-American female
performer who refuses to stabilize or make transparent her own
meanings.

TALKING ACROSS THEORY AND PRACTICE

Martin's interview with Smith begins a section of "talking withs" in the
sourcebook. The ways in which performers talk about their work is
fascinating to me, partly because their speech tends to cloak more than
it often reveals. Smith, for instance, resists the feminist critique with
which Martin would like her to engage, and insists that her work is
outside of the privileged spaces of certain kinds of intellectual (critical/
theoretical) languages. Hughes, too, in her interview with Rebecca
Schneider, refuses a critical framework Schneider offers from lesbian
performance theory, suggesting that "those chicks" are interested in
creating a lesbian-feminist fairy tale out of her work, trying to preserve

it from the corruptions of a mainstream into which Hughes would like, in fact, to speak.

Resistances to feminism and criticism aside, Smith and Hughes are enormously articulate about the production and reception of their work. Smith provides the contours of a resistant, non-psychological acting theory, describing how she works with students to capture the external markings of person and character, through gesture and appearance, and with linguists to find places in language in which "character" is revealed or crystallized. Her description offers glimmers of a critical, political, feminist acting method, one which might empower feminist actors within and outside of the conventional production venues across which Smith herself has worked.

Hughes' interview makes an aggressive argument about reading and producing lesbian performances based in sexual practice that might speak toward (however confrontationally) a larger audience constituency. At the same time, Hughes clarifies the community impulse behind her work. These performers' relationship to community is a theme threaded through each of the interviews collected here, and several of the articles. While the historical pieces on feminist performance seem to presume a somewhat stable, coherently bounded community of performers and audiences, the more recent, postmodern performance work worries about community in ways fraught with anxiety about who constitutes them and what it means to make work from or with them (especially in Smith's case).

Robbie McCauley, in her interview with Vivian Patraka, is perhaps most sanguine about the relationship of her performances to a community base. She insists that "preaching to the converted," the hostile charge regularly leveled at political theatre work, is not really so onerous: "How much do the converted know?" she asks astutely. McCauley's notion of "participatory listening" offers a way to rethink the relationship between feminist performance and community, as well as larger, audiences. Participation (at least ideologically speaking, if not physically, although this distinction is sometimes collapsed in McCauley's work) implies complicity of a useful sort, along with critical agency, contention, a lack of agreement that might, as Smith remarks, force the issue of difference in performance as an "active negotiation." The "converts" toward whom many of these performers are preaching are already fragmented, coalitional identities, forming tenuous communities often based in political commonality, rather than the historical identifications of identities built on a homogeneous assumption of gender or race. Difference is already operative in these productions and receptions – the challenge becomes how to make it speak progressively, how to represent it without making it the same.

The Interview section of this anthology brings an immediacy to discussions between producers and critics/theorists about the historical context of feminist performance work. Patraka's conversation with McCauley is part of Patraka's developing collection of interviews that position both speakers in a complex relation to a more broadly defined notion of culture and history. The speaking-together represented by these interviews gestures toward the importance of feminist performance's and criticism's interventions in the signifying practices of ideology, rather than simply in the signifying practices of the stage. There's a large reach implicit and necessary here that makes the importance of these dialogues pressingly clear.

Karen Finley's interview with Richard Schechner collected here predates Finley's NEA imbroglio, in which her funding was canceled and the media fed over her in a frenzy. But the specter of censorship is predicted, in the performances Finley was asked to stop at the ICA in London, and in the often violent responses provoked by her work. In another contribution toward developing a new feminist praxis, Finley's interview details her performance technique as anti-acting, yet raises complicated questions about the relationship of her work to other kinds of mediation (such as spirit channeling). She insists on blurring the discrete borders between her self and her role, her performance and her life, suggesting she is the vehicle or medium for the language she angrily spits out. Interestingly, given Finley's lead, Schechner poses several questions in the interview that ask if the meanings of her performances attach squarely to her life. Schechner asks, "Is it you – ? Your dreams, your fantasies, or what? Who do these words belong to?". Ironically, because Finley's description of her work makes these life/performance borders permeable, it becomes dangerously easy for other commentators to make the work personal, rather than social and political, and representative of more than her own experience.

If right-wing political writers can insist that the work is Finley's alone, and disparage her personally, then the issues circulating around feminism and theatre and performance come full circle. If the genre started with activist women's groups insisting on the centrality of experience ("Is it us?"), the concept of experience as *individual* is now used by the media and dominant audiences, in effect, to contain the work. As Hart's article details, Finley became the "chocolate woman" in the smear campaign launched by Helms and other anti-NEA Washington homophobes; but was there something in the form or style of her work already that lent it to such an individualized, voyeuristic reading?

The differences between Hughes and Finley have always been significant, in ways their interviews and texts and the theoretical work by Davy and Hart reprinted here tease out further. Hughes walks perhaps a different side of Finley's line, representing female sexuality as a threatening site of resistance in dominant culture. Hughes' work ironizes, while Finley's work accuses. Finley's fragmented, broken narrative figures the violence of sexuality within a post-Freudian nuclear family system; Hughes rewrites the family dynamic in a lesbian-structured space, in which the mother (in *World Without End*, especially) becomes sexual guru, and pleasure, rather than violence, becomes most dangerous to the larger body politic. Finley's is ultimately an auto- (or anti-?) erotic dialogue with herself, into which spectators can dare themselves to gaze. Finley cants,

> Let me tell you how I look at young men in blood-soaked costumes. Let me tell you how I look at young women undressing behind closed doors.
> Let me tell you how I look at children dancing in their parents' blood.
> I'm your voyeur.

Hughes is more insistently homoerotic; her cackling language spills out into the audience as a challenge to configure desire differently – "looking with a reason." Desire, for Finley, can only be part of a destructive structure of exchange on a capitalist marketplace intimately connected to sexual abuse. Not many customers frequent the shop in which Deeluxe and Michigan stage their relationship in *Dress Suits*, but in Hughes' lexicon, it takes two (lesbians) to circulate desire off the heterosexual commodity exchange.[23]

The matter of looking is central to *Dress Suits* in ways that provoke reconfigurations of feminist investigations of "the gaze." *Dress Suits* rewrites the geography of female/lesbian desire. If the play resonates with the European absurdist tradition of Beckett and Pinter, the stakes in what separates inside from outside of the unmarked, ambiguous clothing shop are very different. If Deeluxe and Michigan appear to be waiting for some other Godot, the governing system is not a theological or ontological question here, but one about the body as territory, about writing gender and sexuality out of the duplicity of male hegemony. The form might recall absurdism or the American, empty ironies of Shepard, but not the language:

> One look at you and my pink pulp starts pounding. (*DEELUXE begins to unzip her gown.*) Wanna know something? They're gonna get bigger. That pink is gonna go all the way into red. Then you watch out. My sap's running from the heat of your eyes. That special blue heat outta the eyes gets the pink ocean stirred up. That's when you squeeze them. Put the muscle on those peaches till my bucks are bucking like I'm riding an invisible palomino.

The body becomes a geography, mobile, constructed, criss-crossed by desire, that challenges a stable ontology or a static, essentialized female relationship to nature. Adding her own opinions to the debate over context and shifting meanings in her interview with Schneider, Hughes says, "I feel real strongly about putting lesbian work out.... I really feel like I don't want to preach to the converted. I really feel that it's very important for women's work to be seen in a more general context".

It is not surprising, somehow, that this particular text should generate so much anxiety over its performance context. *Dress Suits* is a much more writerly text, among a history of feminist and lesbian work that never aimed for "good" writing. Yet even so, the text is essentially different without the bodies of Weaver and Shaw to complete it. Debates about *Dress Suits'* aesthetics and audiences indicate the distance feminist performance discourse has come since Rea's discussion of the value of women-only performances. Now that authors, performers, and critics are aware of the work's status as commodity and property, and the different stakes this creates, the pleasures (and the anxieties) are very different.

Within these texts and the writing that theorizes them lies the potential for profoundly (if only temporarily, if only in the present absence of performance) altering signifying systems. The struggle to rearticulate dominant meanings links work in feminist performance to cultural productions in other media. *Dress Suits* offers that the mysterious, omnipresent, male-identified Little Peter, represented as a gloved hand at the end of Peggy Shaw's arm, "may be a dick but he's not a penis", which prompts Schneider to ask Hughes, "Are you trying to manipulate penises to be less of a power-filled image – to rewrite the penis?". To which Hughes replies, "I am interested in talking about sexual pleasure and what it could mean for women". By spinning the sign system (seducing it through a strategy of appearances, as Case might argue), Hughes offers female redemption through rearticulated sexualities.

I have not wanted to make an evolutionary tale out of this work, but intended to draw something of a fragmented historical circle around a feminist notion of praxis, which these collected articles, interviews, and performance pieces represent. The performance work cited by Hart and Phelan is not more advanced than that described carefully by Rea or Sisley; it's simply differently situated in a history of aesthetics and politics. All of the work offered for critical contemplation here is full of intelligent, emotional response, motivated by exploratory energy. The context shifting around it is historical and cultural, and in many ways illustrates the difference between a modernist and a postmodernist impulse and style in United States culture on which feminism has drawn. This is an important distinction between the 1970s and the 1990s, one that an anthology such as this encounters in its 20-year span of selections. This collection gathers articles that are pedagogically important as they help historicize the discourse of the field.[24]

NOTES

1. See, for example, *Performance and Cultural Politics* (Routledge, 1995), edited by Elin Diamond, on cultural studies and theatre studies, which collects papers presented on a series of panels called "Cultural Studies, Theatre Studies" at the 1992 MLA Convention. Stacy Wolf's 1994 University of Wisconsin-Madison dissertation on theatre audiences is one of the few full-length studies I know of that uses cultural studies methodologies to investigate aspects of performance and theatre.

2. See Elizabeth Zimmer, "Has Performance Art Lost its Edge?" *Ms.* (March/April 1995): 78–83, for a discussion of feminist performance art in the 1990s.

3. My article, "In Defense of the Discourse," included here, details some of the debates staged at the Women and Theatre Program conference in San Diego in 1988, which represented the earlier, fraught, argumentative, and outlaw history of the organization and of feminist performance theories. See also the special issue of *Women & Performance Journal* 4, no. 8, 1989, devoted to the Women and Theatre Program.

4. See Ellen Messer-Davidow's article, "Know-How" in Joan E. Hartman and Ellen Messer-Davidow, eds., *(En)gendering Knowledge: Feminists in Academia*, Knoxville, Tenn.: University of Tennessee Press, 1991, 281–309 for a provocative discussion of the ways in which feminist scholars and teachers can continue to promote activist thinking while inhabiting a powerful, institutional space. I know from my own experiences how my description of the centering of feminism in the discourse of theatre studies shifts historically and continually.

5. Nancy K. Miller, *Getting Personal: Feminist Occasions and Other Autobiographical Acts*, New York: Routledge, 1991.

6. For a cogent history of *TDR* up to the early 1980s, see Brooks McNamara, "*TDR*: Memoirs of the Mouthpiece, 1955–83," in Brooks McNamara and Jill Dolan, eds., *The Drama Review: Thirty Years of Commentary on the Avant-Garde*, Ann Arbor: UMI Research Press, 1986, 1–26.

7. I should note that I worked with Michael Kirby as the managing editor of *TDR* from 1981–1985. Although he wasn't interested in developing a critical methodology for feminist or any other kind of theatre and performance, he was always supportive of our efforts to document this work. Under his editorship, Kirby also provided quite a lot of in-kind support to *Women & Performance Journal*, which started in the Performance Studies Department at NYU while I was managing editor at *TDR*. Phones and typewriters and paper were always accessible to us because of Kirby's support and generosity.

8. In the years covered by the theory articles collected for this anthology, *Women & Performance Journal* and *Theatre Journal* were also viable options for publishing feminist work. *Women & Performance* published its first issue in 1983, virtually out of the same editorial office that published *TDR*.

Theatre Journal, on the other hand, has always been a more obviously institutionalized site for publishing in theatre studies. From its beginnings, this journal has been affiliated with the preeminent national theatre studies organization: first, the American Theatre Association, and now, the Association for Theatre in Higher Education. Its first explicitly feminist issue was published in October 1985, although certain editors had courted feminist scholarship much earlier. When Sue-Ellen Case became the editor of *TJ* in the late-1980s, it marked a decisive turn to the left and toward theoretical and feminist studies for a publication with a longer record of empiricist, historical scholarship. Selections of articles from Case and Timothy Murray's editorship of *TJ* are published in *Performing Feminisms: Feminist Critical Theory and Theatre*, Sue-Ellen Case, ed., Baltimore: Johns Hopkins University Press, 1990.

9. For an elegant theoretical discussion of the relationship between postmodern feminist performance work and the modernist tradition of Beckett, Brecht, Pinter, and Genet, see Vivian Patraka, "Binary Terror and Feminist Performance: Reading Both Ways," *Discourse* 14, no. 2 (spring 1992): 163–185.

10. For an argumentative engagement with the notion of performativity in critical theory and its relationship to performance and its studies, see my "Geographies of Learning: Theatre Studies, Performance, and the 'Performative,'" *Theatre Journal* 45 (1993): 417–441. For a discussion of performative feminist criticism, see Peggy Phelan, "Reciting the Citation of Others; or, a Second Introduction," in Peggy Phelan and Lynda Hart, eds., *Acting Out: Feminist Performances*, Ann Arbor: University of Michigan Press, 1993, 13–29.

11. Chinoy's article was later published in *Women in American Theatre*, Helen Krich Chinoy and Linda Walsh Jenkins, eds., rev. ed., New York: Theatre Communications Group, 1987. This anthology was the first important book in the United States to gather writing about women and American theatre. This present anthology is in many ways the progeny of Chinoy and Jenkins.

12. This article has been widely reprinted, but is most recently available in the following: Adrienne Rich, "Compulsory Heterosexuality and Lesbian Existence," in Henry Abelove, Michele Aina Barale, and David M. Halperin, eds., *The Lesbian and Gay Studies Reader*, New York, London: Routledge, 1993, 227–254.

13. Kate Davy's recent work on WOW also explicates the ways in which the space has always been implicitly defined by whiteness. Her two papers – "Making (W.O.W.) Girls: Communing with Culture" (presented at the Association for Theatre in Higher Education conferences, 1993) and "Outing Whiteness: A Feminist/Lesbian Project," *Theatre Journal* 47; no. 2 (May 1995): 189–205 – persuasively articulate the sometimes unacknowledged racial politics circulating in this space.

14. See Kate Davy, "Fe/male Impersonation: The Discourse of Camp," reprinted in Moe Meyer, ed., *The Politics and Poetics of Camp*, New York, London: Routledge, 1994, 130–148, for an argument about the differences between lesbian and gay male productions of camp. See also Sue-Ellen Case, "Towards a Butch–Femme Aesthetic," in Lynda Hart, ed., *Making a Spectacle: Feminist Essays on Contemporary Women's Theatre*, Ann Arbor: University of Michigan Press, 1989, 282–299, in which she argues

that camp does in fact provide a liberatory stance for the butch–femme lesbian subject.

15. John Fuegi's new book, *Brecht and Company: Sex, Politics, and the Making of Modern Drama*, New York: Grove Press, 1994, although much maligned; argues that Brecht might not have written all the work attributed to him, and that the women in his orbit in fact did much of the writing and labor, without being properly credited or appreciated. Authorship, of course, doesn't much matter in this context, but in terms of Brecht's relationship with women, feminism's borrowing from his theory now has taken on a new and different tint.

16. See Elin Diamond, "Mimesis, Mimicry, and the 'True-Real,'" in Phelan and Hart, eds., *Acting Out*, 363–382, in which she asks similar questions around feminist mimesis.

17. See Lynda Hart, *Fatal Women*, New Jersey: Princeton University Press, 1994, for an extended reading of various cultural texts – Deb Margolin, Peggy Shaw, and Lois Weaver's *Lesbians Who Kill*, the film *Thelma and Louise*, and the story of serial killer Arlene Warnous, among them – using psychoanalytic feminist strategies.

18. Peggy Phelan, *Unmarked: The Politics of Performance*, New York, London: Routledge, 1993.

19. See, for example, Herbert Blau, *To All Appearances: Ideology and Performance*, New York, London: Routledge, 1992, in which his nostalgic and melancholic ruminations on presence and absence in performance resonate with Phelan's, yet illustrate the difference between a feminist writer determined to draw out a complex, shifting nexus of political meanings and a humanist writer whose final attachment to modernist traditions keep him reaching for a differently unmarked, transcendent universal.

20. In subsequent issues of *TDR* Holly Hughes and Sue-Ellen Case exchanged letters to the editor about this event that many feminist performance scholars and practitioners found very damaging, partly because of the vituperative nature of the exchange and partly because they thought *TDR* was not the right venue for such matters.

21. See Liz Kotz, "An Unrequited Desire for the Sublime: Looking at Lesbian Representation Across the Works of Abigail Child, Cecilia Dougherty, and Su Friedrich," in Martha Gever, John Greyson, and Pratibha Parmar, eds., *Queer Looks: Perspectives on Lesbian and Gay Film Video*, New York, London: Routledge, 1993, 86–102, for references to the "theft-based strategies" of postmodernist videomakers that might resonate with work by postmodernist feminist performance artists. For example, discussing Abigail Child, Kotz suggests,

> Child's found footage and reconstructed materials offer a strategy of appropria-tion and erotic reinscription of pleasurable *and* problematic images from an array of sometimes deeply misogynistic mass cultural sources – a strategy based on reconstructing and refiguring these images, rather than trying to produce an "affirmative image" of female or lesbian sexuality.
>
> (1993: 91)

22. In fact, the Tony Awards committee debated long and hard about whether *Twilight: LA, 1992* constituted a play when it was performed on Broadway,

or whether it was a documentary record that Smith didn't write, since it consisted only of other people's words.

23. The concept that two lesbians are required to enter the symbolic as "a" subject is teased out by Case in "Toward a Butch–Femme Aesthetic," and by Teresa de Lauretis in "Film and the Visible," in *How Do I Look?*, Bad Object-Choices, eds., Seattle: Bay Press, 1991, 223–263, and in her "Sexual Indifference and Lesbian Representation," in Case, ed., *Performing Feminisms*, 17–39. Given that both Case and de Lauretis theorize the necessity of what Case calls the "dynamic duo" to feminist subjectivity, it's appropriate that lesbian performance work should be represented in this volume by Lois Weaver and Peggy Shaw in a text on which they collaborated with Holly Hughes. Weaver and Shaw's butch–femme performances secure their space as the most notorious couple on the American lesbian theatre scene.

24. I want to dedicate this article to all those learning about feminism and theatre and performance, and from whom I have learned so much: the students and teachers and colleagues and practitioners who continue to teach each *other* about the possibilities of our field.

PART I History

1

ART VERSUS BUSINESS

The Role of Women in American Theatre

Helen Krich Chinoy

In the decade or more since the women's movement began, a number of books on the female experience in literature, art and architecture, film and dance have been published, but no comparable attempts have been made to identify a women's tradition in the complex art of theatre. Some excellent volumes of plays by women and some about women, some interesting articles on individuals and on the new feminist theatres, a symposium or an interview here or there have appeared. With the exception of the reissue of Rosamund Gilder's classic, *Enter the Actress*, however, no overall study has tried to see how women have used and have been used in theatre.

Yet questions about women's participation in all aspects of theatre have become more insistent. As women with new self-awareness and enthusiasm try to use theatre to explore what it means to be a woman, they also look back in the hope of locating themselves in some female tradition that will help them understand their problems in the present as well as plan for the future. Despite the public life of theatre, we know very little about the role that women have played. It has not been easy to see a female network in the composite art of theatre or to find a sense of "we-consciousness," as Simone de Beauvoir calls it, among actresses, playwrights, designers, directors, and producers.

As a starting-point, there is the striking evidence of women's continued and extensive participation in theatre. Acting, of course, has been the obvious career for women. If you were pretty but poor, or well-born but hard-up, with no useful skills but your feminine attractions to offer, the stage was always a possible way to earn a living. In *Aria Da Capo* Edna St. Vincent Millay neatly satirizes the easy link of women and acting. When Columbine complains that she can't act, Pierrot answers: "Can't act? Can't act? La, listen to the woman! ... You're blond, are you not? – you have no education, have you? Can't act! You underrate yourself, my dear!" In addition to their obvious but crucial function as actresses, women – often starting as actresses – have been involved in greater numbers and in a greater variety of jobs than are indicated in the theatre history books that usually mention only the big names who made it on Broadway.

Many of these unsung women were born into theatrical families where they learned to do all that was necessary. Some added management to acting on the death of their fathers or their husbands; others started their own theatres, often the first in an outlying area, out of the need to earn a living for themselves or their children or a desire to enrich the life of a community. There were those who were the power behind the scene, managing actress daughters or enriching, or almost ghostwriting, the plays of their husbands. Various strong, independent women served theatre on their own terms, whether that meant playing male roles to satisfy their own sense of power and authority or alternatively exploiting their female sexuality in defiance of the "flabby sanctimoniousness" of good women who, they chided, dwindled into "nonentities" on marriage.

Liberated by their work in the very public, often vulgar world of theatre, they wrote plays for themselves or for others to star in, courted commercial success or struggled for personal expression. They organized companies, trained young performers in their troupes and later in notable studios and schools. They experimented with chemical and physical laws to devise new scenic effects and directed the plays they wrote to ensure that they were staged properly. They have been casting and dramatic agents, producers, financiers, and lawyers for theatre. Especially since the turn of the 20th century, women have made their way into all the specialized positions in theatre, where they can be found if you have a mind to look for them and some sense of where they are most likely to be located.

For although many women have made their mark in theatre, it hasn't been easy for them to do so on Broadway or in the mainstream of theatre. In show business as in other businesses and professions, women have not easily or regularly come into positions of importance or power in the major institutions. They have been restricted by the blatant prejudice against letting women have any say where big money and decision making have been involved, as well as by their socialization into a passive but emotional self-image.

To the usual limits on female career aspirations – marriage, family, appropriate submissive behavior and acceptable feminine appearance – theatre has imposed further restrictions by being socially and morally suspect in puritanical, middle-class America. In a country where theatre was thought of as Satan's haunt and actresses often equated with harlots whose "lascivious smiles, wanton glances, and indelicate attitudes" threatened the ideal of "womanhood," the women who worked in theatre had a difficult time. Defined in this way by society, they could exploit their erotic attractions before an often largely male audience and make a rather free and easy life for themselves outside the limits of good society. Or, anxious to get on, they could fit themselves to the stereotypes acceptable to the popular audience – the innocent ingenue, the noble wife, the fallen woman. From the beginning, however, some women challenged the debased image of theatre and of women in it. Attracted by the stage, they tried to reform it and to raise the moral and aesthetic level of the profession. Although they were sometimes snobbish, prudish, even priggish – reflecting what was thought appropriate when a "lady" turned to theatre – these women, through their efforts over the years and in response to changing values, eventually transformed their defensive attitudes into a dynamic idea of theatre in America.

Uncomfortable in the commercial theatre or barred from full partici- pation, important creative women have insisted that their theatre must be more than "amusement ... prostituted to the purpose of vice," to quote Mercy Otis Warren, our first woman dramatist, or "more than an amusement" to quote a Sunday *New York Times* headline about Zelda Fichandler's Arena Stage. In an earlier day women dramatists and actresses spoke of themselves as "reformers" who would grace the theatre with "their own pure and blameless lives" or with the "benign influence of a noble womanly spirit," to quote Anna Cora Mowatt, the lady who wrote *Fashion*.

Olive Logan, actress, writer, and bluestocking, suggested that theatre could become "a worthy channel for gifted, intelligent, and virtuous young women to gain a livelihood through" if producers would only get rid of the "leg business" made popular in hits like Ada Isaacs Menken's "nude" *Mazeppa* or *The Black Crook*. In her fascinating series of essays, *Apropos of Women and Theatre*, written in 1869, Olive Logan argued that a career on the decent, serious stage was one of the few in which women cold earn equally with men and was therefore worthy of an aspiring, independent woman. Julia Marlowe, for example, was such a young woman who deliberately prepared herself by hard work and careful study of Shakespeare to be a "moral force" in acting his plays. She conceded that what impelled her as an actress was "the dramatic attraction of the woman who stays pure." Her contemporary, Mary Shaw, equally idealistic, was impelled by the possibility of using the stage for a feminist vision. "Women exert a tremendous and virtually irresistible influence over the stage," she insisted. "Aristocrat of the arts and child of religion," she told the International Congress of Women in London in 1899, the drama "is a field for women." With Jessie Bonstelle, actress and director-manager of important stock companies, Mary Shaw projected a Woman's National Theatre devoted to communicating "distinctive feminine feeling or opinions," one of several such theatres planned in the early years of the 20th century.

By 1931, Eva Le Gallienne, actress-director of the Civic Repertory Theatre, could look back on this heritage of high-minded activism when analyzing "Women's Role in the Theatre" in the *Alumnae Quarterly* of Smith College, which had just given her an honorary degree. Her point of departure was an attack on women by Gordon Craig, who had written that "to achieve the reform of the theatre, to bring it into the condition necessary for it to become a fine art, women must have first left the boards." Miss Le Gallienne's defense began in an apologetic familiar vein, noting the absence of women in ancient theatre and the use of only "lower types of women" in "orgies of licentiousness" during the "degenerate days of Rome and the Renaissance." The modern movement in theatre, however, disavowing sexism and show business, was created by both men and women. Indeed, Le Gallienne suggested, at first somewhat hesitantly and then in stronger terms by the end of her comments, the modern theatre was in many ways the accomplishment of women. Looking at the achievements of, among others, Miss Horniman in Manchester, Lady Gregory in Ireland, Irene and Alice Lewisohn, Mary Shaw and Minnie Maddern Fiske in New York, she pointed out that, as she saw it, women were really the "doers" in the development of the modern art theatre.

Looking today for what seems especially to distinguish the contributions of notable women, for a female network or feminine consciousness in American theatre, we find ourselves reinforcing Miss Le Gallienne's suggestion that, counter to Craig's perverse admonition, serving the art of theatre has in many ways been the special function of women. The women who have made major contributions to American theatre have tended to identify themselves – whether they were actresses, playwrights, directors or producers – with an idea of theatre larger than that of Broadway. In the 1920s Edith Isaacs, editor of *Theatre Arts Magazine*, the journal of the art theatre movement, dubbed this alternative theatre "the tributary theatre." In her important essay, she rejected commercial New York theatre as "not an artist's goal," and urged Americans to go to "the four corners of the country and begin again, training playwrights to create in their own idiom, in their own theatres." In declaring that theatre must have a "relation, human or esthetic, to the life of the people," she sounded a call to which women have responded with unusual dedication.

The association of women with regional, institutional, little, art, and alternative theatres is striking. Think of Susan Glaspell, who became an innovative playwright after founding the Provincetown Players with her husband, George Cram Cook; of Theresa Helburn, executive director for many years of the famed Theatre Guild; of Edith Isaacs, for over 25 years reviewer, editor, and manager of *Theatre Arts Magazine*; of Rosamund Gilder, her disciple and associate, critic, historian, activist in the National Theatre Conference, ANTA, and voice of America through the International Theatre Institute; of Cheryl Crawford, co-founder with Harold Clurman and Lee Strasberg of the Group Theatre, and later collaborator with Eva Le Gallienne and Margaret Webster in the American Repertory Theatre; of Hallie Flanagan Davis, creator of the Vassar Experimental Theatre and the Smith College Theatre Department and head of the great Federal Theatre Project; of Margo Jones, director-producer in Dallas, "high priestess" of the post-World War II regional theatre movement; of Nina Vance of the Houston Alley Theatre; of Zelda Fichandler of the Arena Stage; of Judith Malina, guru of the Living Theatre; of Ellen Stewart, "La Mama" of the whole off-off-Broadway theatre movement.

Most of these women turned their backs on making it on Broadway. They rejected what sociologists consider the male preoccupation with power and climbing the ladder in the "cash nexus world." Their concerns have tended to be with the values of what has been called the "status world" in which love, duty, tenderness, individuality, and expressiveness are central. Their activities belong to the tradition of female rites in which, as Linda Jenkins has pointed out, performance events are used primarily for family and social bonding rather than largely for entertainment and profit. Eva Le Gallienne, to stick with her instructive experience, turned against what she felt was the "stultifying effect of a successful engagement" as a leading lady to try her hand at special matinees of "better" plays. Her determination to stage Ibsen, Hauptmann, and Chekhov led to the founding of the Civic Repertory Theatre where the satisfactions of ensemble playing, repertory scheduling, low prices, and free training for performers replaced the triumphs she could have easily had as a star. Other leading actresses also freed themselves from being "commodities" in the hands of producers to head their own companies or join institutional theatres or even just tour an individual production that would allow them to perform personally and culturally meaningful plays. Think of the great Minnie Maddern Fiske, who was called the "most civilizing force" of the stage of her day, of Katharine Cornell, Lynn Fontanne, Helen Hayes, Julie Harris, and Irene Worth, among others.

Many of these women tend to look on their companies as family units within a larger community group, sharing, supporting, learning, and teaching. They reject the "atmosphere of hysteria, crisis, fragmentation, one-shotness, and mammon-mindedness" of the Broadway system as inappropriate for the "collective and cumulative" art of theatre, to quote Zelda Fichandler. They tend to turn away from the "nameless faces and the anonymity" of New York, as Nina Vance confessed she did when she opened her Alley Theatre in Houston, where she had a "feeling of roots." They tend to work for a theatre "which is part of everybody's life ... where there is a theatre in every town providing entertainment and enlightenment for the audience and a decent livelihood along with high artistic goals for the theatre work," as Margo Jones put it in her book, *Theatre-in-the-Round*. This sampling of quotations, it should be noted, antedates the new feminist theatres where these nurturant, supportive, cooperative, community values have become the basis for a new kind of theatre that can even call itself, as one feminist troupe does, "It's All Right To Be a Woman."

Much of what women did was dedicated to realizing a dream of a different kind of theatre. Perhaps this concluding sketch of the career of one woman will capture the essence of the special spirit that seems to have animated many of the women in American theatre.

During the "full, lean years" of the Depression, a tiny woman in a fedora hat cast a huge shadow that covered the whole land with the vision of a different kind of theatre. Hallie Flanagan Davis during the few short years of the Federal Theatre Project made the tributary the mainstream. The educational, regional, experimental, art theatre became our national people's theatre.

When Hallie Flanagan Davis was appointed National Director of the Federal Theatre Project in August, 1935, the *New York Times* wrote that "the boys – the local gentry for whom the theatre does not exist outside Manhattan – did not quite know what to make of that." To them the appointment "represented 'art'.... There was headshaking. What this project needed, they said, was an old-line Broadway manager who knew the commercial theatre's devious ways."

There were many reasons why Harry L. Hopkins with President Roosevelt – and, we might add, Mrs. Roosevelt – supporting him wanted someone outside the commercial theatre, but here we only want to ask what were some of the qualities that Hallie Flanagan Davis brought to the job.

Born in South Dakota and brought up in Grinnell, Iowa, she belonged to the vast reaches of America that Broadway thought of as a "dumping ground" for some of its products. Although she eventually became part of the eastern scene, she always recalled, in often lyrical prose, the great quiet prairies and the "long summer days and long winter evenings" of a "serene childhood" and youth spent in the spacious west.

At Grinnell College she, like the rest of her group, was "imbued with the Grinnell conception of public service," and she developed a strong sense of the importance of being "part of an institution." She wrote of herself that "I can't imagine just being a floating rib someplace." She could not imagine theatre apart from the life of a group.

She started her first work experience like a latter-day Nora, trying to earn money in secret for her ailing young husband by giving drama lessons, one of the few skills this young wife had. When her husband died, she thrust herself into teaching to earn money for herself and her two children. Her first notice came as a playwright when she won a prize offered by the Des Moines Little Theatre Society in a regional contest open only to Iowans. This success plus her effective productions at Grinnell College led her to Professor George Pierce Baker's Workshop 47 at Harvard, where she earned a Master's degree. With her small son Frederick, Davis went east to learn the art of theatre after suffering the death of both her husband and her 7-year-old son, Jack. Professor Baker, she recalled, "believed that I should give up everything and write plays. But I couldn't – I had a family to support!" All her active life she was concerned to support herself and her family; her work was for her no fanciful creative outlet, but a serious economic commitment. But the work was also more than just a job.

She went back to Grinnell where she used all she had learned at Harvard. A production at her Grinnell Experimental Theatre of *Romeo and Juliet*, into which she confessed that she "secretly" poured her remembrances of her young husband, won the attention that led to the award of a Guggenheim Fellowship, one of the first given to a woman. It also won her a position at Vassar College, where President Mac-Cracken asked her to set up another experimental theatre.

With her Guggenheim Fellowship she traveled to Europe to see the *Shifting Scenes*, as she would call her book about the journey. Her exposure to the innovations of Craig, Reinhardt, Stanislavsky and especially Meyerhold sharpened her awareness of and commitment to theatre as a dynamic instrument to serve the people as they change the world around them.

In the next few years at Vassar, she and her Experimental Theatre became the "dynamo," to use another word that would become a title of one of her books, that "releases youth's burning energy . . . into the power of creative change." She foreshadowed the later Living Newspapers in her Depression documentary and call to action, *Can You Hear Their Voices?*, and she found ways of transforming classic dramas into contemporary actions. Her innovations attracted the attention of educators, artists, and critics, as well as government officials, and led eventually to her appointment as the National Director of the Federal Theatre.

When this "soft-spoken slave driver," as she was admiringly called, took on the Federal Theatre Project to employ unemployed performers, she tried to realize for the nation the values of the kind of theatre in which she had worked. With her associates she tried to create a regional, popular, educational, art theatre in which, as Harry Hopkins told her in urging her to take the appointment, "the profits won't be money profits."

Without arguing the success or failure of the Federal Theatre or the mistakes or limitations of Hallie Flanagan Davis, we can observe that she brought us nearer to the realization for the nation of the dream widely shared by other women. In her Federal Theatre, the profits were human. An actor, a playwright, a designer, or a technician had a job, even if the salary was only 25 dollars a week. The roots were regional. The theatre tried to "explore sources of native American life." The accomplishments were national. Theatre became for a new audience of millions an artistic medium "of free expression," an "access to the arts and tools of civilization," and a "bulwark of the democratic form of government."

2

WOMEN FOR WOMEN

Charlotte Rea

Women's theatre groups are seeking new forms – forms that have not been derived from the male-oriented and male-dominated theatre that now exists. A search for new content also characterizes these groups, but their most important aspect is their relationship with their audiences. The theatre done by these groups is aimed at a specialized audience and often is performed exclusively for that audience – women. Almost all of the women's theatre groups reserve at least one of their performances for women only, and most prefer to play only for women, even when they admit men.

While women's theatre groups exist in many cities throughout the country, New York provides a base for a large number of troupes. Many of these groups maintain themselves by touring colleges, universities, and women's centers throughout the United States and Canada. For the purposes of this article, we will be examining the work and ideas of Sue Perlgut of It's All Right To Be a Woman Theatre, Roberta Sklar of the Women's Unit and consultant to the Womanrite Theatre, and Lucy Winer and Claudette Charbonneau of The New York Feminist Theatre. Each of these groups is basically a collective working out of New York City. All, except the It's All Right To Be a Woman Theatre, use a director some of the time.

The It's All Right To Be a Woman Theatre develops pieces directly from the lives of its members. Calling the form "Stories from Our Lives," the members translate stories into theatrical terms but leave the story intact. The Womanrite Theatre uses personal material, too, but incorporates it into the Cinderella myth with its message that each woman can be "saved by a kiss." The Women's Unit, a group that began working at Bard College, uses personal material but casts it into the form of testimonials, scenes, songs, and stories. The New York Feminist Theatre, however, works entirely from a script without the improvisational methods of the other groups. The playwright and director are members of the group.

The goals of these groups can be summed up as wanting primarily to reach women by doing theatre. But "reaching women" means different things to each group. The New York Feminist Theatre avowedly wants to awaken women to the politics of their oppression. Winer states:

> Feminist theatre reaches out to women: "Get angry, get upset, look at how you live." It's probably the best way to arouse women ... and to force them to see how they live, what their options are, and, more importantly, what they aren't. How they've been oppressed; why they're slaves, regardless of whether they're rich or poor.... When you begin to see sexism, [you see that] it's everywhere ... in the kitchen, at schools, in the bedroom.... The pan that you pick up every morning to cook an egg for your lover or husband, that's a political act in so far as it expresses the way in which you are oppressed as a woman. We'll have to look at very different actions, a whole different area of life, all of life, to find out in what kinds of ways women are oppressed so that perhaps they'll ... see it, hate it, and stop – and so will the rest of the world.

Winer sees her troupe as a potential "arena for all kinds of women doing all kinds of things artistically – if they have ... something to say artistically about what it means to be a woman."

Sue Perlgut feels that women in feminist theatre are trying to say,

> Look this is who we are and we're going to show it because nobody else will. I want to show there are alternatives and if we need to struggle to get them, we can get them. I feel committed to doing things for women; there is a woman's culture and I want to be part of it and support it.

Sklar comments on the goal of women's theatre:

> Women's theatre is created by women who are in a state of experiencing the fact that they are women in new ways. What they want to do as they create is share this experience with other women, bringing them into this new state of awareness.

Sklar believes that it is important to determine whom one is addressing:

> The general audience is the male-oriented audience. If you say that the society is male-dominated and that art has grown up in male traditions, then anything that is a sort of general thing is, in fact, coming out of that tradition. If you're going to talk to women, you have to think about that and make choices that way. If you're successful at it, men are going to come away saying that they liked it but didn't quite feel moved by it, or there's something cold in it, or it was funny but it wasn't deep enough – because they are not the persons being spoken to.

In addition to affecting the kind of material developed for performances, the intention to perform for an all-female audience gives the performers greater freedom in developing material that they might feel uncomfortable portraying to a mixed audience. The Women's Unit has specific pieces that are censored for mixed audiences because members of the group want to avoid the possibility of being looked at with prurient interest. The censored material is concerned in part with women's bodies and women's feelings about their own bodies.

Perlgut relates that their group censored one of their early pieces called *Saggy Breasts* because it showed drawings of the breast. The group felt that the material was something which "men could guffaw at and ridicule instead of identify with.... That's why there are consciousness-raising groups without men, so we can talk about those things with each other – our bodies, our breasts." Some of the women in the group also feel exposed in mixed audiences when they discuss lesbianism.

The dream-plays of It's All Right To Be a Woman Theatre, in which the members of the troupe act out the dreams of spectators, are limited strictly to the dreams of women. In fact, one man insisted once, according to Perlgut, on having his dream enacted but was refused. Perlgut claimed the group understands women's dreams "because we are women; we don't understand men's dreams."

The presence of men in the audience also appears to affect the reaction of women in the audience. Perlgut says that their group is

> strongly dependent on the audience – if the audience is there for us, we become more there for them; ... [when the] audience doesn't understand us, we don't give such a hot performance.... When women come with men, they worry about what the man is thinking – does he like it or not? Women often come back on all-women nights so they can dig it by themselves.

In one of the pieces done by It's All Right To Be a Woman Theatre, Perlgut portrays a girl who has been made to feel evil by the adults around her; during this scene, she says, "I'm evil, don't come too close" and expresses her anger. She found that in an all-female audience, she would get cheered because the audience understood, but in a mixed male–female audience, people would become very quiet and would withdraw. When she showed less anger, there was less withdrawal.

Sklar observes:

> Certain material played in a mixed context comes off one way. It may come off funny and theatrical. But in the context of only women, it comes off in a much deeper, more penetrating way. You see the audience responding differently.

Why does the presence of men change that?

The answer isn't related to theatre. Why does the presence of the male change the way in which we relate to one another in any setting? Then you can shift it to a more intense situation: a man and a woman have come to the theatre – they are in the context of what one might call a date, an evening out together; they're a closed unit. They're also in a situation in which there may be something going on between the performer and the spectator but the potential, for example, for sexual interaction is between the couple who has come to see the play. The potential for intimacy is between those two people.

Therefore nothing important can happen to the woman?

Definitely not, because if one of the insights the woman has is one which distances her from men and makes her feel closer to women or more identified with women, what does she do with this feeling when she's already committed to the course of the evening?... There's always, at some remote place, the possibility of interaction between a man and a woman that precludes women getting along with each other.

The New York Feminist Theatre troupe, however, feels that the boisterous, "hooray for our side" response, which is sometimes elicited at the all-women nights, can work against the audience's full under-standing of the play. A skit that usually gets a strong positive response in all-women audiences is a lesbian scene. Charbonneau says

If someone immediately cheers when [a performer] says, "I'm a lesbian and I'm proud," I understand that but I also want to say "Hold it a minute and see what's going to happen because it's a heavy scene and we have to go through first being attacked and pushed and pulled before we can get to that point and understand [the positive aspects]."

She feels that the audience must go through the pain and depression of being a lesbian in a society that condemns lesbianism before they can experience the enthusiasm.

According to Winer, the mixed audience is sometimes more attentive because:

The men are usually better educated and better able to laugh at themselves – it's part of being a master in a slave society. Often, in a mixed audience, there will be a greater spontaneity about laughing in the appropriate spots, about relaxing, "What have we got to lose? So this play is clever, so they're pulling it off – so what?"... However, that [reaction] finally recharges the necessity for performing for only women.

Politically, we prefer to perform for women. However, sometimes mixed audiences pick up on things better than all-women audiences where the women sometimes come with preconceptions about what we're trying to say – but when an all-women's audience gets it, they get it far better. Women have a better opportunity of understanding and responding when there aren't men present.

The responses of the all-female audiences are often expressed outside the bounds of the performances – in after-the-show discussions, in letters, and by individuals coming up to one or more of the performers. Sklar said:

> I know so many women who say when they first saw It's All Right To Be a Woman Theatre four years ago that it changed their lives. They don't mean, "I felt something." They mean they changed their jobs or got into consciousness-raising groups – concrete things. I don't know any man who says his life changed after he saw It's All Right.

The Women's Unit performed for groups of women in prisons, and found the responses to be positive and enthusiastic.

> No one is saying to us "I don't think you go deep enough, or this is a really fun play, but I've thought about all these things already." People are saying "I've thought about these things." But they've thought about them in different ways. They want to know more about why you're thinking about it in this way. They're also feeling like you're "coming out" in a sense when you speak against the male-dominated society. The attitude is "You're really right on, and it's really great for you to do it." They also corroborate some of the things you've said.

Although the idea of a specialized audience for a particular type of theatre generally presupposes an already convinced audience, Sklar feels that the effect of women's theatre groups on the lives of women audience members may be even more penetrating and long-lasting when the women are not convinced of the validity of the ideas behind the women's movement.

> If you say that a woman's [theatre] piece is a consciousness-raising experience, then you can't do that so well with women who have already had the same insights that the performers and creators have had. It doesn't do it half so well as when you're speaking to women who have not been directly involved with the women's movement.

A negative response to the material being presented is often indicative of the effect of the material on the audiences. When the Women's Unit performed for a Hadassah group on Long Island – definitely a group not entirely persuaded by the ideas of the movement – the audience was both divided and vociferous in their reactions to a piece called "Obscenities." "Obscenities" is not performed for mixed audiences. Part of it involves women describing some of the abuses and mistreatment women suffer in public places – verbal abuse and obscenities, molestation, exposure, etc. Again, the effect of the material on a specialized but unconvinced audience can be seen. Sklar says:

> We found that the primary identity of the women in the audience was the identity of mother. . . . In the Hadassah situation, a real dialectic developed between the younger mothers and the older mothers in the audience. . . . There was actual argument. The conflict involved the willingness on the part of the mothers to recognize that these things [molestation, exposure, etc.] have happened to their daughters. And if you recognize that it happens to your daughter, often times you have a willingness to recognize that it has happened to you, too. You identify with your daughter as a sister, not a daughter. What happened [was] that the women in their fifties refused this and ... they started getting up, walking around, not leaving but chatting. A couple of women literally turned their backs. Other, younger women, got angry with them and confronted these women, not *en masse*, but we heard people saying, "Sit down, stop talking, turn around." Afterwards, there was an informal exchange [among the audience and performers] and the older women said, "This didn't really happen." Not "Did it?' but an attitude of "I can take so much but this part you're just making up." On the other hand, the younger women had the shock of recognition. There was lots of "This happened to me, too."

The New York Feminist Theatre troupe also documents the strong reactions of audience members, particularly to one of the first pieces in their play – a scene about birth control, which is concerned with the fact that there is no means of birth control that is both safe and reliable and the fact that doctors continue to prescribe pills and IUDs, despite evidence of their harmful effects on women. The reaction during the scene is often "terrific silence," but women, in discussions after the play, often indicate depression or even tears because of being forced to confront a chronic problem in their own lives – the unresolved problem of birth control.

More spectacular was the reaction of many women in Canada during the group's tour this past summer. Women in some of the towns The New York Feminist Theatre performed for actually left their homes and joined the troupe. Winer said: "The show is important in a human way – it is important for women to feel that they can be part of something and plunge in – it is a risk – and do it." She also described the group's effects on the audience as being "consciousness-raising crammed into a few hours. Finally, it means going back to their lives with a kind of anger and energy – saying they will try to change their lives."

Not only do the women often find their lives changed by their responses to the women's theatre groups, but audience members are beginning to have certain expectations about the material they see performed. In particular, as in the larger women's movement, the gay women expect to see their problems and their lives portrayed on stage. Sklar:

> In New York, if you do something and it has a kind of homosexual content to it, the gay women in the audience openly appreciate what you are doing; they thank you for being direct, etc., and if you don't, which the Women's Unit didn't, you get confronted. "Why aren't you raising these issues? Are there any gay women in your group? If not, have you considered why? Why aren't you talking about your own homosexuality?"

In the It's All Right To Be a Woman Theatre, according to Perlgut, the gay women feel there should be something lesbian in their plays, but the straight women feel likewise that there should be something that heterosexual women can respond to. The group consistently maintains material that explores the problems of both homosexual and heterosexual women. Perlgut says that when gay women go to an all-woman night, and there is nothing lesbian, they can become outraged.

In the New York Feminist Theatre play, the lesbian scene attempts to meet the issue head-on. The group claims, "We do not feel a lesbian/ heterosexual split. In fact, we specifically stage the scene so that every member of the cast, lesbians and heterosexual women, assumes the lesbian role at one point or another. At the end of the scene, the entire cast declares their lesbianism." The lesbian scene evokes much laughter of recognition and encouraging remarks on the all-women nights.

In addition to the sociological or human importance of the women's theatre groups for the audiences, these groups are also beginning to explore theatrically – and to use as raw material for their plays – an area of experience that is virtually unknown in theatre history: the conscious-ness of women as seen through women's consciousness. Winer says:

> Women are half the species and they have had an experience totally different from men's.... It's not that they're a fairly small minority.... Now, if there ever comes a time, and it won't in our lifetimes, when women can express themselves without fear and have a life to express – which they do now – or a tradition, one which they can grasp and put forth, there's all the art in the world for them to create. I think Virginia Woolf puts it very well [when she discussed the reasons why] we'll have difficulty for a long time to come. She said that we'll be too angry, too busy answering, too busy imitating, and finally too held down in shackles of poverty and several other things, if we're trying not to conform, to be able to create very much. But finally we have to create. And I do think

that male art is more or less finished, that the patriarchy has come to a dead end that I don't find exciting and, looking back, I find less and less of what I loved to be exciting. And it was always a kind of qualified love, in that I wasn't included. My whole life was ignored, misunderstood, condemned, looked down upon – women were. And even when being cherished or scorned, laughed at or praised, they had nothing to do with me – the attitudes of men toward women, so even in the greatest writers and artists, I felt a kind of qualified response.

Perlgut comments:

We are dying to know more about ourselves.... [So far] it has all been through the eyes of men – how men saw women, the heroines, what heroines were like. And we know that we're not those heroines; and we know that we're different and we know that there's another kind of woman and one way of showing that is women's theatre because men are not going to write about it [women's experience] and women are – because we know who we are and we know we don't have to be a prostitute; we don't have to be a mommy.... We're much more complex; we've got many more ideas and we will talk about them. I wish I had women to look up to that I felt were more complex. I wish I could go to the movies and see a woman I could completely identify with and relate to. I've almost stopped going to the movies ... or doing a lot of things because I couldn't stand the way I was being portrayed. And women in women's theatre are trying to say, "Look we're different, and this is who we are and we're going to show it."

Even though women's theatre groups are exploring the new material of women's experience, there is yet a great uncharted area of experience that neither the groups nor the current women playwrights are reaching. Sklar amplifies:

There is other content [than the material being developed by the women's theatre groups] that hasn't been touched by women's theatre, but some of it, for example, is rarely touched in our lives as women, and I'd like to get to that. For example, theatre that is stimulated by men can often have a religious aspect to it, like the ritual theatre of the past years.... Women, if you ask them if they ever had a religious experience, often look at you as if to say, "What are you talking about?" There are certain experiences that we've hardly been allowed to have, and there are some experiences that we've had which have been pushed into a place that is different from the place we really experience it. For example, childbirth. I think that the experience of childbirth – the awesomeness that's in it – has not been explored to any great degree. The whole thing that the primitive world has been focused on has been demolished in the twentieth century [because of] the twilight zone, anesthetic, childbearing. And now that a lot of women have been conscious while they have given birth, they have a sort of secret experience.... Nobody knows about it. One of the things I think would be really interesting to get into in terms of new content for women's theatre is some more of the unknown experiences that we've had ... experiences we've had that have not been given their rightful due. And they're not areas that are about rejecting men or being hostile about having been oppressed.... [They're about] re-establishing the meaningfulness of certain events in our lives. If I wanted to think about the piece in which the central event in it, or the central stimulation, was childbearing, for example, my feeling at this point would not be to spend a lot of time on how the society has made me look at it in a certain way. But rather what was it and what's my fantasy of it ... to get into a different range of the emotional and, if you will, spiritual experiences of women. I have been interested personally in honing down from my prior experiences what things are really typical to woman's experience ... to separate out the things that don't apply to women but women do anyway. [For example], on the one hand, the theatre today puts a demand on the use of the body in a highly active, flexible way. On the other hand, women are pretty much locked into certain senses of their bodies as being too this, too that – the beauty scale is a crucial measuring stick that a woman carries around with her all the time. So, if you ask people to be totally flexible and responsive with their bodies, it seems to me you have to recognize what the psychological baggage is that's holding them down. In teaching a lot of the physically freeing stuff that developed in the late sixties in experimental theatre, I found it important to focus on where women's minds were as they worked with their bodies. Let me be concrete: a woman often thinks of a certain type of physical movement as calisthenics, as exercise for how her body's going to look. And if that's unshakeable, then it's worthless to do those things with women actresses. If the goal is to free the tension in the body and to develop flexibility, but the head is working on a smaller waistline, it's a useless thing to learn to do the headstand, etc. ... unless you can break through the calisthenic mind set.

The exploration of women's mind-sets is primary material for the theatre groups; however, the question of creating new forms for the content they are discovering and developing has become important to several of the groups. Sklar, in describing the work of the Women's Unit, discussed the mode of presentation as one aspect of creating new forms for women:

One of the things we did was take things that might be highly emotional, and we presented them under great control. There was a line of tension between how you had experienced the thing and how you communicated it. The men simply experienced this as not moving, whereas the women

> [spectators] recognized it as a requirement that had been put on them, that they had certain experiences which had to be held down, repressed.... [They recognized] their own experience of having held back, of not [being] allowed to share certain kinds of emotion. Let me give an example. One of the performers tells a story about a girl in a neighbor's swimming pool and the father in this family offering to flip her into the water and in doing so, he keeps on grabbing her crotch. Meanwhile, her own father is watching at the side of the pool, and the girl feels that he knows what's happening, but he's pretending he doesn't.... "My father's watching the whole time." This story is told in a kind of remote way, in a way that doesn't overtly articulate the emotional experience. The women identified both with the experience and the holding back. We made careful choices about how we used emotion in the piece ... because of the whole issue of how the female is socialized emotionally.

Doesn't form necessarily transcend male–female barriers? Isn't form perceived in an androgynous way – with no relation to sex. Sklar comments again:

> I'm not sure. First of all, maybe we'd have to know what we mean by form ... form doesn't come out of the head of Medusa that way. Form evolves over the history of civilization. Nothing is totally new but is an outgrowth of something. So, if you go back to the idea that form as we know it is out of a historically male tradition, i.e., the male experience, sometimes informed by the female experience, but not predominantly from the female experience. Then you have this special difficulty – if women are trying to work both in content that comes out of their experiences and forms, they have to find ways of extricating themselves, not from all form that they've worked in coming out of the male tradition, but from those portions of it which are truly the male experience.... For me, another side of it is to try to discover, in a very careful way, the forms that do appeal to women, the things women experience as things they need to do. And it has to do with a certain kind of analysis. As a group we analyzed the emotional composition, the socialized emotional composition, of the female. In [doing] that, we made certain decisions about directions we wanted to work in. We developed what we called, as a loose term, a grotesque or ugly esthetic. People wanted to spread out one end of the spectrum, to be able to work with anger, ugliness, aggressiveness, noise, looking very unpretty. Not to name this as good or bad, but [to] be able to do it, to have that as part of our range.
> I think that behavior on stage is part of structure, of the esthetic. We began talking about an esthetic that would include a different range of behavior than the ones we already had – that came out of an analysis of what kind of emotions we are permitted to have and what kinds of ways

we are permitted to express them, through our socialization.... We all knew that we had anger, for example, but as far as that being explicated in our lives or being expressed on a stage, that's very limited and we wanted to explore that and make it a part of an esthetic, not just something I want to know and make better about myself.

Another thing was wanting to be able to control and shape and sharpen how we presented emotions so that the tension between expressing a highly charged experience and repressing it to a certain degree and then sending it out became a part of the ... acting form that was being evolved.

Winer also sees a development of a woman's aesthetic or form, but in a direction that heightens and uses the traditional emotional behavior patterns of women. She states:

We can't use men's forms to express our content.... One of the things that can happen with women is the very thing that we've always been told is wrong with us and we can use it – our emotionalism, our irrationalism, that whole horrific archetypal horror picture of the woman. That's how our art should be – all encompassing, sucking in, surrounding, embracing, not linear, not clear-cut, not sequential. Somehow related, in fact, to what men very recently have begun to touch upon, men as different as Marshall McLuhan and Andy Warhol and several others – that male happening thing, but [that's] something that's done artistically only for the effect – because they have so little left to believe in or say. We can use that surrounding, happening everywhere, bringing together all kinds of contradictory art forms, contents, feelings, so that the audience really is submerged in the experience of being a woman.... Film, slides, music, puppets, actresses, dancers, everywhere, on top of you, below you, around you. That would be women's theatre – a circus feeling throughout the play, a circus that people could enter, complete with side show, cages, animals, human animals ... a monolog coming through speakers. A side show would be part of it, so that the whole motif of living our lives as creatures in a circus, various kinds of freaks, would really come through. And it would be a spectacle that totally surrounded one so that audience couldn't relax, they couldn't be comfortable with what was happening up there, because they shouldn't be.

3

THE WOW CAFE

Alisa Solomon

The WOW Cafe is a force more than a place. Unlike many East Village performance spaces, WOW, at 330 E. 11th Street, did not begin as a location seeking work to produce but was born the other way around. Women who had been producing a vast variety of work all over the East Village sought a permanent home. Recently, during one of their weekly open staff meetings, the 15 or so women who make up the Cafe's anarchic organizing collective spoke about the origins of their cafe. In typical WOW fashion, women periodically wandered in and out. The Cafe's oral history, recounted at this meeting for the first time, is rich – and long enough that the tellers disagree about the details of their story. At the same time, WOW's creatively amorphous organization includes enough newcomers that some women were surprised to hear there was an extensive past.

WOW began with a dream shared by Lois Weaver and Peggy Shaw. Touring in Europe in the late 1970s with Spiderwoman Theater and Hot Peaches, they met several companies who wanted to perform in the United States. They also attended many women's theatre festivals in Europe and thought it was about time one took place in America. "It became clear," says Weaver, "that if it was going to be done, we were going to have to be the ones to do it." They began to mention their vision to European companies, making it clear that the American system did not permit conditions equivalent to the ones they enjoyed in Europe; they would be unable to invite groups into a theatre that could pay even a small fee or accommodate them. "You would have to come and produce yourselves; that's how we do it," Weaver told them. Peggy Shaw, tossing in wry interjections throughout Weaver's narrative, adds with a sigh recalling exhaustion, "We didn't think they'd really fall for it. We said we'd do it, and then, all of a sudden, we had to."

And all of a sudden is how it happened. They had the idea in May 1980, and the first Women's One World (WOW) Festival took place the following October. Without any personal capital or funding, and not enough time to apply for grants, Weaver and Shaw, forming "Allied

Farces" with Jordi Mark and Pamela Camhe, began to work fanatically to create a festival that would feature international groups but also highlight national and New York women performers. Acknowledging that music and dance already had healthy circuits in place, they concentrated on theatre, with the European Festival as their deliberate model. There, one could pay one admission to see two or three shows, a movie, sit in a café and talk, and dance afterwards. "We wanted to create that sort of multimedia environment," says Weaver, "so we did. God only knows how."

One tactic was to amass a crew of volunteers, who became the backbone of the project. Throughout the summer of 1980, they produced benefits, usually in the form of wild costume parties, in donated spaces. In addition to giving the Festival exposure, these benefits acquainted the women with the vagaries of producing, accustomed them to the technical demands of their performance space, and collected a following. "We didn't raise much money," Weaver says, "but it did give us a lot in the long run in terms of exposure and experience, and we developed an audience."

Working out of the Allcraft Center on St. Mark's Place (the old Electric Circus), Allied Farces had to put up their sets right before they went on and break them down the same night. By the time the Festival arrived, they had acquired an adept technical crew. The Festival ran for two weeks with two, sometimes three, performances a night and occasional afternoon shows. Groups came from Europe, paying their own way and sleeping on floors of friends of the Festival. "We couldn't offer much," Weaver explains, "but just having a spot to perform in New York was a big deal for them. And we got them some press. That actually generated enough interest that they could come back on their own later, as Beryl and the Perils did." "We couldn't pay them," Shaw adds, "but they got a lot of attention and made a lot of contacts."

When the Festival ended, the Allcraft management, pleased with its success, offered its organizers the space to keep going. "'Why don't we do *what*?,' we said," explains Weaver, "but space was at a premium, and we felt that if someone was offering us a women's performance space, we couldn't very well refuse." They stayed until March.

In the ensuing months, they produced dance, theatre, and poetry by women every Wednesday night and sometimes on Thursday nights, splitting the receipts with the performers. As word about the space got out, résumés and brochures from performers barraged them. But just as their reputation was growing and their procedures were taking shape, they got locked out of the Allcraft Center. One night the Flamboyant Ladies, a black lesbian group, performed a show that Weaver describes as "very, very hot, very sensual." "It was beautiful," says Shaw, "but a little too sexy for the Center." It happened that near the end of the show there was a fire in the building next door that had nothing to do with the performance, but it caused some damage to the Allcraft. The next time the WOW staff came to the space, they found padlocks on the door.

There is no animosity between WOW and the Allcraft manager; the women understood that Allcraft had been under investigation by the CETA Board that funded them and were afraid of losing money. "There had been some growing tension, some homophobic kind of tension, because of that," says Weaver, "but they really had been generous. We did pay them a portion of our proceeds but not nearly as much as they could have made if they had rented the space out."

Weaver, Shaw, and the current WOW organizers do not seem disconcerted by the implicit indirect censorship from the CETA foundation. They had, after all, if not by design, acquired a reputation for producing lesbian work and expected certain attacks. Though their policy was to produce any work written or directed by a woman, or that presented a woman's sensibility, many of their benefits depended on creating environments that, depending on the theme, might include such attractions as kissing booths. However, they made no deliberate attempt to appeal exclusively to lesbians. "You didn't have to be a lesbian to get into the shows," explains Shaw, "but most of the people who came were." Then she adds jokingly, "Most either came that way or ended up that way."

Locked out, in any case, but booked for the next three months, the WOW brigade searched for a space and eventually found the ballroom at the Ukrainian Home on 2nd Avenue. It was difficult to create a congenial atmosphere in the cavernous, 86-year-old theatre, but bringing in platforms, folding chairs, and electricity enabled them to produce a month of Wednesday performances and some benefits. In the meantime, they made a connection with the University of the Streets when it was still, in Shaw's words, "just a tacky little storefront," and they staged benefits there as well.

By now it was April 1981, and time, they felt, to plan another Festival. This time, they knew they wanted to include an all-day café space where performers and spectators could hang out, and they immediately made arrangements with University of the Streets. Wanting to expand the Festival's scope, they also booked other spaces. Again they worked without substantial funding: the October 1981 WOW Festival budget amounted to $2–3,000. Each of its 11 days was packed with performances: "Pasta and Performance" at University of the Streets every day at 6.00 p.m., mainstage shows at 8:00 and 10:00 at the Ukrainian Home, 11:00 performances at Theatre for the New City, midnight Cabaret at the Centre Pub, and occasional films at Millennium. After a year, WOW had

become a full part of the international network of women performers and
attracted groups from Finland, Sweden, New Zealand, and all over
Europe. Some got money from their own countries, but most came over
on their own just because they had heard about the previous WOW
Festival.

After the second Festival, artists felt that something was missing and
realized that they did not want to give up the inspiration that working
together had generated. "It was like there was just energy left over,"
Weaver explains.

> There had been a place where you could just drop by and always run into
> someone you knew. Not only people who had been working, but also
> people who had been spectators really missed the energy after the Festival
> finished.

So this arbitrary group of people – including a huge production team of
designers and technicians – who had come together for the Festival,
began having brunches together on Sundays and talked about creating a
permanent café. According to Weaver, "This was something we always
hoped would happen, and it seemed like the perfect outgrowth of the
Festival."

This ad hoc brunch committee began to organize benefits at Club
57: costume affairs like the Freudian Slip party to which guests came
dressed in lingerie, a Debutante Ball, and "X-rated Xmas" – which
brought back one of the most controversial performers from the
Festival. Diane Torr, a performance artist making her living as a go-go
dancer in New Jersey, created a piece with her colleagues in which
they danced and talked about their lives. Many women were upset
by the show, Shaw thinks, "because they didn't know how to act,
how to react, or how to be with these women. A lot of women loved
it, but many objected to it politically." Never shying away from
controversy, they invited Torr to work on a benefit in which she
performed for an all-women audience and invited them to participate.
Other benefits included a Medical Drag Ball attended by people in
costumes dripping with blood and gore, who danced with their IVs.
Club 57, an old horror movie house in the basement of a church at
57 St. Mark's Place, was one of the first clubs in the area to feature
crazy theme parties. Appreciative of WOW's purpose and zaniness,
they rented them the space for $75 a night.

These benefits had financial, albeit modest, success. "All of a sudden
we had five or six hundred dollars in our hands that had been raised for
a café, so we started looking for spaces," says Weaver, "and one
afternoon we found 330 E. 11th. We had to talk the landlord into renting
it to us because he didn't really want any little lesbian theatre in his

building." "We told him we wanted it for a women's resource center," Shaw explains, "but," adds Weaver, "he took one look at us and said, 'Oh. I have a son who's gay.' We had learned by then that you have to be up front right from the start because we didn't want to put our hearts into something and end up disappointed."

Since opening in March 1982, the WOW Cafe has presented innumerable poets, performers, plays, films, videos, and art exhibits. Continually reconsidering the Cafe's purposes, the staff molds its flexible shape to meet its constituents' changing interests and needs. They began literally as a café, serving coffee and toasted brie sandwiches, simply, as Mo Angeles says, "because we had called it a café. So we had to serve coffee."

The space was named "WOW at 330" to signify both its address and the hour, as Weaver puts it, "when girls get out of school and go out looking for fun." It was open from 3:30 until 11:00 p.m. – a feasible prospect since everyone on the staff had a key – and truly became a social center. "But what we really wanted," says Weaver, "was a women's performance space. We also wanted a hangout, a girls' social club." Unsure of their institutional identity, the dozen or so amorphously organized staff (anyone who showed up to an open staff meeting automatically joined the staff) argued over whether to have a pool table, what color to paint the ceiling, and whether paintings should be left on the walls during performances. "We eventually learned," Shaw says, "that you could do anything you wanted in the space when nobody else was there." Every time they would come in, they explained laughingly, someone else's paintings would be newly hung.

Without explicitly declaring their intentions for 330, its organizers expressed their plans when one of the first things they did was to construct a platform stage at one end of the room and hang a curtain. The stage, like the entire space, is barely 10 feet wide. With its floor of octagonal ceramic tiles, patterned along one side, the room seems like it might have been someone's vestibule or, even earlier, half of a dining room. Now, impossibly narrow and maybe 20 feet long, it hardly contains a dozen or so rows of folding chairs. The homemade lightboard of household dimmers sits in the center of the room, controlling a handful of small, outdoor-type reflector lamps – all the electrical system can accommodate. The backstage area is a 10 feet by 10 feet jumble of old props, bits of costumes, and chunks of sets. The Cafe's original excuse, an enormous coffee-maker, is stashed in a corner.

In its early days, the Cafe kept afloat by selling food and memberships. For $60 a year, members got half-price admissions to performances. Although this was not much of a bargain since performances were not yet very regular, it offered patrons a way to support the Cafe where they "hung out." Membership reached 120 within a few months. Performance booking remained erratic until Holly Hughes emerged to take on the management of the Cafe. She instituted a number of regular events that increased the Cafe's visibility, brought more regular customers, and attracted more writers, comics, and actors. She orchestrated a number of brunches, for instance, and created the popular "Talking Slide Show," where artists would show their slides and talk about their work. Variety nights also caught on, providing opportunities for many inchoate artists to work on material without having to face the risks and mechanics of mounting entire productions. Countless East Village performers got their start in these casual shows. Hughes herself developed her first piece, *Shrimp in a Basket*, at the Cafe, and then *Well of Horniness*, which went on to become a popular Lower East Side cult piece, playing at the Pyramid Club, Limbo Lounge, and on WBAI Radio. Tammy Whynot, a character in Split Britches' most recent play, *Upwardly Mobile Home*, first appeared at a talent night. And Carmelita Tropicana, a persona created by Alina Troyano, was born almost by accident. Troyano, drawn to the Cafe because of its sense of humor, went on for an emcee who did not show up one night and, she proclaims, never came off. Recently she performed at the Chandalier and the Limelight.

After about a year, Holly Hughes was exhausted by her non-paying, full-time management of the Cafe and decided to leave. Therefore, in the spring of 1983, the roughly 15 women who still comprised WOW's collective management called a retreat to determine their next steps. "What happens, unfortunately, when one person is in charge of all the details," Weaver says, "is that the collective sort of vanishes and leaves all the little decisions up to that one person. So we had to regroup. This meeting was really a turning point for the Cafe."

The women who gathered for the weekend were tired and knew that something had to change. "We were no longer just a café," says Weaver. "Now we wanted to be serious about being a performance space, a cultural center." So they sat around a big table, and each person recommended what she would like to see happen in the coming season. They drew up a month-by-month list of the suggestions – and produced every one of them the following year.

Worried about Hughes' departure, the WOW collective remained uncertain about the Cafe's definition and wondered whether all of its functions could coexist gracefully. "We wanted to be an art space, a theatre space, a hangout, and have as much input from the community as possible," Troyano remarks, "but how do you maintain that?" As usual though, things fell into place. Because they had sketched out a calendar for the season, Weaver believes, "each month just materialized. It wasn't as if anyone was there holding us to it, it just sort of happened because the calendar had to be filled in each month ahead of time, so we just did it; it was pretty magical."

That magic was replaced by a less ethereal if equally powerful force in fall 1983 when Susan Young took over as booking manager. "I had just moved here," she relates.

> I didn't know any of these women, I hadn't seen any WOW Festivals or really knew that they had existed. But I came here and saw Split Britches perform and knew immediately that this was where I wanted to work.

Since then, she has been designing WOW productions and carrying out day-to-day managerial tasks. Under her direction, informed by the collective, the Cafe has turned in slightly new directions. While continuing to book anyone who requests space, Young has also set up some regular events whose management she turns over to the groups involved. Each Sunday night from September 1984 until Christmas, for example, is directed by the Asian Lesbians of the East Coast. "Instead of taking individual bookings for a jam session here, a film showing there, we decided that this group would put together its own evenings. The outcome has been incredible: films, videos, poetry readings, music." This arrangement also serves a growing aim of the Cafe – to reach out to a more racially mixed audience.

At the same time, cafeniks are beginning to rethink their policy of allowing anyone with an interest to book the Cafe, not only because they want to put their energy into producing their own work, but also because they are sometimes displeased with the results. "We still want to provide a producing service to the community," says Young,

> but women come in expecting a great deal and don't give anything back to the space. There are a lot of women who aren't regulars here who come in and perform, put holes in the wall, break our light-board, and split, and don't even think of ever coming to a staff meeting or even to a performance by another woman.

More abstract issues such as the risks that works will be artistically bad, politically inconsistent with the Cafe's tacit feminism, or just poorly executed increasingly concern the staff. Yet they would rather tolerate occasional disasters than audition women for the space; that, they believe, would amount to censorship. "We're always criticized for not auditioning," Shaw complains. "We're told, 'Now that you've been around you have to have quality work.' But we feel the minute you start auditioning you become just like anybody else."

These issues may become less pressing as the Cafe moves toward its year-long goal of putting on work from within its own community – a priority not as cliquish as it may sound since anyone who hangs around is absorbed into that community. Facing some of the difficulties posed by outside performers, Young explains, "We wondered, why are we breaking our backs producing so many other women when our own work is not a priority?" This past season they decided to rectify the situation and to make concrete proposals for in-house bookings. Just as booking a calendar the year before provided the structured impetus to keep the Cafe going then, this new commitment generated creative work and pushed WOW women toward inventing and finishing new projects.

The most experienced of the WOW regulars is the Split Britches company, comprised of Lois Weaver, Peggy Shaw, and Deborah Margolin. Their recent work-in-progress, *Upwardly Mobile Home*, has been shown twice at the Cafe, once in the spring of 1984 and again, further developed, in the fall. Though there is probably no such thing as a typical WOW performance, Split Britches crystallizes some of the distinguishing qualities from which one might be able to infer a WOW sensibility.

Upwardly Mobile Home takes place in 1986 after Reagan's re-election. Three actors in a theatre company, who are preparing a production of a 1920s hit, *Shanghai Gesture*, are camping out under the Brooklyn Bridge, homeless. There, one woman peddles her old clothes, another sells instant coffee over the phone, and all three fantasize, argue, and rehearse their show. A bizarre sense of humor combines with a barrage of intersecting ideas to create a complex criticism of American myths. Formally inventive, the piece follows a day in the life of these actresses, with overlapping monologs, songs, and play-within-a-play sequences.

Other WOW productions so far lack Split Britches' dramatic sophistication. But *Heart of the Scorpion*, "a lesbian Harlequin Romance" by Alice Forrester, also reflects some of WOW's typical energetic zaniness. Forrester's production also came out of the Cafe's recent push to produce more in-house work. Another reason for this shift in emphasis is that the Cafe might lose its lease at 330 E. 11th when it comes up for renewal in March. "We wanted to be sure we would still have definition even if we lose the space," explains Weaver, "so we created a number of regular projects to fall under the umbrella of WOW Productions." In addition to Split Britches' and Forrester's work, these projects have included the Lower East Side Girls' Chorus, a loose collection of women who got together to sing; "Holl's Dolls," a group directed by Holly Hughes that is currently working on a new version of *Bye Bye Birdie*; "High Fiber Comedy," featuring the comic Reno; and the Working Girls Repertory, a newly formed ongoing women's repertory. Working Girls Repertory premiered in December with an adaptation of Hans Christian Andersen's

The Snow Queen, adapted by Shaw and directed by Weaver. Incorporating storytelling techniques with dramatic representation, the play offers a subtly feminist revision of the fairy tale.

If the Cafe has not declared any manifestos to define the nature of WOW productions, some common themes and aesthetics have emerged. Feminism and lesbianism appear in the shows not as issues but as givens. If there is an overriding artistic impulse, says Young, "it's simply to invent from what we have. We can't afford to go out and buy things, so our limits determine our creativity." What is true literally of the sets and costumes applies equally to the material of the plays – it is drawn from the women's lives. The stylistic result is an attention to detail, an approach Weaver calls "a feminine aesthetic because its details are often forgotten or stepped over in male-dominated works. But little parts of our lives are as important as the big climactic events that usually make dramas." Often, for instance, they work from simple images or from examining a single day in a character's life. Their method of working also reflects a feminist intention with its implicit rejection of mainstream hierarchy; jobs are defined and individuals take responsibility for specific tasks, but everyone contributes to creative processes in discussion, and anyone can become part of the Cafe staff simply by choice.

Working within limitations may be a fruitful challenge, Shaw is quick to point out, but she thinks they would do just as well with plenty of money and a big space. But chances are they won't ever have to worry about money cramping their creativity because they have slim prospects of ever acquiring much cash flow. Members of the WOW staff disagree about applying for grants. Some, like Troyano, believe that no one wants to bother sitting down to write proposals. Angelos likes the idea of grants, but found when she did some research that "the kinds of things I thought we might be able to get money for were not really the kinds of things we wanted to do." And Shaw worries that "grants change you. You get grants, people come in and *judge* you, and you start thinking that you better not do anything that will make them take your grant away." "Butch and femme night?" someone chimes in referring to a past extravaganza, "Forget it."

To compensate, WOW still throws benefits now and then; some of the best ones, the staff claims, have been rent parties. And some of them have been known to beg on the street, in Shaw's words, "guilt-tripping our friends into writing checks." It does not help that the Cafe has been robbed periodically. "Don't publish that we just bought a new projector," Angelos jokes. The life of Cafe property has averaged three or four months. They had speakers for only a month and have lost many bicycles. Shaw says, "They used to come here and even drink our beer, throw the cans on the floor, and leave the toilet seat up. But that stopped many months ago. Things feel safer."

The Cafe is even safer in a figurative sense. Anyone is encouraged to get up and perform at WOW and, says Weaver, "that encouragement creates a freedom to express oneself. Once a performer feels safe, you can train her." Troyano agrees and considers the support she gets from her WOW colleagues a crucial element of her progress. "People here will be critical of your work," she says, "but they'll criticize in a positive way that's helpful when you go out to perform in the other theatre world."

Though several of the WOW women refer to "the real theatre world," they do not really feel isolated or illegitimate. A number of WOW technicians and designers are hired by Equity productions, and the Cafe is known as a resource for good stage managers and technical people. But what gives WOW its strength is its independence: It needs no external sanctioning in order to survive because it has a loyal, critical audience of women of various backgrounds who consider the Cafe vital. "We do want criticism," Weaver points out. "We don't want to be ghettoized, but we also like the safe, growing atmosphere." "It's a place to learn the craft," says Troyano, "while you're doing it." Above all, Weaver continues,

> the WOW Cafe is community theatre in the best sense – it's creating theatre of, for and by the community. If we have a big show to put on, we don't go outside to find a more talented actress, for instance, or a more talented and expensive lighting designer. We pull all the resources from the community as it continues to form itself.

That's why WOW will survive even if they have to leave 330 E. 11th. WOW's community is defined by a force bigger than geography.

4

NOTES ON LESBIAN THEATRE

Emily L. Sisley

What *is* lesbian theatre? One may cite any of the following operational definitions:

- Lesbian theatre is about lesbians – i.e., content is structured around a theme that deals with the experiences, thoughts, and/or "lifestyles" of lesbians.
- Lesbian theatre is by lesbians – i.e., plays written by lesbians are lesbian plays regardless of theme.
- Lesbian theatre is played by lesbians – i.e., plays are lesbian when they feature gay women, whether out or closeted (like so many of the "greats" everyone knows about but no one talks about).
- Lesbian theatre is feminist theatre – i.e, because of its focus on woman/woman relationships, all feminist theatre is essentially lesbian theatre.
- Lesbian theatre is distinct from feminist theatre – i.e, lesbian plays concentrate on lesbian relationships rather than woman/woman relationships in general.
- Lesbian theatre is part of, but not the same as, feminist theatre – i.e., the shared focus differs from the sharp distinctions between "gay (male) theatre" and "straight (male) theatre."
- Lesbian theatre is consciousness-raising in performance – i.e., the lesbian audience requires theatre specifically dedicated to clarifying points concerning oppression, the validity of woman-to-woman relationships, and heroism divorced from male identity.
- Lesbian theatre is part of gay theatre – i.e., themes concerning homosexual relationships may apply to either gender and/or to shared elements of homoesthetics of homoeroticism.
- There is no such thing as lesbian theatre – i.e., theatre is theatre, whether gay or straight.

There is an element of truth in *each* of the above-noted definitions; the most accurate definition could probably be made from bits and pieces of all of them, with additions and/or corrections invited from any and all sources.

At the risk of offending some sister-lesbians, one may borrow a definition written by a man. With the word "lesbian" substituted for the words "gay" and "homosexual," the following is quoted from William Hoffman's Introduction to *Gay Plays: The First Collection* (Avon, 1979), "I define [lesbian] theatre as a production that implicitly or explicitly acknowledges that there are [lesbians] on both sides of the footlights." Such a description allows for a wide range of approaches. One can hold that lesbian theatre is basically feminist theatre because the latter "explores the dynamics occurring between women," to quote Clare Coss. Or, as Atthis Theatre's Keltie Creed puts it: "the dividing line between feminist and lesbian is quite elastic." At the same time, one might agree with feminist-theatre pioneer Sue Perlgut. Perlgut thinks that lesbian theatre is "very much about lesbians, their lesbianism, and their relationships." Too, such a general definition also permits inclusion of Jane Chambers' sentiment about gay plays: "The world calls them that, and producers call them that. As far as I'm concerned, they are *plays*."

Lesbian theatre as we know it today must inevitably be tied to the great surge of feminism associated with the 1960s and early 1970s. Two of the first woman-identified theatres were Caravan Theatre (Lexington, MA), founded in 1965, and Omaha Magic Theatre, founded in 1969. In view of common problems such as collectivism vs. hierarchy, message vs. entertainment, specialized audience vs. general audience, etc., it is particularly noteworthy that these ongoing companies have survived with their original founders. This is not the case with two other organizations almost as venerable. Neither Synthaxis Theatre (South Pasadena, CA), 1972, nor the Rhode Island Feminist Theatre (Providence), 1973, retains any of its original members.

In New York City, 1969 saw the birth of the New York Feminist Theatre with Lucy Winer and Claudette Charbonneau. In 1970, feminists founded the Westbeth Playwright's Feminist Collective and also It's All Right To Be a Woman Theatre [see *TDR*54], with theatre-activist Sue Perlgut maintaining that women's culture deserved to be shown and "nobody else will [show it]." Womanrite Theater Ensemble and Women's Interart Center started in 1972. Roberta Sklar, then at the forefront of feminist theatre, remains extremely active [see *TDR*86]. Along with Clare Coss and Sondra Segal, she founded the Women's Experimental Theatre in 1977. The three women share authorship of *Elektra Speaks*. This play (Part III of *The Daughters Cycle*) is not called a lesbian play, but its theme – woman learning to be her own, independent spokesperson – holds considerable appeal for lesbians, explicit or implicit, on both sides of the footlights. The work was again produced in the late fall of 1980 at The Women's Interart Annex in New York, and extensive excerpts were published in the *Union Seminary Quarterly Review* (spring/summer 1980).

The growth of feminist theatre has continued – with some, such as At the Foot of the Mountain (Minneapolis, 1974), producing successfully over a period of years. However, more than two dozen companies have been dormant for varying periods of time. These companies include Women of the Burning City (sometimes erroneously cited as being the *first* troupe to explore the real lives of women), New York's The Cutting Edge, the New Feminist Theatre, and It's All Right To Be a Woman (although Sue Perlgut is forming a new group, with a production planned for the spring of 1981).

With some collaboration by Phyllis Mael and Beverly Byers Pevitts, Rosemary Curb of Rollins College published an extensive "Catalog of Feminist Theatre" in *Crysalis*, no. 10. This material, which Curb continues to update, provides a useful rundown. Another source, published late in 1980, is *Feminist Theatre Groups* (Jefferson, NC: McFarland & Co.) by Dinah Luise Leavitt. With such references available, it seems unnecessary to pursue further listing here – except to note women's theatre groups that have *specifically* identified themselves as lesbian.

They are relatively few.

Starting in 1973, two associated groups emerged in Minneapolis: the Lavender Cellar and the Minneapolis Lesbian Resource Center. They first produced Pat Suncircle's *Prisons* and then, following a series of revue-type presentations, did the full-length play *Cory*, also by Suncircle. The script (which is on file at the Lesbian Herstory Archives in New York) portrays the dilemma of a 16-year-old girl trapped between her self-acknowledged lesbianism and the pressures of a hostile world.

> ... the play focuses on the character of Cory and her fear and frustration, [but] it also deals with related aspects of the same problem through Denise, who has not come to terms with her homosexuality, and Susan, who has. Society's rejection and misunderstanding of lesbianism is shown through the students who giggle about it, the school psychologist who regards it as mental illness, the mother who cannot even discuss it and the father who believes that sexual intercourse with a male will cure it. Sex-role stereotyping is presented through Cory's parents, who attempt to make a young lady of her, and through Susan's parents, who found motherhood under any circumstances preferable to lesbianism.
>
> (Feminist Theatre Groups)

Of course, not all lesbian plays view lesbianism in terms of grief, frustration, and inner struggling against outside rejection. For example, Kate Kasten's *On the Elevator* (also preserved by Deborah Edel and Joan

Nestle at the Lesbian Herstory Archives) features two characters called Dyke 1 and Dyke 2:

> Initially repelled by the frankness of the conversation between Dyke 1 and Dyke 2, other elevator passengers back away. Then, slowly, one by one, each acknowledges her or his own homosexuality: the old woman, the hard-hat, the waitress, the child, the businessman, the teenager, and the janitor. The skit celebrates the coming-out process.

Another of the many scripts on file is *December to May*, a play by Jane Staab in which husbands must confront their wives' falling in love.

But, for the moment, less of plays and more of theatre companies.

Other "early" groups plainly identifying themselves as lesbian rather than feminist started in the mid-1970s and, like the Minneapolis organizations, seem not to have survived. The Red Dyke Theatre in Atlanta, Georgia, was founded in 1974. According to Curb's listing, their main purpose was "to entertain lesbians and celebrate their sexuality, *not* to educate straight people about lesbians and gay issues." On the other hand, the Lesbian-Feminist Theatre Collective of Pittsburgh (organized in 1977) set about to dispel "myths about lesbians for straight audiences." *Medusa's Revenge* (New York), 1977, aimed to explore "a homoesthetic sensibility" in theatre that played to women-only audiences.

Other lesbian theatre groups have survived and several have been started in the past year. Companies currently producing include – among others – the Lesbian Community Theatre in East Lansing, Michigan; the Washington Area Feminist Theatre (Judith Katz); the Cambridge (MA) Lesbian Theatre, with Sequoia as artistic director; Atthis Theatre in Toronto, Canada; and The Whole Works, a collective in Berkeley, California. More than 20 other groups identify themselves as "lesbian/ gay theatre companies" and perhaps half a dozen are described by the Gay Theatre Alliance as "not specifically gay theatre companies, but either regularly do gay plays, or are closely related to the concerns of gay theatre." Still others are on no special list. For example, it seems highly unlikely that either Georgetown University or Alabama's Tri-State University would care to have themselves classified as lesbian. Yet both these institutions performed Jane Chambers' *A Late Snow*, described in the *Gay Theatre Alliance Directory of Gay Plays* (New York: JH Press, Terry Helbing, editor) as follows:

> Five women are snowbound in an isolated cabin: Ellie, a college professor; Perfect Peggy, Ellie's first lover; Pat, an antique dealer, Ellie's last lover; Quincey, a college student, Ellie's current lover; and Margo, a novelist, Ellie's next lover.

Thus at this time, it seems that the production of lesbian theatre need not necessarily be confined to groups that specifically define themselves as lesbian. This lends some strong support to those who have maintained there is really no dividing line between what is lesbian and what is feminist. In 1974, Charlotte Rea quoted the New York Feminist Theatre's explanation:

> We do not feel a lesbian/heterosexual split ... every member of the cast, lesbians and heterosexual women, assumes the lesbian role at one point or another. At the end of the scene, the entire cast declares their lesbianism.
>
> (*The Drama Review*, T54)

During the same era, the It's All Right To Be a Woman Theatre consistently explored problems they felt applied to both gay and straight women. And as recently as late November of 1980, Sondra Segal explained that by "unearthing what's suppressed' and by being "woman-identified, woman-centered, and addressed to and derived by women" feminist theatre can be equated with *coming out*, hence reflecting the special experiences and sensibilities of lesbians.

What are some of the other ways in which lesbian theatre can be compared with feminist theatre? In both categories, most groups – especially in "the early days" – started out as collectives. Many worked not with scripts and not with directors, but tended to pool their individual experiences into material they believed would reflect both the uniqueness and the universality of women's lives.

Somehow the collectivity did not always work – especially when theatre took a back seat to feminist rhetoric. More and more, theatre groups have returned to written scripts (even when, as with *Elektra Speaks*, early readings incorporate audience feedback and a gradually built script emerges slowly over a period of time). A number of companies have also returned to the use of directors, people trained in acting, and more sophisticated staging techniques.

Other comparisons can be made with the ways in which both lesbian and feminist theatre draw from the experiences of women as *women* experience them (not as men think they do); the importance of woman/woman relationships (mother/daughter, sister/sister, aunt/niece, friend/friend, lover/lover); an emphasis on personal, internal reality; retelling old stories (e.g., classic myths, socio-political history, societal expectations) from a female or feminist perspective; and a reliance on other women for support.

These shared aspirations can perhaps be neatly summarized by quoting a few lines from a chart prepared by At the Foot of the Mountain (Minneapolis) after the group became an all-female, feminist theatre collective:

Male Patriarchal Values	Female Matriarchal Values
Product	Process
Codified	Changing
Competitive	Supportive
Abstract ideas	Concrete images/details

What are some of the ways in which lesbian theatre can be compared with just plain theatre? In February 1980, *Last Summer at Bluefish Cove* by Jane Chambers opened at a small theatre in the Chelsea area of New York City. That spring it moved uptown to Mainstage Two. By late fall–early winter, it graduated to the Actors Playhouse in Greenwich Village. *Last Summer at Bluefish Cove* takes place at a lesbian vacation spot on Long Island. Seven women, old friends, have gathered in their usual summer cottages preparing as best they can to enjoy what they all know will be Lil's last summer. Through a "slip-up" on the part of a realtor, one of the cottages is rented to Eva, a straight woman who has just left her husband. Lil and Eva fall in love and their relationship heavily affects the entire group.

The play – produced by The Glines and directed by Nyla Lyon – was remarkable in its capacity to draw not only lesbians and gay males but also a general audience of straight people ranging from teens to senior citizenry. Chambers says that "nobody seems to be concerned that it's about a love affair between two women. They seem most concerned that it's two hours of good entertainment."

Commercial success – along with a broader, general audience – also came to Chambers after *A Late Snow* was published in *Gay Plays: The First Collection*. Until that time, the play had been produced only once – at the Clark Center (New York) by Playwrights Horizons in 1974. Hoffman's book was released in 1979, and by December 1980 *A Late Snow* had been produced not only at Georgetown and Tri-State Universities but also by the following companies: the Lysistrata Women's Group (Madison, WI); Third Base Productions (Fayetteville, AR); The Painted Ladies Theatre Company (Winnipeg, Canada); the Rochester (NY) group first called The Up Front Production Company then Rising Productions; The Celebration Company (Urbana, IL); Helena Fesbians (Helena, MT); The Out-and-About Theatre (Minneapolis); Atthis Theatre (Toronto, Canada); and the Lesbian Community Theatre (East Lansing, MI).

No matter how one chooses to define lesbian theatre, both *A Late Snow* and *Last Summer at Bluefish Cove* are very much about lesbians – yet both also hold their own as commercial successes with a general audience.

So if lesbian theatre shares much with feminist theatre and much with theatre-in-general, what needs to be added about it that makes it special? Let's check with representatives of currently functioning companies that define themselves as *lesbian*.

The Atthis Theatre in Toronto is a small, nonprofessional group that "grew from and grows around a particular audience: a lesbian audience." Keltie Creed further explains that the group is comprised of "lesbians using theatre for expression more than thespians focusing on lesbian-ism."

As has been true with a great number of such companies, Atthis Theatre conducts open discussions after performances, and audience participation has yielded a number of themes and issues that are dealt with in workshops and explored through work-in-progress productions. A few examples are child custody, dual-family merging, coming out ("emotionally, socially, politically, and sexually," Creed elaborates), harassment, sexuality, roles, and relationships.

For Atthis Theatre this scheme has worked well because Creed and her associates have experienced difficulties in their script searches. This is ascribed partly to "lack of quality material, partly to lack of contacts, and partly because scripts have been confiscated by [Canadian? USA?] postal customs officials." On the latter, Creed observes: "This has never happened to me in my straight theatre experience."

Creed is among those who find "much of feminist theatre ... to be lesbian." Atthis Theatre presents only works written by women. "I don't choose to pour my energy and the energy of the women with whom I work into the expression of a man's conception of our life when so many women are struggling to find media for their voices." Then Creed adds a little wistfully: "I just wish that we could connect with more of those voices."

Like many women in theatre, Creed complains about the absence of "a network to plug into" (as well as a lack of resource people and money). But when *A Late Snow* was published, Creed directed a production in 1979 with a cast that included Lyne Waddington (with Shelagh McNally as alternate), Shelagh MacGillivary, Sheila Miller, Kate Swann, and Marcia Cannon.

Speaking for The Whole Works – a lesbian theatre group in Berkeley, California – Eliza Roaring Springs echoes Creed's complaint about the difficulty in obtaining suitable material: "We write our own material largely out of necessity. Since it is so difficult to get material published to begin with, the amount written has been limited, and access to it is next to impossible." Roaring Springs also agrees that "feminist theatre as a larger category also encompasses our form of lesbian theatre." She defines lesbian theatre as "theatre performed by lesbians, primarily for lesbians, [presenting] our experience of life from a lesbian perspective." However, she notes that "lesbian theatre encompasses many different forms. Ours is shaped by our strong socialist and feminist consciousness."

During the spring of 1980, The Whole Works toured the West Coast rather extensively (as far north as Seattle) with *Ain't It Something*. Using a wide variety of theatrical styles (ranging from song and dance to tragedy and satire), the play takes on a number of socio-political issues: occupational health, tenants' rights, gay oppression, and others. One skit involves two lesbians at their respective office parties: one is out, one is in the closet.

Sequoia, artistic director of The Cambridge Lesbian Theatre, would probably agree with Roaring Springs' statement that "lesbian theatre encompasses many different forms." While hardly oblivious to the more "political" aspects of lesbian/feminist theatre (the subtitle to her play *First Lover* is "the Anti-Death-Culture Scream"), Sequoia celebrates the sheer joy of declaring lesbianism. "To get on stage and cry, sing and laugh out loud that you are a lesbian, that you believe in lesbianism, that you are *happy* to be a lesbian" is an experience Sequoia believes to be especially liberating. She decries the long years of silence and cites Diana Davies (author of *The Witch Papers*), who calls her show "the voices of women whirling through the silence."

The question of searching for scripts remains essentially unanswered. Obviously publication of *A Late Snow* propelled the play into a number of productions. Also helpful are various lists (such as Curb's) and some reasonably thorough collections (such as that of The Lesbian Herstory Archives). Yet Sequoia mentions several lesbian shows performed in New Orleans in 1977 and 1978 (*Dyke Drama Drag Show*, *Outlaw Music* and I'm Gonna Live To Be an Old Womon Theatre's *Free Womon*) that seem to have escaped notice. There are probably countless others. And although some organizations have sought to collect lesbian scripts, how many theatre groups have ready access to, for example, The Lesbian Herstory Archives?

In the *Directory of Gay Plays* – omitting mixed authorship (i.e., a woman and a man), "lost plays," and works that have seen only British productions – the female–male ratio is startling.

Female Playwrights	Male Playwrights
15	250

However, scanty as the references that have been given here may be, evidence indicates that we can all be perfectly certain that there are hundreds of lesbian plays out there – many of which have never been produced but, clearly, including a sizeable number that have been staged.

One thing that is very much needed is a complete cataloging of all lesbian plays (as distinguished from feminist plays that do not specifically state their lesbian orientation). The compilation could begin with plays that have been produced – anywhere and under whatever circumstances! – and be supplemented by a listing of unproduced works the authors of which, singly or collectively, consider ready for presentation on stage.

Another educational tool for creating heightened general awareness would be more of the kind of work done by writer-director Terry Wolverton. At a Lesbian Art Project held in May 1979 in downtown Los Angeles, Wolverton and a dozen collaborators presented *An Oral Herstory of Lesbianism* with storytelling, magic, and theatre. As a kind of journey into lesbian consciousness, the women sought to answer theatre-related questions such as: Is it performance? Is it art? Is it theatre? Is it therapy? The resulting 24-scene revue (to quote the *Directory of Gay Plays*) "[explores] issues such as coming out, coming on, mothers, racism, homophobia, incest, team sports, butch and femme roles, sexuality and lesbian future visions, combining music, dance, performance and video." Also helpful would be more festivals or congresses where people are able to *see* lesbian theatre. The sheer availability of so many and such diverse productions would also offer the added advantage of inviting critical commentary by viewers whose expertise can further increase awareness. Case in point: Rosemary Curb has written and lectured abut her reflections on the First Women's Theatre Festival. This festival was held in Boston in May 1980 and featured more than 20 women's groups – some of them explicitly lesbian. Similarly, in the 22 January 1981 issue of *The Advocate*, Jane Chambers describes her reaction to several performances given at the Women's One World Festival (New York, October 1980). Sponsored by the Allcraft Foundation and Allied Farces (a group that includes two members of Spiderwoman), the festival presented 49 theatre events. Uncloseted lesbian representation was quite prevalent, with companies such as The Radical Lesbian Feminist Terrorist Comedy Group and performers such as Robin Tyler and Pat Bond.

While – just as in straight theatre – companies come and go, it seems clear that lesbian theatre is here to stay. It's theatre that, according to Keltie Creed, is attracting women who "had never seen a play before." Thus people involved with theatre in general might want to show particular support for attempts to explore and describe the genre.

And for lesbians in theatre, better understanding of the specialness and/or nonspecialness of lesbian theatre should lead not to constraints but rather to greater artistic freedom and increased access to the *stage* side of the footlights.

After all, isn't making the implicit explicit a shared aim of *all* theatre?

WOMEN AT THE HELM

In Leadership Posts Once Reserved for Men, They're Challenging Our Assumptions About Sex and Power

Misha Berson

It has been so gradual a revolution, so long overdue, so inevitable, that very little media hype has greeted it. Yet slowly, quietly, without manifestos or banners or victory marches, a changing of the guard has begun in the American regional theatre movement.

Women artists are, at last, breaking through the glass rafters, and taking charge of some of the country's largest nonprofit theatre establishments.

This is news – at least in terms of recent changes, and serious numbers validate them. From the pioneering 1960s through the consolidating early 1980s, the artistic directors who guided the creative affairs for most of America's major resident nonprofit stages – the "anchor" institutions with the heftiest budgets, longest subscriber lists, most generous endowments, and widest community visibility – were largely men. Yes, women held the top administrative posts at many major theatres, and filled other key jobs – literary manager, production manager, even associated artistic director. And a few gutsy female directors – Zelda Fichandler at Arena Stage, to name one of the most visible and dominant – did start their own high-profile regional reps, and remained at the helm as their companies solidified and expanded. But there seemed to be room at the top for only a few women leaders – a few exceptions, like the sprinkling of female faces in the US Senate.

Tremors of change stirred in the late 1980s, when a generation of entrenched male founder-artistic directors began to retire or move onto new pursuits. And surprise, surprise: waiting in the wings was a platoon of well-schooled, dynamic and (in some cases) controversial female theatre artists who had risen up through the regional ranks and were ready, willing and able to take over.

During the last five years, Emily Mann succeeded Nagle Jackson as the leader of Princeton's McCarter Theatre Center for the Performing

Arts. JoAnne Akalaitis inherited founding producer Joseph Papp's mantle at the New York Shakespeare Festival. Anne Bogart was chosen as Adrian Hall's replacement at the Trinity Repertory Company in Providence, RI, and Irene Lewis assumed Stan Wojewodski's top post at Center Stage in Baltimore.

Each one was the first woman to be granted the chief artistic job at those theatres. The same can be said of Sharon Ott at Berkeley Repertory Theatre; Carey Perloff at San Francisco's American Conservatory Theater; Libby Appel at Indiana Repertory Theatre; Margaret Booker at Florida's Asolo Theatre Company; Josephine Abady at the Cleveland Play House; Tanya Berezin at Circle Repertory Company in New York; Timothy Near at San Jose Repertory Theatre; and Mame Hunt at San Francisco's Magic Theatre – all of whom took the wheel within the last decade.

But numbers tell only a fraction of the story. What does this gradual yet pronounced gender shift really signify, if anything? Certainly it reflects an overall trend of increased executive opportunities for American women in the arts, as well as in other professions. And surely it is, to some degree, a by-product of the modern feminist movement, which encouraged more women to study and train as directors, start their own alternative drama companies, seek out and compete for coveted positions of authority in arenas where men had long reigned, and challenge the antiquated perception that these jobs were somehow beyond a woman's reach.

Yet once women do rise to the top, does the theatrical landscape change in some fundamental way?

On the surface, perhaps not. Some of the women who have recently moved into positions of authority at the larger theatres are flourishing; others have vividly floundered. Nothing surprising there: men also succeed and fail.

But there are provocative unspoken questions hovering over this entire breakthrough generation of theatrical women, questions that their male peers do not routinely face. Questions like: What impact does gender have on one's executive successes and failures? Have anti-female bias and gender tokenism really been vanquished, or do they continue to pop up in subtle and subversive ways?

Does the diverse crop of new female artistic directors really share common ties beyond basic biology? Are they accepted on the same terms, judged by the same standards, viewed through the same microscope as male counterparts doing the same job? Or are there actually intrinsic, fundamental contrasts in male and female aesthetics and leadership styles – or just intractable double standards in the way each gender is perceived in power roles? Is the playing field truly level yet?

Libby Appel

A NATURAL SEGUE

It's a difficult and often wrenching experience for many, but Libby Appel found the transition to artistic director to be "a very natural segue." Her unique career path led her from a long stretch in academia (which included five years as head of the acting program at California State University at Long Beach and eight years as Dean of the Theatre School at California Institute of the Arts) through a frenetic four-year period freelance directing all over the country (during which time she crowded seven shows a year into a killer schedule) to her current position as artistic director of Indiana Repertory Theatre.

"One of the great things about doing all that freelancing was that I got to see and experience many theatres. I really felt as if I understood an awful lot about what the job was about. It didn't feel very far afield; in fact, it felt like I belonged in that job."

In the barely two years that she has been at the Indiana Rep (she was hired when former artistic director Tom Haas was killed in a traffic accident), she has moved swiftly to enhance an already healthy theatre and take it in some new directions. Appel has begun to fulfill her mission to bring diversity to every aspect of the theatre, reinvigorate the theatre's approach to the classics, increase dialogue with the community ("I've been the keynote speaker at a million functions"), expand the theatre's commitment to young people, and increase the commissioning of new projects.

In the conservative Indianapolis where, according to Appel, "paternalism of government and industry is rampant," a woman in a position of power is not a given. But Appel has not found this to be a problem for her. "I feel extremely welcomed by my board and by the community." For the first year of her tenure, she ran the theatre with two other women, managing director Victoria Nolan (now at Yale Repertory Theatre) and associate artistic director Janet Allen.

"I think the city was kind of excited about the idea of the female triumvirate. In a funny, reverse kind of way, I think the fact that I'm a woman allows me to do certain things that they haven't done here before. I don't know if that's true, it's just something I sense."

Douglas Langworthy

Or is the stage still raked – at angles not always immediately apparent?

It's hard to look squarely at these matters, let alone answer them adequately, in a time when the "gender snarl" (as some academic thinkers like to call it) has never seemed so impenetrably tangled. On the one hand, a number of young, well-publicized neo-feminist pundits like Naomi Wolf and Kate Roiphe are pushing the idea of "victimless" feminism, and researchers, such as social scientist Carol Tavris, are trying to debunk popular notions that women are, in Tavris' reverberant phrase, "the better sex, the inferior sex, or the opposite sex." On the other hand, news events like the Tailhook affair, the continuing disparity in male and female earning power, and the everyday experiences of women in the world remind us that one's sex still counts in the workplace, and in big ways.

It would take a nationwide study spanning several decades, as well as a socio-political treatise from a latter-day Simone de Beauvoir or Betty Friedan, to plumb the depths of these matters. But there is already plenty of anecdotal evidence to consider, when pondering the fascinating and enigmatic impact of gender on the power circles of American regional theatre.

And there is no shortage of women artistic directors willing to discuss the topic. For this article, I spoke with many women directors, but focused on an informal sampling: Carey Perloff at ACT and Emily Mann at the McCarter, both in the midst of their second seasons running those companies, Mame Hunt, who moved into the AD role at the Magic Theatre last year, and JoAnne Akalaitis, whose controversial dismissal from the New York Shakespeare Festival in 1993 made national headlines. These women candidly addressed a many-tentacled subject which they say often goes undiscussed at their theatres because it is considered too emotionally loaded, politically divisive, or just plain rude. And once they warmed to the topic, each had a lot to say about the potent lingering assumptions, the question marks and conflicts, that swirl around women as they enter the top levels of the regional theatre hierarchy.

Assumption #1: Women are new at this game.
I didn't think of myself as a feminist, but I have always been free.
Zelda Fichandler, director and educator

Anyone with a thorough grasp of American theatre history can easily disprove the idea that women are newcomers to leadership posts – but can we take historical awareness for granted in these post-literate times?

As the landmark 1981 sourcebook *Women in American Theatre* (Crown, 1981) (edited by Helen Krich Chinoy and Linda Walsh Jenkins and reissued by TCG in 1987) and many other, more recent works of feminist scholarship have made abundantly clear, several key women directors were instrumental visionaries and creative "matriarchs" in the earliest stages of the nation's regional theatre movement.

In fact, it's no exaggeration to say the American regional movement was largely the brainchild of women. In 1947 Margo Jones founded the highly influential Theatre 47 in Dallas and Nina Vance began the Alley

Theatre in Houston, two of the first nonprofit, professional alternatives to Broadway commercialism. Three years later young Fichandler followed suit, when she converted an old Washington DC movie house into Arena Stage.

Intrepid women were distinguishing themselves in the actor-manager capacity much earlier, too. During the 1850s, Catherine Sinclair took the alimony payments from her former husband, the famed actor Edwin Forrest, and plowed them into running the Metropolitan Theatre in San Francisco, where she became (most probably) the first female to independently manage a professional American playhouse. Soon after there arose a number of dominant women stage stars determined to control their own careers: one was Minnie Maddern Fiske, whose directing skills and producing savvy led her to create the Manhattan Theatre Company and defy the economic stranglehold of the Theatrical Syndicate.

In 1926, performer-director Eva Le Gallienne formed her visionary alternative to Broadway, the Civic Repertory Theatre. In the lively 1930s, Cheryl Crawford joined with Harold Clurman and Lee Strasberg to create the influential Group Theatre, and in the next decade, former Vassar Experimental Theatre founder Hallie Flanagan was tapped by President Franklin D. Roosevelt to spearhead the government-subsidized Federal Theater Project.

As Helen Krich Chinoy has written, "The association of women with regional, institutional, little art and alternative theatres is striking." And the back pages of American theatre are filled with female artist-manager role models, if you search for them. Yet something shifted in our culture after World War II, the same shift responsible for a retro-realignment in other professions: women receded into the background, or made important contributions from the fringes, while men clustered at the top echelons. Blame the GI Bill, which directed educational subsidies primarily toward returning male war veterans. Blame the unliberated Eisenhower Era, the postwar baby boom, the images of nuclear family tranquility and rigid gender roles piped into millions of homes via television. Blame fluoride in the drinking water, if you want to.

Whatever the matrix of causes, male artists mostly commandeered the regional theatre frontlines, where the real money was raised and large audiences congregated. And though women were instrumental in founding the anti-commercial, renegade troupes that sprang to prominence in the 1960s and 1970s like a vast field of wildflowers – such dauntless women as Judith Malina, Ellen Stewart, Megan Terry, Joan Holden, Olympia Dukakis, Lyn Austin, Julia Miles, Susan Loewenberg, Margaret Booker, Vinnette Carroll, and Lynne Meadow, to name a few – it took another dozen years for the directorships to open at those multimillion-dollar, multi-facility, community-entrenched anchor theatres, and for women to be deemed qualified enough to run them.

Assumption #2: Women artistic directors largely owe their jobs to affirmative action policies and tokenism.
I'm accustomed to thinking that I'm always going to have to knock at the door and hope that somebody will let me in, rather than thinking that I have a right or that I have a key. I don't have the key.
Roberta Levitow, director

Ask the McCarter's Emily Mann about this persistent (if largely unspoken) notion, and she gets adamant. "I was in training for this job for years," Mann declares. "Everything I've done has been preparation for me to do this job." Her résumé backs her up: it lists a degree from Harvard University, a Bush Fellowship at the Guthrie Theater, a stage-manager post at the Guthrie and the distinction of being the first woman to direct on the theatre's main stage, and a resident directorship at the BAM Theatre Company at the Brooklyn Academy of Music, not to mention her many achievements as a playwright.

Mann's background is typical of her female colleagues at other, comparable theatres – not in the particulars, but in the thorough apprenticeships most have served before snagging a status job. Sharon Ott spent years as a resident director at Milwaukee Repertory Theater, and freelanced at theatres around the country. JoAnne Akalaitis was a founder and crucial member of the experimental troupe Mabou Mines for more than a decade, then a freelancer with major credits at the Guthrie Theater, the Mark Taper Forum, and other high-profile establishments. Before taking her post at the smaller-budget Magic Theatre (which nonetheless has a big reputation for generating new plays), Mame Hunt served as a proactive dramaturg and literary manager for numerous companies associated with new play production, including the Los Angeles Theatre Center and Berkeley Repertory Theatre.

This is not to suggest that women artistic directors are any more qualified than their male counterparts. But, on the whole, they appear to be every bit as qualified, judging by the breadth and length of their experience in the field. And many speak gratefully of the men (and it was usually men) who recognized their talent, mentored and encouraged them, and recommended them for the positions they now hold.

"We've paid our dues, all of us," declares Hunt. "There are no miracle stories here, no shortcuts. We all worked shit jobs, apprenticed ourselves, watched the guys do it and learned from them."

And it's the same raw ambition men rely on, she suggests, that finally catapults women into these jobs.

> Look at the type of women who have been promoted to positions of authority and you'll see that most are seasoned, driven and extremely ambitious people, who've gotten where they are by putting themselves out there very forcefully. I think that's what boards of directors identify and see when they're looking to hire. That's the turn-on, not gender.

Irene Lewis

MOIST VERSUS DRY?

Irene Lewis bristles at the suggestion that her work may be influenced in any tangible way by her sex. "I think that posing 'gender questions' to women artistic directors diminishes the larger issues we face – those associated with the art we produce," argues the artistic director of Center Stage, a two-theatre complex with a budget of more than $3 million.

After having served as associate artist for five years and acting artistic director for six months, Lewis assumed the helm of the Baltimore company in December 1991 following the resignation of Stan Woje-wodski Jr.

Lewis has consistently balanced a freelance directing and teaching career with artistic staff positions at a series of institutional bases. Prior to her long association with Center Stage, she served as artistic director of the Philadelphia Drama Guild and associate director of the Hartford Stage Company, where she was affiliated for eight years.

"What prepared me for the artistic director job? Everything and nothing," Lewis declares. "My past experience has given me an enormous amount of knowledge for certain aspects of the job, but nothing prepared me for the *daily* tension of being a director of plays on one hand, and running an institution on the other. One of the biggest problems I face is when to be pragmatic in solving a problem and when to just insist on the art."

Among the new initiatives Lewis has brought to Center Stage are audio-described and sign-interpreted performances, a subscription series for parents offering babysitting services and a reduced subscription for adults under 30. She is as quick to scoff at the notion that any of these programs might stem from a feminine (or feminist) sensibility, however, as she is to criticize those who insist on heightening the influence of her sex on her work.

"The *Village Voice* reviewed Stan's first show as artistic director at Yale Repertory Theatre, and my first one as acting artistic director at Center Stage," Lewis notes. "One conclusion the reviewer drew was that my work was 'moist' while Stan's was 'dry.' Unbelievable!"

Stephanie Coen

> *Assumption #3:* Women are running regional theatres because a lot of highly qualified men don't want to anymore.
> *As women, our historical role has been to clean up the mess.*
> Marsha Norman, playwright

An artistic director who shall remain nameless sardonically suggested to me recently that there are more top-level theatre openings for women now because "the guys" are bailing out of the business. Her offhand comment struck a loud chord.

Let's face it: running a regional theatre in 1990s/information highway/ Beavis and Butt-head/tax-revolt America – even a theatre in tip-top fiscal and artistic shape (and how many of those are there?) – is obviously no bed of orchids. Probably it never was, not even in the glory days of William Ball and Tyronne Guthrie and Joe Papp.

But what's different today is that the average AD devotes at least as much (often more) of his or her time to fundraising, board schmoozing, community politicking, and managerial demands as to artistic tasks. The era of the 20-year tenure may be largely a thing of the past: recently two well-entrenched male heads of West Coast theatres resigned, one ostensibly because he wanted to devote more energy to acting and directing, another because Broadway opportunities were beckoning. More have moved on to better-paying, potentially glitzier opportunities in film and television, while others grew jaded or just needed a break from the nonprofit boogie.

The new wave of women (and men) replacing the old guard often walk into landmine situations. Carey Perloff, for instance, assumed control at ACT soon after an earthquake critically wounded its longtime venue, the Geary Theatre. She's still struggling to find the $24 million to repair the place. Josephine Abady, until recently the artistic head of the Cleveland Play House, inherited a crippling deficit along with her spiffy title. And by the time JoAnne Akalaitis stepped into Joseph Papp's enormous shoes, the New York Shakespeare Festival was unfocused and in financial disarray.

"Women are picking up the pieces," contends Akalaitis.

> I knew what the deficit was, and what I was getting into. But I believed in the theatre, and felt this was an opportunity to help out. I was innocent in the best sense, but I often said, "no one but a woman would be dumb enough to do this."

Remarks Perloff,

> I do think it's absolutely true that a lot of men aren't interested in these jobs anymore. It's not out of some great generosity that they've given the

reins over to women. Men tend to gravitate to where the main sources of power are, and unfortunately the status of theatre has diminished in this country. If women had the same access to the Hollywood success men have had, they'd probably be trying to make it there too. But Hollywood isn't really open to women directors, and theatre is.

While the women artistic directors I've talked with tend to concur with Perloff's acerbic analysis of the situation, they also share her excitement about "the great opportunity" this mini male exodus has created for younger artists, women, and people of color in the regional arena.

"Men are jumping ship," asserts Akalaitis,

> not because they're unfeeling idiots, but because they want a car, a house, the money to take care of their families better. There's also a kind of fatigue, brought on both by spiritual and financial institutional crisis, that just isn't part of being an independent artist.

> But women are coming aboard in the hope that there's some possibility for renewal,

she continues. "We have the energy and desire to pursue that."

Seconds Mann,

> I know the strikes against theatre, but I have an enormous stake in keeping it alive. I think theatre is essential to a civilized society, and as the world dips into a new state of barbarism I feel what we do on our stages really matters. There was a period of great despair and cynicism among some of our burned-out male leaders for a while, and it transferred over onto the boards of directors too. I think it's our role now to bring new life, new optimism and sanity back into these theatres, where it's really needed.

This same idealistic sense of mission is echoed by Hunt. She believes that women have not simply fallen into these positions by default, but because they believe fiercely in the medium.

> Ultimately I don't think it matters why these jobs are given to us," she says. "Maybe boards are so desperate, they're willing to try anything – even hiring a woman. But the bottom line for me is, I love this job. And what's the alternative? I'm just not interested in being a story editor on a Hollywood film.

Timothy Near

SAILING BEAUTIFULLY

Never mind her years as a freelance director, including interim artistic directorships at the Alliance Theatre in Atlanta and Stagewest in Springfield, MA. Never mind her years as an actress, which garnered her an Obie for her performance in Emily Mann's *Still Life*. When asked to describe what prepared her best for her current position as artistic director of the San Jose Repertory Theatre, Timothy Near hearkens back to more distant roots.

"As far as wanting to relate art to community, that really started when I was a child. We lived in a very small town, and my sister [activist folksinger Holly Near] and I were asked to sing all the time for Lion's Clubs and garden clubs. So we were always creating art to speak to a particular group of people. To me that's the most important preparation."

Near's commitment to community and activist's desire to do the impossible emboldened her to take on the San Jose Rep's enormous problems seven years ago. When she assumed leadership, the Rep built its scenery in the high school gym, had no permanent managing director or costume shop, and performed in a town hall shared with four other groups. It had a deficit of $650,000 and was about to be evicted from its offices.

"I took the job," Near remembers, "because I wanted to save a theatre for the 75,000 people that attended every year. The vision was not only to keep the boat from sinking but to put together a ship that would sail and sail beautifully."

Seven years later, captain Near has transformed the tugboat into a graceful ocean liner. Because of her success at putting the theatre back on its feet financially and cementing its importance as an artistic presence in the city, the local redevelopment agency, with the full support of San Jose Mayor Susan Hammer, is building the Rep a stunning new $16-million facility. Near has also spearheaded a creative coalition of arts groups, the Silicone Valley Arts Stabilization Campaign, through which 11 arts groups will raise $20 million and eliminate all of their debts.

How does her being a woman make a difference in her work? "I think that as a woman I'm very sensitive to human issues – human rights and equality. And as much as possible our productions reflect that."

Douglas Langworthy

Assumption #4: Women run the show differently than men do.
I believe that our aesthetic sense, whether in works of art or in lives, has overfocused on the stubborn struggle toward a single goal rather than on the fluid, the protean, the improvisatory. We see achievement as purposeful and monolothic, like the sculpting of a massive tree trunk . . . rather than something crafted from odds and ends, like a patchwork quilt. . . .
Anthropologist Mary Catherine Bateson, in *Composing a Life*

The question of the differences in power styles between women and men should be raised gingerly, and considered without the romanticism or denial that often clouds our perceptions about gender. Women who have achieved some authority tend to be understandably reluctant to make blanket generalizations vis-à-vis female behavior. Yet the differences, they will assure you, exist – and they matter.

"I do think there's a contrast in the ways women wield authority," Hunt says.

> I see it in the different work cultures of myself and my male managing director. I like lots of people to be involved in my decision-making, lots of group brainstorming. He prefers to solicit information one-on-one. Sometimes our styles are so different it drives the rest of the staff a little crazy.

Couldn't we just chalk that up to disparate personalities? Yes – if Hunt's peers didn't offer strikingly similar observations about their own work habits. Many say they are (at least theoretically) more interested in collaborative, cooperative management structures and lateral decision-making processes instead of the top-down, trickle-down authority structure that's standard in American businesses of all kinds.

"I found ACT very hierarchical when I arrived," Perloff reflects.

> It was very much an organization that had been run for a long time by a brilliant, autocratic man, and power was invested in the withholding of information. I was interested in a new structure, with much more communication. We have a policy team now, and the seven of us meet weekly.

Akalaitis goes a step further in her assessment:

> I can't imagine it isn't a different institution with a woman at the top. I do think women are more open, more playful, more responsive to change, more emotionally expressive. I know that sounds like reverse sexism. But those were my assets as an artistic director. And I didn't have to bear the burden of Western civilization on my back, like all those guys do. I could say, "I don't know."

Saying "I don't know" and being constantly open to change does not always inspire confidence in others, Perloff quickly learned. "One of the things that is associated with weakness is changing your mind. To say I've rethought it, let's do it differently – that's considered a terrible thing."

A place where ideas flow freely, where uncertainty and change can exist without panic – yet also a comfort zone where an extended family of artists is welcomed, appreciated, and trusted. That's a common ideal for women artistic directors, even if it's frustratingly difficult to achieve. Mann isn't the only one who speaks of turning her theatre into an "artistic home" for colleagues, an image that connects to female conditioning and responsibilities through the ages. "One of the best compliments I get is when someone who comes to work here tells me, 'I love the feeling in your theatre and that must be due to you,'" she reports. "I wanted to make the kind of place for artists to work in that I wished I'd had when I was a freelancer on the road."

In the writings of earlier women artistic directors, as well as in casual conversation with contemporary ones, the notion of making the theatre a magnet, a haven, a focal point for the surrounding community also arises again and again. It's in Flanagan's dream of a nationwide network of theatres responsive to their times and constituents, in Fichandler's bold idea that young, working-class, and ethnic-minority patrons were a vital part of her potential audience.

"During my two years at the Public, I think the theatre became a community center, a place where a lot of things were possible," observes Akalaitis about the New York Shakespeare Festival's theatre building in lower Manhattan. "It's something I miss now that I'm on the road again. What I always wanted to do was create a social, political, artistic community in a great theatre."

> *Assumption #5:* Women artistic directors favor plays written by women.
> *Playwriting will change not just because more women are doing it but because more women are doing other things as well.*
> Caryl Churchill, playwright

While women are still statistically underrepresented as artistic directors of the larger playhouses, consider the status of female playwrights. In the mainstage lineups especially, it is still very common to find six-play seasons in major regional companies that do not include a single work by a woman. And of those that do produce works by women, a startling few feature two or more within a given year.

Progress is being made toward greater inclusion of women writers, as well as ethnic minority authors of both sexes – but for a bevy of aesthetic, cultural and economic reasons, the change is not happening at the speed of light. And those expecting the new female theatre heads to redress the gender balance of the repertoire, and change it pronto, are barking up the wrong tree: A glance at the 1993–1994 rosters for a group of the larger women-run theatres reveals no greater number of women's scripts

Sharon Ott

DON'T FENCE HER IN

"A real problem in the American theatre is how hard it is to prepare someone for the job of artistic direction – it's something you have to learn on the job, and that's tough," says Sharon Ott, who has filled that difficult job at California's Berkeley Repertory Theatre since 1984. During her tenure the theatre's budget has more than doubled, and she now oversees a $3.8-million operation with managing director Susan Medak. "I think that's one of the reasons that first year is such a challenge for some artistic directors," she adds. "You really never know what's happening at a theatre until you live in it."

Ott began her career as an actor, working with, among others, the Kraken Company (whose members also included actor-director Bill Irwin and director-designer Julie Taymor) and the international troupe Camera Obscura. After cutting her teeth as a freelance director, she settled in Milwaukee as associate director of Theatre X and later as resident director at the Milwaukee Repertory Theatre. It was at the Rep that she developed a close working relationship with then artistic director John Dillon and managing director Sara O'Connor.

She refuses to attribute any aspects of her management or leadership style to gender alone, but Ott recognizes that being a woman may affect her artistic choices. "I do focus on bringing some new voices – women playwrights and directors – to the theatre. But I don't consciously take that as a mission – although I do think I often pick plays that specifically relate to questions I may be asking as a woman."

Ott objects to the kind of "ghettoization" of women artistic directors which leads to writing articles like this one. "The simple fact that we still *have* to write articles about women artistic directors shows that it's still an issue. It proves there's still some way in which we're regarded differently. It's subtle. There's a kind of focus on the individual and a pressure to succeed that is perhaps more intense because of it."

Does Ott see this situation changing in the next decade? "I think that's the hope – that when there are enough of us in all positions, we'll just be regarded as people and artists, period, and not as representatives of a minority group."

Michele Pearce

scheduled on those main stages than in male-driven institutions.

That's due largely, perhaps, to the general nature of repertoire at the majority of resident houses – the familiar "balanced" formula of revived modern and older classics (mostly by men), local premieres of recent Broadway and off-Broadway successes (try to name New York commercial hits by women, not counting anything by Wendy Wasserstein or Anna Deavere Smith) and, maybe, a world premiere or two of a new work.

The women I canvassed declared without apology that they feel no special obligation to produce women writers. "When you do a new play you're more likely to find women writers on the shortlist," Emily Mann comments. "But if you present as much classical work as we do at McCarter, you won't see as many women on the list. So many, many factors go into planning a season. Ultimately all you can do is follow your gut, and look for the pieces that are most exciting to you."

Though you'd be hard-pressed to forge a common aesthetic among women artistic directors at the larger theatres, all of them have displayed a fairly eclectic taste in stage literature. And none has devoted herself primarily to the works of other women.

Observes Perloff – who made her mark staging works by Strindberg and other venerable writers at New York's Classic Stage Company – "It takes generations to compile the body of work that white men have developed for the theatre. Men have had 2000 years to develop as playwrights and women have had, what – 50, 100 years? They're making progress, but it's not going to happen overnight."

In the meantime, Perloff says she focuses more on female characterization than female authorship:

> It comes down to getting pleasure from stories about people who interest you, and I tend to be most interested in works with three-dimensional female characters. That's why I was so eager to have us do *Hecuba, Antigone, Duchess of Malfi.*

Yet Perloff did tap female playwright Timberlake Wertenbaker to translate and adapt the version of *Hecuba* she will mount next season at ACT, with Olympia Dukakis in the title role. And the first grants from ACT's new commissioning program went to Elizabeth Egloff and other women dramatists.

Even though, as Mame Hunt bluntly puts it, women ADs "don't feel a responsibility to produce plays by women," they are commissioning a record number of them, and presenting them more often in second-stage and workshop settings than most of their male counterparts. Hunt has also cultivated a cluster of up-and-coming women writers (Claire Chafee and Marlane Meyer, among others) at the Magic Theatre – a company which has specialized in new plays for three decades, but primarily plays by men. "It's not a mandate," Hunt says of her own script selections.

> I just like the way women write. I don't know if that's because we're seeing the world from a similar angle or what. But most of the women writers I enjoy and want to produce look at the world with a diversity, a circularity, a complexity that I admire.

As for the day when mainstage subscribers at LORT companies will see as many women's names under the title as men's, it probably won't occur within our lifetime. But with more women in charge, we're probably steaming toward that destination faster.

> *Assumption #6:* The expectations of women artistic directors – by boards of directors, subscribers, the press – are no different from those that men face.
> *A token woman in a group of men will feel highly aware of her femaleness, and so will the group. Almost everything she does will be attributed to her gender, which is why she is likely to be accused of being too feminine (thus not "one of the boys") or too masculine ("trying to be someone she's not") – but what's really at her issue is her visible difference from the majority.*
> Carol Tavris, in *The Mismeasure of Woman*
>
> *Innovators are always controversial.*
> Eva Le Gallienne, director and actress.

When JoAnne Akalaitis reflects on her turbulent two years running the New York Shakespeare Festival, and her sudden (and very controversial) dismissal, she keeps coming back to the subject of Hillary Rodham Clinton, the accomplished and constantly-under-fire First Lady.

"One of the things we women do is rush to be liked, to do the right things, say the right things, wear the right things," Akalaitis contends.

> You can't often respond honestly in the work situation and the public arena if you're female. You have to think two or three times before you react, and use a more manipulative mechanism to deal with things. I mean, Hillary had to come up with that chocolate chip cookie recipe during the Presidential race. That cookie – it's a code for our standards of social behavior for women. You have to come up with the cookie, or you're damned.

In view of Akalaitis, one of the things that lost her the directorship of the Shakespeare Festival was her failure to deliver something equivalent to Hillary's cookie – some kind of primal assurance to those who considered her unsuitable for the job from the outset, and those who were responding to her media image which Akalaitis considered false and misleading.

"The elements of that picture were: here's this downtown, avant-garde woman who wears black, has short red spikey hair, who is smart, outspoken, honest and cold," Akalaitis recalls mordantly.

Mary B. Robinson

SHE KNEW WHAT SHE WANTED

Mary B. Robinson was barely out of her teens when she decided unequivocally what she intended to do with her life. "I wanted to run a theatre from the time I entered college – my eye was on it all along," she confides during a break from *Othello* rehearsals at the Philadelphia Drama Guild, where she's been realizing her early aspiration since 1990.

The path to her goal was deliberate: after Smith College came five years as associate artistic director at Hartford Stage Company, then another five years of far-flung freelance directing. "I wanted to be a free spirit, live in New York, get a sense of the field overall. I felt that when the right opportunity came I would sense it."

It came in the form of an offer from the venerable Philadelphia company, which in 1990 sported a solid subscription base, no deficit and – after the departure a year earlier of nine-year artistic director Gregory Poggi – no clearly enunciated sense of mission. "There was something of a blank slate quality about it," she says of the company, which performs in the capacious 900-seat Zellerbach Theater at the Annenberg Center.

"As one of several very interesting companies in Philadelphia, we have to carve out our identity very carefully and clearly – and repetitively, I've found. Before I arrived, the theatre tended toward an American repertoire of Miller–Williams–Albee, but now we're doing far more classics. We also do culturally diverse work – African-American and Latino plays, to tap into the diversity of Philadelphia. Receiving a Lila-Wallace grant in 1992 enabled the Guild to hire associate director Walter Dallas, who has gone on to become artistic director of the Freedom Theatre, an African-American company – which is a wonderful link. We've commissioned a play by Samm-Art Williams which will be presented at the Freedom. And, of course, we hope that will translate into *Othello* audiences."

Robinson makes sure a "strong female voice" is heard in every Guild season, whether that means staging plays by women, hiring women directors (Gloria Muzio, Melia Bensussen) or selecting works with woman-centered themes, such as last year's *Nora*, the Ingmar Bergman adaptation of Ibsen. "None of these decisions are particularly conscious," she reasons. "They're pretty instinctive."

Jim O'Quinn

What was missing from the portrait was the visionary, intuitive artist, open to new challenges. I think my experience at the Public was disturbing and demoralizing to the theatre community in general. It sent a signal about what happens to women who assume too much power.

One can regard the Akalaitis affair as an isolated occurrence triggered by a nexus of explosive factors – the replacement of a legendary producer with a Broadway outsider, the wrath of a powerful critic, the inheritance of an overwhelming debt and a nervous board. Or one can see it strictly as a bad match of institutional personality and individual artistic temperament. But much of what Akalaitis says about the social images forced on women executives also resonates with her colleagues. And similar vibrations were stirred by the recent abrupt dismissals of Josephine Abady after six seasons at the helm of the Cleveland Play House, and Margaret Booker after four at Florida's Asolo Theatre Company.

> "I've gotten a lot of sexist stuff since I came here," says ACT's Perloff. "People wonder: 'Is she in control of this organization? Can she cope with the heat? Does she really know what she's doing?' The perception is that women have no ability to deal with money, so the minute you're running a large organization there's this terror that you won't be able to keep things together financially. I don't think there's that same level of anxiety with a man."

Mann believes women still have to walk a very thin emotional tightrope in public in order to succeed: "We have to make sure we don't sound shrill, or overly expressive, or angry, so that we aren't too threatening to anybody. We have to learn how to censor ourselves."

The tension stems partly from the fact that this group of ground-breaking women are part of a demographic "swing shift." As baby boomers, they (and their male peers) grew up with the rules of the 1950s ringing in their young minds – "don't overshadow or threaten men, be feminine, don't reach too far or too high professionally." But theirs was a restless girlhood in a time of great cultural upheaval, and these same women began challenging and rewriting the gender rules in the late 1960s. Still, as Akalaitis puts it, "sexism is deeply rooted in this culture, and it keeps on reappearing in all kinds of forms."

An example: Akalaitis (who has two grown children) recalls going head-to-head with her board over retaining maternity leave for NYSF employees. Perloff (the mother of an infant and a toddler) has pressed her own board unsuccessfully for day-care facilities. Are these battles men would have chosen?

Perloff remains impassioned about her crusade:

> One of the reasons for the theatre's failures is that we're the only profession in this country that never deals with childcare. You can't go to a political meeting, or an American Bar Association convention, or an academic meeting anymore without finding some provision for childcare. Yet how many theatres offer it to their employees or audiences?

While there can be such lobbying on occasion without affecting the balance of power, Hunt believes that "women have had to learn and speak the language of men to get hired and to survive in this very competitive profession." And Perloff complains of it being lonelier at the top than it is at the starting gate. When I go to meetings of artistic directors from the "big seven" arts institutions in San Francisco, I'm the only woman in the room. In many ways, I feel very, very alone in this job.

While acknowledging the special pressures on women, Mann prefers to put a positive spin on their struggles:

If you're a woman in this job you'll have a harder transition to power, have to prove yourself more, and you can't make as many mistakes. Given that, I think it's an extraordinary accomplishment that we've all done this, and it's a very, very good sign for the theatre.

Women started this movement, then they sort of disappeared for a generation and a half. Now we're back. We're rediscovering the reasons these theatres exist, and revivifying this movement. We're part of the change that has to happen.

"If nothing else," Akalaitis sums up,

it's a matter of justice to have more women in power. I happen to believe in women's sense and sensibility, our spirit of adventure, our openness, but it's also about balance. Our theatres need the real picture – which means we need everyone involved.

PART II Theory

6

BEARING WITNESS

Anna Deavere Smith from Community to Theatre to Mass Media

Carol Martin

Anna Deavere Smith's process is by now well known, even celebrated. For well over 10 years she has created performances, usually concerning race, gender, and politics from taped interviews in response to actual events. Smith edits the interviews and constructs them into a multi-perspectival, multivocal replaying of a crisis for communities in which the events occurred. Her most commercially successful works, *Fires in the Mirror: Crown Heights, Brooklyn and Other Identities* and *Twilight: Los Angeles, 1992,* however, departed from this method: they were created for larger audiences not directly connected to the events or to the communities under consideration.

What happened to Smith's work as she moved it from specific communities to professional theatre to television reveals much more than Smith's well-deserved success as an author and performer. As her performative identity was wrought differently in different contexts, it became clear that Smith's subjects were not the only ones being interrogated. As she changed venues and audiences, Smith's own identity within her performances shifted.

Because struggle with identity is at the core of Smith's work, changes in her performative identity have a bearing on the arguments of her work. Rather than try to put forward a single analytic conclusion about the merits and mistakes of Smith's different styles and modes of production, it might be more useful to explore how different sites of production have impacted on Smith's work.

Approaching her work from this perspective, one can see how Smith's visibility in her performances as she moved her work from community stages to professional theatres to mass culture was increasingly eclipsed in favor of full "characters" in the conventional theatrical sense. These characters and their stories tended to obscure Smith's complex subject position as both author and performer of the work. What had been a radical example of Brechtian *Verfremdungseffekt* ("alienation-effect") became a more ordinary theatrical experience. Smith, who previously fascinated us by not quite transforming into the persons whose voice and gestures she represented, was now more an actress capable of playing many roles sequentially. What jumped to the foreground were the events and people of Crown Heights and Los Angeles. To some, this signaled an improvement over Smith's earlier work, a recognition that theatre is basically enacted storytelling. To others, it was a surrender of the performative complexity of author, performer, interviewer, and inter-viewed centered in Smith's identity as an African-American woman. In the earlier works, Smith's "voice" was heard along with all the other voices she simulated. In the later works, Smith's personal voice receded.

Apart from Smith's formidable skills as a performer, both her fluidity and her ability to portray many characters from many ethnic and racial backgrounds are attributable partly to the fact that she is light-skinned enough to pass. In addition, Smith does not elaborate on or retell the stories she hears, but scrupulously and in full detail repronounces what others tell her. This re-enunciation is not done in Smith's own voice or in her own ordinary body, but as closely as she can make it in the voices and bodies of her informants. Smith works from a documentary basis, her ear and eye for popular culture possibly adapting some techniques from TV news broadcasts and other on-the-spot reports. But she does not narrate from the authoritative position of the "voice-over." All that she provides her audiences with are the voices, faces, and bodies of her subjects uncannily reproduced and represented.

Smith collaborates with her informants, with those she interviews in their own homes or offices, on the streets, or wherever. Together Smith and her collaborators create chronicles, veritable "local histories." Seen this way, Smith's ability to swiftly shift roles seems to transcend race, class, gender, and other subject positions even as she presents these markers as determining signs. Her ease of adaptation shows the truth of Judith Butler's claim that gender and personality are constructed; and Adrian Piper's demonstration that race itself is at least partly an imagined reality (see Butler's *Bodies That Matter* [1993] and *Gender Trouble* [1990], and Piper's performance piece, *Cornered* [1988]). Smith exposes and represents the structures of racism and sexism while simultaneously using performance as a means to play with the mutability of identity. This is furthered by the fact that, although she identifies as an African-American woman to those who do not know her, she is not immediately identifiable as such. Similarly, because she is tall, slim, and angular, when she dresses in men's clothes and pulls her hair back, she can effectively represent maleness.

Smith crosses sex and gender. And she effectively represents clan, region, age, class, religion, and dialect. Her theatrical specialty is shape-shifting, a morph without aid of digitization. Slippery identity and morphing are very powerful because they conjure the extreme fluidity of social and personal identities and the fears such fluidity arouses. This fear forms the bases of some types of fundamentalism and racism. Smith's ability to move within and throughout various identity categories gives her performance a powerful double edge, at once magic and familiar.

Throughout all this, an audience never directly gets Smith's own viewpoint or opinion, though one can detect a certain kind of liberalism, an openness to multiple interpretations. And in choosing whom to interview, her performance of the tension between identity and socially constructed images registers her sympathies. While dramatic conflict usually pits difference against difference, Smith's ability to perform opposite points of view brings them closer together even as she documents the deepest and strongest expressions of antagonism, fear, and anger. If classical Hegelian tragedy concludes with some kind of resolution of conflict, Smith's work builds into its core small and personal "resolutions." These are not in the words and gestures of those speaking, but in the consciousness of the spectators who receive, in rapid succession, and in the most personalized way, conflicting attitudes and opinions which clearly cannot all be "right" or "wrong." The postmodern reality of multiple simultaneously existing actualities is registered in Smith's work not as abstract theory but as concrete information. In *Fires*, for example, by convincingly performing a disillusioned black male teenager in one moment and a highly educated Jewish female author in another, Smith makes a performative argument not only for the compelling reality of such different persons but for the graphic ways in which their differences cannot fade. In this way Smith's performance argues with her text. The "raw texts," if simply read on a page, often reveal hatred and intolerance (along with humor, warmth, and personal, value-derived opinion); but Smith's performance clearly signals that racial and gender hatred cannot be accepted as the end of the story.

Smith first relocated her work from community-based performances in conference rooms and lecture halls to the theatrical stage and eventually to television when *Fires in the Mirror* was commissioned by the New York Shakespeare Festival's Public Theatre. In 1993 *Fires*, one part of Smith's series of performances titled *On the Road: A Search for American Character* begun in 1982, was videotaped for broadcast as part of the PBS American Playhouse. In this series of performances, Smith tape-recorded interviews with members of each community or group who commissioned her work. While listening for passages that reflected the psychological and social through-line of each speaker, Smith selected verbatim sections to memorize and shape into performances that addressed the often controversial issues and situations embroiling the communities.

Early parts of *On the Road* were performed in lecture halls in front of the audiences who commissioned each work. To create transitions between characters, Smith used a variety of different telephones to simulate her interviewees speaking to her. The resulting performances were Smith's look, from the outside, at the multiple subjective realities which, when taken together, produced complex and compelling repres- entations of the community's tensions. Most often, these tensions centered on race, gender, and class (Richards 1993; Bean 1993; Martin 1993; Case 1989). Smith's power of performance, and the fact that she was able to stage personalities that the audience knew, elicited general delight from the community. But was this something more than collective narcissism, a community's enjoyment at seeing its own reflection refracted with such skill? In addition to narcissism, and perhaps transcending it, was the critical stance Smith built into her performances. Like Augusto Boal's "forum theatre" – in which communities enact what is bothering them and often reach, through theatrical actions, decisions about specific alternatives – Smith's virtual realities give to those watching a view of themselves that otherwise they could not purchase: a view that might empower them to make changes. This is because Smith's enactments are not edited by the speakers but by Smith. She is the one selecting what is to be distinct during the performance; she is the one who makes public the peculiarities of each speaker. Smith's representations are accurate but selected, true to the person but edited. In that selection and editing, a sharp socially critical mind is at work. Smith's presentations are neither puffs nor roasts, but constructive, re-presentations seasoned with a critical consciousness.

About Smith's performances in nontheatrical environments Sandra Richards has observed:

> Because many of the people represented are personally known to viewers, audiences often greet these episodes with uproarious delight at the accuracy of Smith's rendition of speech patterns. Yet, because she is replaying volatile issues that have threatened to rupture their semblance of community, they also get caught in their own laughter, suddenly shocked or hurt by what this near-image reveals of their individual and collective shortcomings.
>
> (Richards 1993:37)

Similarly, as Sue-Ellen Case has pointed out, Smith's process of selection is an active part of her performances. Spectators view Smith's portrayal of different members of the community, some of whom they probably know personally, but also "what she chose to enact, what she ignored, whom she portrayed and how she portrayed them became as much a part of the performance as the characters themselves and their own content" (Case 1989:20).

With a telephone receiver in hand Smith imitated those she interviewed and simultaneously represented herself as the receiver of the call. This simple device emphasized Smith's presence even as it exposed her basic interviewing technique. She could mimic the voice of those she interviewed while showing the facial expressions of the receiver of the information. Smith's presence as the receiver of the call was a pivotal critical presence, an important but mercurial reference, which cued the audience as to how they might respond to what they were hearing. Smith thus became a quasi-member of the community she was performing even as community members became quasi-performers in Smith's show. At the same time, Smith interjected an ironic presence that underscored incongruities in the narrative of events and/or emotions. This irony separated Smith from the people/characters she brought to the stage and served to underscore her position as the author of the work: not only author, but commentator as well.

The visibility of Smith's particular kind of shared ethnography, her selection of characters and text, and her often ironic performance style, revealed her process as an author and performer, as well as her relationship to the communities she represented onstage. The complexity and problems of her research were part of the performance. While Smith positioned herself as the unifying force of the narrative, she allowed contradictions and conflicts between different stories and realities to remain intact. However, as compelling as Smith's representation of different characters was, it was her presence that was not only incontestable but sought after. She became both respected and famous for her work.

Fame meant Smith was increasingly asked to perform, and by new clients. However, when Smith accepted the commissions from the Public Theatre and eventually PBS, the community in question was separated from the producers of the work. This shift, this split, is decisive. Smith no longer represented the community to itself; she now showed a community to the public-at-large. This change in receivers brought with it an alteration in her performance style.

In *Fires*, the piece commissioned by the Public Theatre while JoAnne Akalaitis was still the artistic director, and premiered in the spring of 1992, Smith explored the racial tensions that fueled the riots between blacks and Jews in Crown Heights, Brooklyn, in the summer of 1991. The circumstances Smith dramatized were well known to many New Yorkers: on 19 August 1991, Gavin Cato, an African-American child, was hit and killed by a car that was part of the Lubavitch rebbe's motorcade. By the end of that day Yankel Rosenbaum, a young Jewish scholar from Australia, was murdered in retaliation. Riots broke out.

Fires was different from Smith's earlier work in a number of ways. In her community work, Smith directed herself. *Fires* was directed by Christopher Ashley (whose work had also appeared at New York Theatre Workshop, WPA, Manhattan Punch Line, and many regional theatres) as a stage play. As such, *Fires* included the same extraordinary range and number of personages as Smith's community work. Their portrayal, however, was markedly different. For *Fires* Smith "improved" her previous technique of portraying her informants by simply receiving phone calls. Props, a set, lighting, and costume changes were used to present Smith's interviewees in different settings – the street, a living room, an office, a library, a youth center. Seated in an armchair, or at a desk, donning a yarmulke, a cap of African kente cloth, a spangled sweater, or a raincoat, Smith enacted 29 characters, including Angela Davis, Ntozake Shange, Reverend Al Sharpton, Leonard Jeffries, Rabbi Joseph Spielman, Letty Cottin Pogrebin, and Rabbi Shea Hecht. From a theatrical point of view, Smith performed in the "poor theatre" tradition of minimal sets and costumes. Conversely, from the point of view of her earlier work, Smith began to "realize" characters fully, not simply "represent" them by means of their voices. Also for *Fires* Smith investigated two communities, suspicious of each other to the point of murderous violence and riot; earlier she had dealt with one community at a time. The irresolvable contradictions of the stories of the 29 people Smith impersonated in *Fires* did not mitigate one another; they were not resolved nor consolidated into a single point of view.

Smith abandoned critical irony in favor of a transformational perform-ance style that sought to evoke the multiple realities of the personages portrayed. Discussing her creative process at this stage in her career Smith told me:

> The point is simply to repeat it until I begin to feel it and what I begin to feel is his song, and his song helps me remember more about his body. . . . I become them. I become the them that they present to the world. And you know the performance of ourselves has very much to do with the self of ourselves.
>
> (Martin 1993:57)

In the Public Theatre version of *Fires*, an overhead screen displayed the name of the person Smith was performing, just in case spectators would not know who it was. Such a bald identifying device would not have been necessary for Smith's earlier work in which the audience was the community being performed. Indeed, the audiences for *Fires* were very different from those for Smith's previous community work. When the spectators regarding the performance at the Public Theatre recognized different personages, they were recognizing not members of their own community, but newsprint and media personalities. The intensely personal shock and delight at seeing in a new light someone one personally knows – a quality of Smith's community-based work that impressed both Richards and Case – was no longer present. In *Fires* testimony was resituated away from the community and presented to a theatrical audience with theatrical concerns. *Fires* was a work that could be reviewed by the press, evaluated as any other "theatrical product." Nor was *Fires* the only work of social import on the boards that year. Tony Kushner's *Angels in America* (also originating at the Public) was enjoying an enormous success on Broadway. But Smith's work was fundamentally different from Kushner's: the sources of Smith's entertainment were actual people, and were actually named. In this regard, Smith's piece was closer to Ron Vawter's celebrated one-actor, two-person show, *Roy Cohn/Jack Smith*. But Vawter's people were dead, while Smith's were very much alive.

The interviews Smith conducted for her new work had the same goal as her earlier work: to investigate, by direct means, a particular social world, a world which she could render in dramatic and theatrical terms. As a stranger in Crown Heights, Smith sought out people to interview according to her interests. But what were these interests? Were they theatrical – looking for the most interesting, the most stageworthy persons? Were they social, seeking the seeds and branches of the discord that roiled the Jewish and African-American communities? Were they psychological, an investigation of the private and intimate forces driving people in a heated, desperate situation? Were they cultural, investigating the apparently irreconcilable divide separating African-American and American Jewish cultures? The answer seems to be: "All of the above." Smith did not abandon her earlier program when she became more theatrical. Rather she added to the mix more cogently theatrical and aesthetic concerns.

As anthropologist Kirsten Hastrup pointed out, although part of the experience of fieldwork is to be unknown to the community studied, the researcher must then find a position from which to speak about her experiences and data, a liminal position both inside and outside the community under study (1992:333). In finding this position, and locating her life at least temporarily at that place, a fieldworker finds her anthropological identity. This process is not without risk. In the case of Smith, the identity is not anthropological but artistic (and to some degree cultural and racial). Although the performance of *Fires* is hers, the words and gestures remain those of her subjects. Though edited and arranged for theatre, these words and acts acquire the status of oral history, a "documentary" of sorts. However, documentary theatre has representational problems of its own.

The suspension of disbelief Smith demanded from her audience – that she was now a man, now a woman, now black, white, Jewish – drew audiences deep into the multiple realities of Crown Heights in 1991. Smith offered audiences the possibility of "entertaining" (in both senses of the word) divergent points of view, of balancing contradictory narratives. The spectators at the Public Theatre, who might be expected to have entered the theatre with their minds made up regarding who was right and who was wrong in Crown Heights, an audience divided and decided, might through Smith's work begin to doubt its own finality. If this African-American woman could so convincingly embody an orthodox Jewish woman and Al Sharpton within the space of a few minutes, might not the stories these very different people tell be regarded differently, as part of a multiplicity of views rather than as irreconcilable "positions" in a race/class/religious war? And Smith portrayed not only the woman and Sharpton, but 27 others, each of whom had their own take on events. Yet Smith's pitch to spectators was not so much ideological as it was aesthetic: the aesthetic absorption Smith's performance generated was so intense that it produced the illusion that the spectator created the multiple insights the work generated.

From the point of view of the interviewees, racial, gender, and religious identity were taken for granted. Part of the pathos of Crown Heights was that people were more or less fixed in particular identities – Jewish, black, men, women. But Smith's performance called such secure notions of identity into question. At one level, all these identities were absorbed into one – Smith's own; at another level, the similarities and fissures among different people were all the more visible for audiences to regard. For example, Al Sharpton seemed to many whites the embodiment of reckless racial politics during the Crown Heights controversy. He was a man whose physical presence – long hair, bellicose voice – both terrified and amused, even as it aroused and solidified some African Americans. Sharpton is put into an entirely different dimension, however, as Smith-as-Sharpton related the relationship between Sharpton and singer James Brown. "The long hair?" Smith-Sharpton declared, leaning back in his chair, "That's me and James's thiiing!" Spectator response depended largely on who one takes Sharpton to be, and whether or not one knows James Brown's story. In either case, the result was a provocative friction between the explicit ideology of Sharpton's narrative and the ideology of Smith's performance; namely that racial identity and history, along with quirky and unpredictable personal occurrences, determine social and political life, even as borders, racial and otherwise, can be, or must be constructed as becoming fluid and negotiable. Smith's point was not limited to her view of Sharpton. It permeated *Fires*: neither a melting pot (we're all really the same) nor multicultural (we're all different and must respect each other) perspectives were sufficient. Something more fluid and complex, more performative, was needed: a process of discovering who we might be as social, personal, political, and historical circumstances unfold within and around us; and as we accept our agency in relation to these circumstances, neither really being their author nor their subject. To put it another way, Smith did not author *Fires* in the conventional sense, nor did she just "find it" or "report it." She both authored the work and found it; and the stories she tells remain in the flux of discovery, even as they are fixed in a particular theatrical rendition.

As different as *Fires* is from its community-based predecessors, so is the PBS *Fires* different from the stage version. In the community phase of Smith's work, she was freer to interject directly her own point of view and underscore her authorship with the use of irony. In *Fires*, Smith's authorship of the work was visible more through transitions than commentary during the performance. Examining the PBS version reveals still further revisions in the complexity of Smith's performance, if not her message.

The PBS/American Playhouse production of *Fires* directed by George C. Wolfe (Artistic Director of the Public Theatre) moved even farther away from the audience-as-source origin of Smith's work. Perhaps this additional distancing was directly due to the involvement of mass media (Bean 1993). One of Smith's strongest qualities as a performer is her ability to transform from one persona to another without the help of costume, makeup, or any other theatrical paraphernalia. The irony of this transformational ability was lost in moving from community-based work to the Public Theatre where the transparency of persona was translated more in the direction of the mask of character. An even bigger change occurred, however, when *Fires* was configured for PBS. For the PBS production, Smith used a wide range of costumes, wigs, and sets. The through-line of Smith moving between different characters was eradicated in favor of an almost complete disguise of her identity with each new character. Viewers lost the subjective and authorial presence of Smith in favor of a beguiling array of completely different people. This loss undercut the sense of shared experience that was such a powerful political tool in the stage production of *Fires*. Fluid identities and morphing were translated through the medium of television as costume change.

For PBS the 29 characters of the stage version were carefully edited down to 19. Characters left out included playwright Ntozake Shange, Wolfe himself, the rap artist Big Mo, and CUNY professor and black nationalist Leonard Jeffries. The broadcast begins with a mini-interview with Smith, in which she talks about her process of making the work. The process that was self-evident in the performance of the community-based work now needed explanation, as if to a college class. Instead of the troubling openness of the earlier work, *Fires* on PBS was given tight closure by a final montage of African-American and Jewish children, too innocent to arouse anything other than a desire for social peace. "If these children are so loving," the final image suggested, "why can't we adults strive to be likewise?" Laudable as that desire might be, and appropriate as it might prove for television, such a perspective begged the question of violence in Crown Heights even as it presupposed a better world. These sentimental images distanced the viewer from the social causes that underlaid and drove the racial hatred in the first place. Faces of sweet children provided closure in the suggestion of hope for a better future. The uncomfortable lack of resolution in the theatrical production was done away with (Bean 1993:11). The stage production ended on a much more disturbing note: Smith's portrayal of Gavin Cato's inconsolably bereft father. Carmel Cato wondered whether the horrific death of his child and the events that followed were the outcome of being "different," not only being African-American, but being "born by his foot" (born feet first). What has the father's karma to do with his son's? Smith depicts Cato being interviewed at night under a dim street light. He wept. Neither the riots nor the pompous political posturing could bring his son back. The devastation of loss and hatred remained naked and barren. The father is still last in the PBS version of *Fires*, but his words are tempered by the visual and musical montage of innocent faces from the same streets in Crown Heights as Gavin. The melee is gone and so are the questions it provoked.

Stuart Hall makes an important argument in relation to the problems of intervening in the way media constructs questions of race. Hall asserts that while ideological statements are made by individuals, ideologies are not the product of these statements. Rather, individual intentions are formed within ideologies that determine social conditions (Hall 1981:31). Individuals must "speak through" ideological positions because oppressive and limiting though they may be, ideology provides a means of making sense of information (32).

A similar point is made by bell hooks in her discussion of *The Waterbearer* by Lorna Simpson, a photographic image of an African-American woman her back to the camera, pouring water from two pitchers (hooks 1995:93). The image appeared in the now defunct *B Culture* with the following phrases printed underneath it: "She saw him disappear by the river, They asked her to tell what happened, Only to discount her memory" (hooks 1995:94). hooks asks us to consider not only the subjugated knowledge these phrases report, but the possibility of provocative African-American female bodies as integral to the production of meaning and therefore history (97). Simpson's photograph renders this African-American female body full of a depth of meaning that forsakes and threatens the transparency of typical representations. The threat is the knowledge of the possibility that black women can embody and relate a credible version of history. But the colonialist must "discount her memory." Why? Because to those in power there is real danger in the emergence of subjugated knowledge that redefines their power and authority. As hooks points out, the intensity of the image of the black woman with her deflected gaze interrogates the rejection of her knowledge that the phrase "discount her memory" suggests. What Hall and hooks suggest is that the performance of our social relations, subjugated though the depth of that knowledge may be, matters precisely because it creates a way of seeing ourselves and therefore informs our actions and our construction of history.

Smith's performances of *Fires* for stage and television are probing versions of a similar quest: an African-American woman telling what happened – according to the experiences of 19, or 29, people who were there when it happened; who, in some cases, helped to make it happen. And though Smith's own voice and gaze, as with the image of the woman in *The Waterbearer*, may be obscured, the intensity of Smith's acting, of her representations, and the logic of the work with its multiple and varied voices, can only emerge from the authority of the storyteller – Smith the "griot" who performs the selected history. Ultimately Smith's knowledge, despite its reconfiguration in different venues and media, is never entirely discounted.

As Philip Auslander puts it,

> we cannot afford simply to dismiss artists' movements from the margins to the center or from the avant-garde to the mainstream as "selling out" any more than we can afford to ignore the significance of cultural expression that originates within the mainstream.
>
> (Auslander 1992:4)

Many I spoke with who had not seen *Fires* in the theatre were very enthusiastic about the airing of the work on PBS. Nevertheless, examining what happens in the process of seeking a bigger audience is tied to the concomitant transformation of Smith's work from community-based to theatrical to mass culture. It would be too easy to cast Wolfe and his penchant for popular and glossy work as the culprit. It is, after all, Wolfe's ability to popularize and make accessible difficult subject matter in works like *Fires*, *Angels in America*, *Twilight: Los Angeles, 1992* (Smith's work on the LA riots following the acquittal of those accused of beating Rodney King), and even Patrick Stewart in *The*

Tempest, that makes Wolfe's project at the New York Shakespeare Festival/Public Theatre so extraordinary.

The PBS version of *Fires* was not a recording of the stage play but a reconceptualization of the work. A repercussion of this choice was the undoing of a delicate correspondence between Smith's subjectivity and that of those she interviewed. In all her works, for whatever audience, Smith draws upon many postmodern techniques: pastiche, appropriation, multivocality, discontinuity, quotation, gender changes, lack of closure. Yet her work is not ambiguous, but demonstrates the dynamics of social crisis and asks for a social change that engages an understanding of complex forces driving contemporary American society. Her works point to the fact that the selection of images and words one borrows can make all the difference. The relocation of Smith's work from community to theatre to television does not retain the complexity of her own ironic presence. But perhaps we should not read this simply as failure but as instruction in the difficulty of the production of certain kinds of meaning for the mass media.

Smith's ability to change venues and attract major producers may indicate mainstream audiences' burgeoning interest in racial issues, or merely Smith's own skills as a performer. Unquestionably, Smith's shift of location for her performances from community-based venues to the Public Theatre and other professional theatres to PBS had a bearing on the work. In earlier works, the swift transformations from character to character underscored fluidity of identity, even as the constancy of Smith's presence provided unity. The tension between the depth of Smith's identity and her transparency – in this case, the means to see the reality of others – created the critical juncture of her performances. The fact that Smith's subjects contradicted one another did not mitigate the passion and conviction of their words.

What was not lost in the move to the Public and PBS was the central place Smith gives to race and gender. She understands these broad categories in their particulars, as performed acts saturated with passionate investment informed by vivid social constructs. Her fluid movement through boundaries of identity insists that no matter how fixed race and gender appear to be in social and political life, they are fluid in imagination and performance. Therefore we are all – performers, subjects, audiences, producers – implicated in the process of creating boundaries . . . and breaking them down.

REFERENCES

Auslander, Philip (1992) *Presence and Resistance*. Ann Arbor: University of Michigan Press.

Bean, Annemarie (1993) "Looking for the Area of Free Play in the Historical Moment: The Performative Fiction of Anna Deavere Smith." Unpublished Paper, New York University.

Boal, Augusto (1985) *Theatre of the Oppressed*. New York: Theatre Communications Group.

Butler, Judith (1990) *Gender Trouble*. London: Routledge.

———— (1993) *Bodies That Matter*. London: Routledge.

Case, Sue-Ellen (1989) "Introduction to Chlorophyll Postmodernism and the Mother Goddess/A Conversation." *Women & Performance* 4, no. 8:20–25.

Hall, Stuart, ed. (1980) *Culture, Media, Language: Working Papers in Cultural Studies 1972–79*, Birmingham: University of Birmingham Press.

Hastrup, Kirsten (1992) "Out of Anthropology: The Anthropologist as an Object of Dramatic Representation." *Cultural Anthropology* 7, no. 3:327–345.

hooks, bell (1995) *Art on My Mind*. New York: The New Press.

Martin, Carol (1993) "Anna Deavere Smith: The Word Becomes You." *TDR* 37, 4 (T140). Also in this sourcebook, 185–204.

Piper, Adrian (1988) *Cornered*. Video installation.

Richards, Sandra (1993) "Caught in the Act of Social Definition: *On the Road* with Anna Deavere Smith." In *Acting Out: Feminist Performances*, edited by Lynda Hart and Peggy Phelan. Ann Arbor: University of Michigan Press.

7

IN DEFENSE OF THE DISCOURSE
Materialist Feminism, Postmodernism, Poststructuralism ... and Theory

Jill Dolan

Ten years ago feminist theatre and performance criticism was something of an oxymoron. Like most avowedly political criticism, feminist work in the late 1970s and early 1980s seemed caught in conflicting demands of aesthetics and ideology. Feminist critics of feminist work teetered uneasily among the desires to support women's production efforts, to investigate the ramifications of an unprecedented switch in gender perspective, and to compare women's theatre and performance with an aesthetic standard that had not yet been formulated. Critics writing for feminist presses usually chose to validate what they saw; those writing in academic venues generally took a sociological approach to theatre's reflection of women's social roles. The bulk of the critical effort was aimed toward redressing the historical invisibility of women in the field.[1]

When French theory began to find its way across the Atlantic it changed the contours of feminist criticism in the academy. Isabelle de Courtivron and Elaine Marks published their landmark anthology *New French Feminisms* in 1981, and suddenly gave American feminist criticism a whole new vocabulary and new territories to cover. Hélène Cixous, Luce Irigaray, and Julia Kristeva, among others, seemed powerful and poetic in their descriptions of female sexuality as a subversive, antipatriarchal textuality. If women could write with their bodies, as *l'écriture féminine*'s florid manifestos proposed, could the body also be a site of a new theatre practice and textual analysis? Could the French feminist pantheon's borrowings from Jacques Derrida and Jacques Lacan give feminist theatre and performance critics new tools for describing the field?

American feminist criticism in the 1980s has also been shaped by the field of cultural studies. The influx of British materialism, with its focus on ideology formation in representation, has allowed critics to dig deeper, farther, and wider in the investigation of representation as an

ideological apparatus with an active role in preserving social arrangements. The materialist approach has moved academic feminist criticism
away from sociological analysis based on assumptions that theatre serves
a mimetic function for the culture, into an analysis of representation as
a site for the production of cultural meanings that perpetuate conservative gender roles. Where sociological criticism considers theatre as
a mirror of positive or negative social images, the materialist emphasis
on representation as a producer of meaning also takes into account the
reception and interpretation of cultural signs by spectators differentiated
by gender, race, class, and sexual preference.

Deconstruction, poststructuralism, psychoanalysis, and materialism
often appear to be unlikely traveling companions along the critical
terrain, but if nothing else, they have prompted an increased focus on
theory over sociology. Feminist theatre and performance criticism, as a
result, has arrived at the end of the decade with its contours shaped
roughly by three different analytical methods based in divergent
ideologies: (1) a liberal feminist insistence on traditional criticism that
supports the play as the basis of the dramatic experience; (2) a radical
(sometimes called "cultural") feminist reification of theatre as a mimesis
that can validate women's identities; and (3) a materialist feminist
approach to theatre and performance as ideologically marked representation, an approach which borrows variously from psychoanalysis, poststructuralism, and Marxist criticism.

These three approaches to feminist theatre and performance criticism
have recently been at odds. At the Women and Theatre Program's (WTP)
annual preconferences, liberal and radical feminist critics and practitioners have butted against materialist theorists' methods and ideologies.
Poststructuralism, especially, seems to challenge many long-held theatrical assumptions that some liberal and radical feminists aren't eager to
release. The heralded "death of the author" (Barthes 1977) displaces the
playwright's primacy and locates the responsibility for producing
meaning in the hermeneutic sphere. The traditional triumvirate of
playwright–director–actor has been disrupted by the spectator's insertion
into the paradigm as an active participant in the production of meaning.

Author's intent has become suspect or irrelevant; the director's
authority challenged; and the actor's position as manipulable object
traded for one of resistance. Poststructuralism's sacrilege, according to
those who deplore its theory, is its unwillingness to idolize the text and
its insistence on the shifting, historical nature of the meanings representation produces.

Poststructuralist theory threatens what some see as feminist criticism's role in validating women's identities in performance. The issue of
identity is particularly vital in theatre, which has historically solicited its

responses based on empathetic identification techniques. The larger struggle in feminism over how to reconcile its conflicting theories of identity and the self, then, is particularly urgent in theatre and perform-ance.

POSTSTRUCTURALISM VERSUS IDENTITY POLITICS

Over the last several years, the popularity of poststructuralism and the prevalence of identity politics in feminism has prompted the develop-ment of opposing feminist theories of the self. Identity politics claims to define women's subjectivity by their positions within race, class, or sexuality, positions which the dominant culture – and often, the dominating voices in feminism – have effectively squelched. Post-structuralist practice suggests that any such coherent conceptions of identity are specious since even race, class, and sexuality, as well as gender, are constructed within discursive fields and changeable within the flux of history. According to poststructuralism, subjectivity is never monolithic or fixed, but decentered, and constantly thrown into process by the very competing discourses through which identity might be claimed.

These opposing feminist camps base their arguments on definitions of experience, as the old slogan "the personal is political" comes back to haunt in unexpected ways. Feminism at this historical moment seems caught between reifying experience as truth, and proclaiming that although experience does dictate a certain material reality, it's a reality necessarily constructed in relation to social ideology and cannot be the basis of any fixed objective truth.

The two camps split on the issue of identity. Radical feminists propose that female identity is coherent and whole, and defined in opposition to male identity. The politics that stem from this position carve out a place in gender, race, and class that is solipsistically unified and that elides the differences within and between women. Radical feminist performance texts, as Elin Diamond has written, tend to romanticize female identity by assuming that a transcendent female self can be mirrored in "woman-identified" theatre (1985).

Asserting a ground of experience from which to theorize feminism is not romanticized or totalized under materialist feminist analysis, which borrows some of its tenets from poststructuralism. Teresa de Lauretis, for instance, cautions that the assertion of identity is not the goal, as it is in feminist identity politics, but a point of departure for a multivalent, shifting ground of subjectivity, a "self-contradictory identity, . . . made up of heterogeneous and heteronomous representations of gender, race, and class" (1986:9). Identity becomes a site of struggle, at which the subject organizes and reorganizes competing discourses as they fight for supremacy.

Materialist feminist performance criticism uses poststructuralism to deconstruct both traditional, male-identified realism and alternative, woman-identified ritual drama and performance art for their belief in coherent, unified identities. If feminist poststructuralism is the tool of this critique, postmodernism is the style that offers potential performance applications. Logically, a postmodernist performance style that breaks with realist narrative strategies, heralds the death of unified characters, decenters the subject, and foregrounds conventions of perception is conducive to materialist feminist analyses of representation.

The intent of the growing, diversifying field of feminist postmodern performance theory is to develop theatre and performance strategies that will create new meanings at the site of representation, which has historically outlawed or silenced women within its frame. Feminist postmodernist performance theories intervene in representation to encourage spectators to think differently about their positions within culture, differently than the comfortable conventions of realism ever persuade them to think. Feminist performance theories give critics a language that unmasks the seeming transparency of performance texts and that potentially articulates the insidious ideology of any representation that presents experience as truth.

Continually watchdogging themselves and their bedfellows, feminist performance theorists have also chastised the commodified brands of postmodernist performance that devolve into an endless plurality of meaning; a chic, politically apathetic ennui; or a retrograde nostalgia for master narratives (see Dolan 1987; Case and Forte 1985). The project of feminist theory is unflaggingly political, as it studies not simply the superficial structure of performance, but its effect on the culture and the search for modes of effective social change.

A wealth of invigorating thinking and criticism has come from pondering the alliance of feminist criticism and postmodern style. But concurrently, feminist criticism's struggle between poststructuralism and identity politics has provoked a metadebate over theory in feminism. Theorists who subscribe to poststructuralist analysis are accused of oppressing radical feminist identity politicians with the privileges of an elite language. Accusations of silencing are hurled about, since this argument takes place in discourse and is very much about the power of language.

STRUGGLES IN DISCOURSE: RECENT WRITINGS AND (MIS)READINGS

Tensions between these opposing camps have been exacerbated by the increasing visibility of critical and theoretical work in feminist theatre and performance. Feminist panels sponsored by WTP at the annual Association for Theatre in Higher Education conferences, as well as at the Modern Language Association conventions, have been very well attended over the last several years, and publishers are beginning to seek out feminist books in the field. Helen Krich Chinoy and Linda Walsh Jenkins' anthology *Women in American Theatre*, originally published by Crown in 1981, was revised and reissued by Theatre Communications Group in 1987; Karen Malpede's collection *Women in Theatre: Compassion and Hope* was published in 1983 (Drama Book Specialists); Helene Keyssar's *Feminist Theatre* was published in 1985 (Grove Press); and Kathleen Betsko and Rachel Koenig's anthology *Interviews with Contemporary Women Playwrights* appeared in 1987 (Beechtree Books).

These four editions essentially reflect the sociological approach to feminist criticism and theatre history. The Chinoy/Jenkins anthology is a valuable sourcebook of information on women playwrights, producers, directors, and actors that provides a solid introduction to the wealth of women's work overlooked in distant and present theatre history. The collection is marked, however, by its early-1980s perspective on feminist theatre criticism as an ill-defined plurality of approaches. The reissued volume surveys more recent critical methodologies in the field, such as semiotics, materialism, and poststructuralism, but shies away from a rigorous investigation of the ideological meanings of different feminist analytical styles.

The Betsko/Koenig collection of interviews is grounded in the liberal feminist assertion of the text's primacy. The book succeeds in providing women playwrights an important, public forum in which to speak for themselves about their politics, their creative processes, and their projects. Like the Chinoy/Jenkins anthology, *Interviews* does not provide an overarching, specific framework for feminism, aesthetics, or ideology. The editors intentionally avoid such distinctions.

Three books published in 1988 take on the task of sorting through feminist ideologies and their various critical perspectives: my own book, *The Feminist Spectator as Critic* (UMI); Sue-Ellen Case's *Feminism and Theatre* (Routledge); and *Making a Spectacle: Feminist Essays on Contemporary Women's Theatre*, edited by Lynda Hart (University of Michigan Press). My book applies critical theory in an effort to investigate the feminist spectator's position vis-à-vis the representational frame and favors a materialist feminist approach. Through case studies of work by Marsha Norman, Richard Foreman, At the Foot of the Mountain, the Women's Experimental Theatre, Spiderwoman, and other performance groups, I attempt to specify the ideological underpinnings of various performance theories and practices.

Case's *Feminism and Theatre* is a handbook that introduces feminist critical theory in theatre and performance. Case rejects the assumption of theatre as mimesis, and argues that theatre history and dramatic literature cannot be read for information about actual women's lives. The book begins with an attack on the Aristotelian, Greek, and Elizabethan theatre traditions as forums for patriarchal ideology that repressed actual historical women. Case suggests that the feminist reader studying *The Poetics* and other canonical texts that gird the Western theatre tradition can "discover the methodology and assumptions of patriarchal production" on which they are based (1988:19).

Hart's anthology mixes liberal, radical, and materialist perspectives under sections that address women playwrights' metaphors, their use of aesthetics and history, and their disruptions of the patriarchal ideology Case describes. Hart characterizes the articles in her collection as documenting the "shift in feminist perspective from discovering and creating positive images of women in the content of drama to analyzing and disrupting the ideological codes embedded in the inherited structures of dramatic representation" (1988:4). The book serves as a focal point for applications of diverging feminist critical thought on contemporary theatre.

The published responses to these books have been somewhat illuminating regarding the debate between poststructuralism and identity politics, and relevant to the dissension among varying feminist perspectives. The anthologies of the early or mid-1980s were generally applauded when they appeared, and were seen as correctives to women's invisibility in theatre history. Keyssar's *Feminist Theatre* (1985) also garnered favorable reviews; her book analyzes plays by women through a more or less traditional critical approach.

Case's book, on the contrary, is a historical/critical/theoretical study with a polemical force that has made it subject to two aggressively unfavorable reviews. Gabrielle Cody, writing in *Performing Arts Journal*, chastises Case for a "lack of intellectual rigor," and an "inability to rise above [her] rhetoric" (1988:117). This attack on her scholarship in fact seems to mask Cody's discomfort with Case's politics. Cody particularly lambastes Case's work on Greek and Elizabethan stage conventions, criticizing her for reducing "thoughts to ideology, literature to sociology" (117).

Cody misreads Case's thesis by attempting to locate her work within the sociological criticism from which Case points away. For example,

Cody challenges Case to investigate Sophocles' and Euripides' women for their strength as characters. In her chapter on the Greeks, Case states explicitly that the feminist critic or historian, reading Greek theatre history through its production practice rather than its texts alone, can no longer view these representations as in any way linked to the lives of real women (1988:25).

Similarly, Cody accuses Case of insulting women by "avoiding the images in Shakespeare (often the only representations of female power in Elizabethan England) by emphasizing his techniques of production" (1988:117). But production is exactly Case's point. She insists these texts be read through living cultural history rather than detaching them into a transcendent sphere. Case's poststructuralist approach does not focus on ahistorical content or images, but analyzes the representational apparatus and the ideology that it enforces through theatre history.

In her parting shot, Cody writes that Case's book "posits that women have been robbed of their own representations throughout theatre history, but a more inclusive mimesis is possible through the creation of a feminist-identified culture" (1988:118). This statement directly contradicts Case's final assertion that "the production of signs creates the sense of what a person is rather than reflecting it (in the traditional mimetic order)" (1988:132). Case's approach is, in fact, antimimesis, and Cody does her a disservice by consigning her work to a radical feminist ghetto of feminist-identified culture in which theatre is a validating mirror.

Joyce van Dyke's lead article in the *Women's Review of Books* contrasts Case's book with the Betsko/Koenig interview collection and Hart's *Making a Spectacle* anthology. Van Dyke applauds the collection of interviews as "energetic, lithe, funny, vivid" (1989:1), then goes on to deplore the "considerable gap between feminist critics and feminist playwrights" (3). She calls Case's story a "lopsided one," and implies that she is more of a semiotician than she is a feminist (3). Van Dyke suggests that Case's work is selectively exclusionary and "does not admit the existence of what it leaves out" (3), such as the women who did perform on the continent during Shakespeare's era, and the wealth of women's theatre work that happened after Hrotsvit and Aphra Behn, on whom Case focuses in an early chapter.

Van Dyke feels Hart's anthology is more "balanced" in its view of contemporary women's theatre and engages her critique particularly with Yolanda Broyles Gonzalez' essay on the women of El Teatro Campesino. Van Dyke's article takes its most ideological turn when she begins to summarize the ramifications of the three books she reviews. She feels that feminist critics place themselves at a remove from work by living writers to focus on their own arena of "critical combat." Suddenly, references to critical militarism ground her review:

There are a number of governing metaphors that shape literary criticism today ... [b]ut the prevailing metaphor is the militarist one, and feminists seem to have adopted it as enthusiastically as other critics. In this climate, the critical vocabulary of attacks, defenses, tactics and strategies seems natural and inevitable. Critics are praised as "brave" and "daring"; "discipline" (with its implications of hierarchy and punishment) and critical "rigor" (not just phallic but suggestive of military bearing, and other life-threatening or lifeless forms) are frequently equated with intellectual respectability.... There are other metaphors available to criticism that would be more in keeping with feminism: for instance, the theatrical metaphor.... It suggests a collectivist enterprise, one that is at least potentially nonhierarchical. It proposes a life-giving and pleasure-giving activity in an arena of liberation from gender and other prescribed roles. It welcomes ... a multiplicity of styles and personal voices.

(1989:3)

Van Dyke's equation of feminist criticism with life-threatening militarism is extremely disturbing. Her suggestion that criticism is male-like unless it's nurturing, "life-giving and pleasure-giving" implies that unless the feminist critic once again places herself fully in the service of the playwright – the ultimate creator, the idealized mother of the dramatic text – she is participating in an imperialistic, nihilistic act that's merely an exercise in power.

As feminist performance critics and theorists move farther into the project of distinguishing the feminisms and their criticisms from the amorphous mass of pluralism, a peculiar backlash has begun to operate. Liberal feminists such as Cody get uneasy when the canon is attacked; radical feminists such as van Dyke refuse to take responsibility for their own positions as critics, since they regard criticism and theory as male-like; and materialist critics get trashed for their willingness to be "daring" and "brave," for attempting to chart new pathways in performance theory's territory. Although my sympathies are clearly with materialist feminist theorists and therefore cloud my so-called "objectivity," it seems to me that the critical attacks on Case's book in particular (despite radical feminist claims to be antiaggressive) are part of feminism's general backlash against theory.

A PERSONAL DEFENSE OF THEORY IN DISCOURSE

Because poststructuralist theory questions the authenticity of experience as truth, many feminist theorists have been attacked as jargon-wielding elitists who have no political project and who trivialize years of political action organized around radical feminist epistemology. This is not the intent, as I know it, of theory. Poststructuralism simply questions the liberal humanist notion that men or women are free individuals capable of mastering the universe, and points out the way in which ideology is masked as common-sensical truth (see Weedon 1987). Poststructuralist performance criticism looks at the power structures underlying representation, and the means by which subjectivity is shaped and withheld through discourse. These are intensely political projects.

But rather than arguing the implications of such a poststructuralist perspective, some feminist academicians and activists attack the project of theory. Black feminist critic Barbara Christian, for instance, in her article "The Race for Theory," reasserts the accusation that theory silences (1988). She believes that theory became popular when marginalized minority writers were successfully clamoring to be heard in academia.

Christian criticizes theorists for ignoring black women writers in their drive to immerse themselves in the verbal gymnastics of famous white men. She implicitly charges that because feminist poststructuralism acquiesces to the death of the author, it's complicit with a reactionary silencing of women authors. Christian is not the only woman to voice these concerns, and from a certain perspective, the point she raises is valid. In theatre, much of the recent dissension over theory comes from a similar unwillingness to unsettle playwrighting as one of women's primary activities. If we agree that the author is dead, how can we continue talking about women playwrights? Feminist poststructuralist theories, however, don't intend to kill off women authors a priori, but to simply enlarge the consideration of texts to take into account the meanings that are constructed in performance as well as on the page.[2]

Christian angles her argument through a racial perspective, insisting that her race theorizes from the basis of its experience as a minority. Other women attack theory by insisting that their experiences of oppression keep them from using its language. How can I, as a feminist theorist, respond to these concerns? How can I negotiate the differences between Christian and myself? Christian says she works in literary criticism to save her own life. I work in theory to save mine. Theory allows me to articulate my differences from a feminism I first learned as monolithic. Theory enables me to see that there is no tenable position for me in the totalizing strategies of radical feminism, and that I can align myself profitably elsewhere.

Through theory, I can articulate the roots of my own identity in the conflicting discourses of lesbianism and Judaism, and know that there is no comfortable place for me within any single discourse. Theory enables me to describe the differences within me and around me without forcing me to rank my allegiances or my oppressions. As feminist critic Gayle

Austin would say, theory enables the divided subject to fall into the cracks of difference and to theorize productively from there, knowing that truth is changeable, permeable, and finally, irrelevant (1988).

The irony of articulating my own experience as a defense of feminist poststructuralist performance criticism is not lost on me. The pervasive glorification of experience, and the testimonial strategies used to enforce it as truth, require that I, too, throw myself back on positions that theory otherwise allows me to detach from.

STRUGGLES FOR IDENTITY IN DISCOURSE: A FINAL EXAMPLE

The antitheory stance of feminists who posit experience as truth and who want to enter representation on the basis of authentic female experience was illustrated at the 1988 WTP preconference in San Diego, for which I served as coordinator. The following account is a testimony to my experience of the event.

The conference was devoted to the intersection of theory and practice. Poststructuralism and postmodernism were employed and discussed. Some participants talked about the contamination of narrative, the subject's decenteredness, and the impossibility of getting outside of ideology. Other participants felt alienated by this language, by words and phrases that appeared impenetrable. Alongside the discourse of theory swelled a nostalgia for a lost female narrative that would nurture, support, and rock women at the bosom of gender.

Despite the intense confrontations that the preconference generated between these conflicting perspectives, three performances were presented that productively illustrated the potential of feminist postmodernism and provided opportunities to examine theory in action. The first was by Anna Deavere Smith – the only black woman of the 100 women attending – who performed an oral history of the WTP. She used the words of black women and white women she had interviewed to editorialize about her subjects and to create versions of their identities and their programs through her perceptions of them as a black woman. The spectators could identify the subjects of Smith's performance – many of whom were in the audience – but were encouraged to see her performing them, to hear her choose their words, and to grapple with the foregrounding of race and ideas.

But some spectators expected mimesis, and railed against their absence from Smith's opaque mirror. Because they didn't see the radical implications of Smith's performance, and because they didn't hear her critique, they proceeded to attack the history of the program instead. Lost in the ensuing struggle among white women was a confrontation with the ideas about race and representation in the performance text Smith constructed. By searching for an "authentic" representation of their own experience, and focusing on their dissatisfaction with its absence, the spectators erased the residue of Smith's commentary on her experience.

At the second performance, Kate Bornstein, a male-to-female trans-sexual, performed her experiences of gender identity. Bornstein delivered a male character's monolog as she once played him as a male actor, aware of her imprisonment in her theatrical and social role. She then performed a female character as she once did as a male actor, protected by the theatrical convention of gender impersonation while her body enacted this impersonation in everyday life.

Bornstein performed a noncoincidence of body and language, a Brechtian, postmodern dissociation of presence and discourse. Her monologs traded among shifting, constructed identities, layered on a body that has experienced all of these constructions. Bornstein hired a surgical knife to allow her to play the gender role she desired in a body that would look the part. Confined by gender construction, Bornstein opted to reconstruct her body to fit herself into gendered discourse. Or did she subvert gendered discourse by her choice to tamper with biology? Watching her perform, I was unsettled by my awareness that Bornstein has no neutral body, that even her biology is not immutable but constructed. Is this the death of character? Where is the truth in this experience?

The third preconference performance was by Marianne Goldberg, a performer/theorist who refuses the traditional and feminist dichotomies that split those terms.[3] She stood behind a lectern and used her body to form words. Her performance was a literarization of the body à la Brecht, not an incidence of l'écriture féminine – in fact, Goldberg insists, "We can claim our bodies only if we stop claiming that they give us truth." Her body became a text written in space, and she played reflexively with the meanings it created.

Goldberg positions herself as the unmasked performer, as a lecturer and demonstrator, as a colleague who refuses the position of "naive art object." Her body, she says, is "in motion and at risk" (see Diamond 1988a), present in a discourse in which she is engaged and competent. She speaks to spectators, and points out that she is exchanging the gaze with them. She is an author who refuses authority, a subject intent on shifting her identity even as she speaks.

These performances illustrated the potential of a feminist postmodern style to concretize the poststructuralist problematics of meaning and experience. Smith performed the spectator, literally blackening Snow White's theatrical mirror. Goldberg performed theory, inviting spectators to theorize with her as they looked at her. Bornstein performed permutations of gender on a body that can't help but editorialize its constructedness, thwarting any attempt to arrive at biological or ideological truth.

These postmodernist experiments happened in the context of feminism, in which the political stakes were very material and quite high. After the conference, Anna Deavere Smith left for a famous regional theatre to perform as a whore in a play by a famous white man. Kate Bornstein returned to a city where she has no job working in theatre. Marianne Goldberg went home to rewrite her performance, since her text is continually in process. An instance of theory had occurred.

Feminist postmodernism happens in theory. Our experiments are conducted at conferences and in universities, and most often on paper rather than on big stages sodden with spectacle. Feminist postmodernism does not play indulgently with meaninglessness or plurality, charges that might be leveled against some postmodern performance auteurs. Feminist postmodernism is committed to meaning, to sifting through the referents of material reality and drawing blueprints of their construction that can be historically revised and changed.[4]

Positions of identity are equally historical. Elin Diamond, on a panel about feminist criticism at the same preconference, remarked that positioning is utterly provisional, that once you have a position, you inherit issues of identity that you want to put into crisis (1988b). My challenge as a materialist feminist performance theorist, then, is to reposition myself constantly, to keep changing my seat in the theatre, and to continually ask: How does it look from over here? To ask myself, how would Barbara Christian see this, and how might she and I prod each other to look differently? Working in theory allows such fluidity, since the only productive position for the theorist is balancing precariously on the edge of the differences between, among, and within women, who are the site of conflicting discourses in which there is no immutable truth.

NOTES

1. This article expands on papers presented at the New Languages for Stage Conference in Lawrence, KS, October 1988, and at the Modern Language Association convention in New Orleans, LA, December 1988.

2. When I gave a version of this article as a talk at Brown University in May 1989, playwright Paula Vogel, who teaches at Brown, pointed out that many women playwrights are still struggling to live, literally, in the mainstream theatre context, which makes the metaphorical death of the author something of a moot issue for them. Poststructuralist theory, she implied, which describes a moment in which authorship is dispersed across various reception strategies, seems premature for women playwrights who have not yet gained access to the author's position.

3. A performance-for-print version of Goldberg's preconference presentation appears as "Ballerinas and Ball Passing" in *Women and Performance* (1987/1988).

4. Because of its concentration in theory, feminist postmodernism has been vulnerable to assimilation by academic critics. The implosion of what might be called "apolitical" postmodernism and the feminist variety poses a very real problem for feminist critics determined to employ theory for political ends. The question resides, once again, in discourse – even publishing an article such as this one in *TDR* makes the movement's issues available to a readership outside its purview. Yet for feminist theory to become familiar and useful to those inside the movement, who have political investments in its utility, it seems important to speak through the public forum journals such as *TDR* provide.

REFERENCES

Austin, Gayle (1988) Comments made on "Elucidating Terms and Issues" panel, Women and Theatre Program Preconference. Horton Grand Hotel, San Diego, CA, 1 August.

Barthes, Roland (1977) "Death of the Author." In *Image–Music–Text*, 142–148. Translated by Stephen Heath. New York: The Noonday Press.

Betsko, Kathleen, and Rachel Koenig, eds. (1987) *Interviews with Contemporrary Women Playwrights*. New York: Beechtree Books.

Case, Sue-Ellen (1988) *Feminism and Theatre*. New York: Routledge.

Case, Sue-Ellen, and Jeanie Forte (1985) "From Formalism to Feminism." *Theater* 16, no. 2 (Spring):62–65.

Chinoy, Helen Krich, and Linda Walsh Jenkins, eds. (1987) [1981] *Women in American Theatre*. New York: Theatre Communications Group.

Christian, Barbara (1988) "The Race for Theory." *Feminist Studies* 14, no. 1 (Spring):67–80.

Cody, Gabrielle (1988) Book review. *Performing Arts Journal* 11, no. 2 (PAJ32):117–118.

de Courtivron, Isabelle, and Elaine Marks (1981) *New French Feminisms*. New York: Schocken.

Diamond, Elin (1985) "Refusing the Romanticism of Identity: Narrative Interventions in Churchill, Benmussa, Duras." *Theatre Journal* 38, no. 3 (October):273–286.

——(1988a) "Brechtian Theory/Feminist Theory: Toward a Gestic Feminist Criticism." *The Drama Review* 32, no. 1 (T117):82–94. Also in this sourcebook, 120–135.

——(1988b) Comments made on "Feminist Criticism" panel, Women and Theatre Program Preconference. Horton Grand Hotel, San Diego, 2 August.

Dolan, Jill (1987) "Is the Postmodern Aesthetic Feminist?" *Art & Cinema* 1, no. 3 (fall):5–6.

——(1988) *The Feminist Spectator as Critic*. Ann Arbor: UMI Research Press.

van Dyke, Joyce (1989) "Performance Anxiety." *Women's Review of Books* 6, no. 4 (January):1, 3.

Goldberg, Marianne (1987/88) "Ballerinas and Ball Passing." *Women & Performance* 3, no. 2 (#6): 7–31.

Hart, Lynda, ed. (1988) *Making a Spectacle: Feminist Essays on Contemporary Women's Theatre*. Ann Arbor: University of Michigan Press.

Keyssar, Helene (1985) *Feminist Theatre*. New York: Grove Press.

de Lauretis, Teresa (1986) "Issues, Terms, and Contexts." In *Feminist Studies/ Critical Studies*, edited by Teresa de Lauretis, 1–19. Bloomington: Indiana University Press.

Malpede, Karen, ed. (1983) *Women in Theatre: Compassion and Hope*. New York: Drama Book Specialists.

Weedon, Chris (1987) *Feminist Practice and Post-structuralist Theory*. New York: Basil Blackwell.

8

MOTHERHOOD ACCORDING TO KAREN FINLEY

The Theory of Total Blame

Lynda Hart

Nineteenth-century criminologists recommended rehabilitating "female offenders" by encouraging them to become mothers or share childcare with other incarcerated women. Such resorts to women's "nature" return in our culture accompanied by spurious appeals to the "real." In the summer of 1991, we witness Madonna's *Truth or Dare*, which purports to show us what the "bad girl" is like behind the scenes. Its primary focus is to reassure us that the sexually transgressive idol has suitably feminine attributes, maternal ones of course. Madonna plays "mommy" to her troupe of gay male dancers and her female backup singers, with special attention to her one heterosexual, and virulently homophobic "son," who needs special attention, threatened as he is by the gay dancers. One of the most prolonged inside views we see is Madonna's visit to her mother's grave; she lies down next to it, imagining herself buried next to her, cradling her head on the tombstone. When she bows down to her father who joins her onstage, the gesture is almost gratuitous; Madonna has already succumbed to the master discourse on femininity through the excessive rendering of the maternal.

In the alternative art world, Karen Finley, who became the media's centerpiece in NEA controversies, appears on the cover of The *Philadelphia Inquirer*'s Sunday magazine (7 April 1991) looking more like a centerfold. The story highlights the contrast between her "beastliness" onstage and her "beauty" offstage, captured in a series of photographs by Timothy Greenfield-Sanders. On the cover, Finley poses in a black shift with a plunging neckline, one thigh teasingly exposed. Inside, she is photographed in half-shadows, her head thrown back in the classic posture of vulnerable femininity, her neck exposed, her eyes closed. Insets show her peeking out from a sari, performing in a low-cut evening gown, emerging from behind a curtain, bikini-clad. These stills make it impossible to see the ways in which Finley subverts such iconic reproductions of women in her performances.

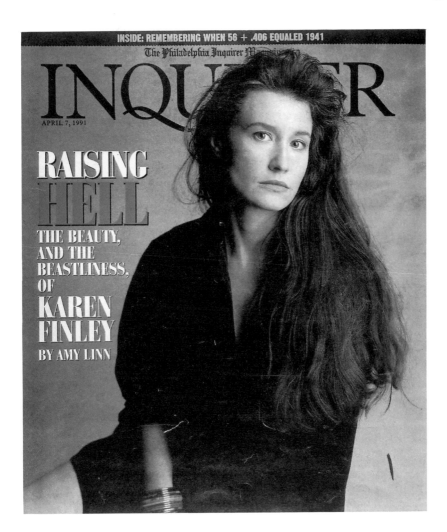

INSIDE: REMEMBERING WHEN 56 + .406 EQUALED 1941

The Philadelphia Inquirer Magazine

INQUIRER

APRIL 7, 1991

RAISING
HELL

THE BEAUTY,
AND THE
BEASTLINESS,
OF
KAREN
FINLEY
BY AMY LINN

Figure 8.1

The accompanying story begins as a typical day in the life of Karen Finley, an "art adventure." Finley walks the streets of New York with her plaid knit cap bobbing up and down as she strides jauntily to the printer's shop, her scarf wrapped "firmly around her pretty, pale neck." "Are you cold?", Finley asks her companion, "wanna wear my gloves?" (Linn 1991:17). She is not only beautiful, but also nurturing. The orthodox Jewish printer recoils from her "immodest" handshake, a fitting anecdote for a performer who ironizes discourses of defilement, pollution, and the unclean, improper body of woman. He attempts to find technical reasons for his inability to print her poster depicting a nude woman with three breasts standing in a garden with a naked man whose snaky penis splashes her with sperm. The caption reads: "Don't Blame Eve." Finley wins the printer over with her exuberant appreciation of the beauty of his stock. Soon the printers are all exclaiming with her about the incredible quality of the paper. The political message of the poster disappears in their mutual love for the aesthetics of the work. Finley explains to them that the poster is art, therefore it is supposed to have some "distressing" qualities. The ironizing aggression of Finley's "It's Only Art" monolog from *We Keep Our Victims Ready* (1990), the title of the monolog being Jesse Helms' last ditch cry for mercy when he is arrested by the confiscation police for making art, is recuperated as an *apology* for Finley. The article emphasizes that Finley is as "normal" as the next person. She might keep up her Christmas tree a little too far into January, but besides such small eccentricities, she lives in a "normal" house, with a "normal" husband, and lives an "incredibly normal life" (Linn 1991:19). This emphasis on her domestic/sexual "normality" comes just a bit less than a year after she was casually tossed in with the homosexual threesome – Holly Hughes, John

Figure 8.2

Figures 8.1 and 8.2 "Karen Finley, the media's centerpiece in NEA controversies, appears in the *Philadelphia Inquirer* Sunday magazine looking more like a centerfold." (Photo by Greg Gorman, used in the *Philadelphia Inquirer* article by Amy Linn)

Fleck, and Tim Miller. The heterosexual family circle strives to reenclose the author of the "Black Sheep" monolog – Finley's assault on the nuclear family as a primary site of oppression.[3]

After Finley's sudden projection into a kind of stardom, albeit one based on notoriety, such efforts to conventionalize her are not unexpected. Nor should we be surprised that some of this rhetoric – "it's only art" – is appropriated, minus the irony, from her own language. Ideology, as we know, often works this way: an appropriation of ideas from one group is made functional by another, even though their interests are in conflict; witness the deployment of radical feminism's valorization of motherhood used by antiabortion activists, or deconstructionists' radical destabilization of identity to justify violence against gays and lesbians.[2] The risk of assimilation is high for a performer like Finley, not only because of her recent push into the limelight, but also because her performances are so provocatively ambiguous. Her politics, as she describes them both on- and off stage, are primarily radical and liberal feminist. Though these are theoretically opposite positions – liberalism for equality, radicalism for difference – such contradictions are pervasive in the politics of US feminists and need not necessarily be reconciled, for both are effective, depending on the context in which they are deployed. Finley's performances, however, occupy politic-aesthetic spaces that are not easily subsumed under either a liberal or radical feminist agenda.

Perhaps due to its relative conventionality, one of Finley's performances has been virtually ignored in all of the media coverage. It is also, however, a work that is obsessively focused on motherhood, which is probably the most hotly contested site for women both inside and outside feminist theories. *The Theory of Total Blame* (1988) more closely approximates a "play" than any of her other work. Set in a realistic modern living room, *Blame* is an easily recognizable American domestic drama, despite a rather unusual cast: Irene, the matriarch, "an alcoholic whose pussy stinks"; Tim, the father, "depressed, comatose, or dead"; Jan, the daughter, who "has asthma but cares a lot about others"; Jack, Jan's husband, "one hell of a guy"; Buzz, a son, who "cares more for a dead dog than a dead dad"; Ernie, another son, "the sweetest underneath but he is a booger eater."[3] Finley plays the mother, Irene, who is cooking a holiday dinner for her reunited family which has come home to share childhood memories and partake of mother's meal. In her performance art, Finley has described herself in terms that suggest a kind of martyrdom as she absorbs, experiences, and transmits the suffering of a variety of oppressed peoples. In *Blame*, however, the pain that she interrogates zeros in on the institutionalization of motherhood. This oedipal play is located squarely within American familial representations, not unlike Sam Shepard's *Buried Child* or Edward Albee's *American Dream*.

Since Finley has said that her performance is in part motivated by a "responsibility to denounce the myths about women and psychology created by Freud and others like him ... to talk about these things until people stop asking me whether or not I'm a feminist" (Robinson 1986:45), *Blame*, so obviously indebted to Freudian/Lacanian concepts, is a particularly risky moment in her career. Finley conceives feminism within the familiar Anglo-American denunciation of psychoanalysis; nevertheless one can see in *Blame* performative possibilities that might only be accessed through, or understood by, the multiple, shifting, and heterogeneous identifications that psychoanalytic discourse both describes and permits. *The Theory of Total Blame* balances precariously between disruption of the Freudian familial model and reification of it, precisely because it overtly confronts *the* master discourse of sexual difference and goes directly to the primary site of patriarchal fear and loathing – the maternal body. Under the influence of certain strains of "French feminism," the maternal body has undergone reclamation as a celebratory space where an essential feminine risks reinstatement. Finley's play, on the other hand, assaults not only a popular reading of psychoanalysis as a discourse that blames the mother for everything and cites her as the individual who initiates the child into culture, but also affronts the totalizing tendency of some feminist theories of the maternal.

In *The Constant State of Desire*, Finley seems to be locked into the Freudian/Lacanian construction of desire. The language of *Desire*, its nonsequential logic, sudden sharp shifts, disjunctions and displacements, its often inchoate rage, imitates the language of the unconscious, foregrounding Lacan's famous claim that the unconscious is structured like a language. Finley reinforces this perception when she enters into a "trance" as she performs, suggesting that she leaves consciousness behind. Nevertheless, Finley never loses the ability to self-consciously perform the unconscious, which enables her to abandon the unity of the humanist "I," to shift around, between, and among subject and object positions, to confound spectators who desire to locate an identity behind the construction of subjectivity. As her title explicitly states, desire in this performance is always deferred; it is a constant pursuit of a lost object. Thus desire is always imbricated in loss, and Finley's "taboo art" interrogates the Freudian/Lacanian incest taboo that is constitutive of sexual difference. Her monologs report the return of the repressed; and as Foucault has argued, this unveiling of sexual fantasies is a compliance with the demand to reproduce sexuality in discourse (Foucault 1980). Finley loudly calls forth the Lacanian transcendental signifier that founds culture, the original lost object, the signifier that has no signified – the phallus:

It is the father in all of us that gives us the Berlin Wall, saves the whales, makes treaties, makes decisions and reasons, bridges and tunnels, cures diseases, ways and means. Politics and disorders. It's the father, it's the father, it's the father in all of us.

(1988:150)

It could certainly be argued that Finley can only rail at her own containment within this system, and while rage can be a satisfying as well as threatening expression, it is also a purifying emotion, a catharsis. Nonetheless, this performance permits transgressions of the unitary, coherent humanist subject. And although, as Derrida states, "even in transgressions and aggressions we are consorting with a code to which metaphysics is tied irreducibly, such that every transgressive gesture reencloses us" (1981:12), Finley modifies the field by performing in an eccentric space that is simultaneously both inside and outside the historical constructs of sexual difference. It would seem that performing art is peculiarly well situated for transgressive, possibly subversive, repetitions; whereas conventional mimesis – with the actor laminated to the character, reproducing the notion of a unified subjectivity, a constant identity – is doomed to subsume differences under some presumed monolithic sameness. As Sue-Ellen Case has argued, in realism "the violence released in the continual zooming-in on the family unit, and the heterosexist ideology linked with its stage partners, realism, is directed against women and their hint of seduction" (1989:297). Classical realism, in fact, is in some ways like hysteria; the action shows us "symptoms" that are transmitted through the bodies of characters who are remembering the *past*, or failing to remember but eliciting signs that nonetheless signify traces of the past. Elin Diamond has subtly explored the question of whether mimesis can be played with a difference (1989), and it is this question that intrigues me about Finley's *Blame*, an unconventionally conventional play. How can a performer signify a space that calls attention to the invisible boundaries shoring up the fiction of a unified subjectivity? I would suggest that Finley uses food loathing as a trope for boundary confusions, and utilizes this trope in concert with the maternal body to make patent cultural constructions of the female body as always already mother.

It has been argued that Finley's work resists comprehension by spectators who are unschooled in feminist theory (Schuler 1990).[4] I don't think a spectator need be conversant with feminist theory to appreciate the fused signification of mothers and food, but perhaps a quotation from Julia Kristeva would clarify things: "... food is the oral object (the abject) that sets up archaic relationships between the human being and the other, its mother, who wields a power that is as vital as it is fierce"

(1982:75–76). Kristeva is the primary theoretician I had in mind when earlier I mentioned the tendency by some "French feminists" to abet the patriarchal valorization of motherhood. Nonetheless, Kristeva's theory can be used for a subversive reading of Finley's *Theory of Total Blame*. Irene is, on the one hand, the masochistic mother who never stops working. We see her constantly trudging back and forth from the refrigerator to the table where she is preparing food. She randomly grabs items from the refrigerator, and mixes them up into disgusting, unconsumable, virtually unrecognizable, messes. Finley uses no instruments other than her hands to manipulate the food, thus she begins to look like an extension of the wasted matter. She digs Jell-O out of the molds and plops the sticky mass onto the table and floor. Her meatloaf ends up all over her body, bits of raw beef hang from her nose, stick to her hair, litter the floor. Ketchup runs down her arms and legs. She shoves uncooked beef into one son's face. Irene has no recipes and she refuses to feed her children. While this "preparation" is in progress, each of the children displays his/her fetishized sexuality: Buzz whips a potted plant with a black leather strap; Ernie strips down to his jockstrap and masturbates as he drips hand lotion onto the back of a chair; Jan undresses down to a girdle and bra and spills milk on the stage. For her children, Irene's body is the hysterical body, a "theater for forgotten scenes" (Cixous and Clément 1986:5), a screen memory. But Irene will not accept total blame. Instead, she claims the ironic power of her marginality, and like Jules Michelet's sorceress (see Cixous and Clément 1986), she reconstructs her own memories, insisting that none of her children's problems are her responsibility.

Unlike the hysteric, Irene is not reenclosed by the family circle. Rather, she disrupts it, ejects its members, even the dead father/comatose husband, and demands the authority of "her house." Irene reverses all of the conventional associations of motherhood with nurturing, and makes them into her own orgiastic rites. If she represents the phallic mother, she does so in travesty to assault the model that constructs her. The discursive body of the patriarchal mother is replaced by Irene's excessive materiality. Whereas *The Constant State of Desire* represents conditions of unmitigated pain, in which the female body is contained and perpetually reinscribed within oppressive cultural formations, *The Theory of Total Blame* moves toward analysis of historical constructs that render women as always already mothers, and hence as origins of cultural horror. Here Finley uses parody and travesty, excessive renderings of the stereotypes, in an effort to swell the models to their limits and explode them. What remains are waste products – spit out, regurgitated, excreted. The ultimate by-product of civilization, the corpse, serves as a constant reminder of the defiled family in the figure of the father whose body is barely visible on the living room sofa. When Irene shakes him "awake," and forces him off stage at the play's end, we are left with the image of a woman who has cleaned her house by exorcizing the products of her body – her children – as well as her partner in making them. *Blame* conjures up the historical allotment of "dirty work" to women – cleaning up excrement, vomit, and other bodily wastes, preparing corpses for burial. But her manipulation of these tasks, and her active making of them, suggests not that she is trapped in the association of women with flesh/nature, but that the wastes signify a violation of the discursive bodies of women/mothers. Seemingly debasing herself, Finley enacts a liminality that threatens the integrity of the maternal body as it has been discursively made. When food appears as a polluting object, Kristeva writes:

> it does so as oral object only to the extent that orality signifies a boundary of the self's clean and proper body. Food becomes abject only if it is a border between two distinct entities or territories. A boundary between nature and culture, between the human and the non-human.

> (1982:75)

If the self's "clean and proper body" is the equivalent of the masculine, coherent identity, then Finley's performance could be read as a disruption of that humanistic (masculinist) body. She uses her female body as an image that merges with the food remainders. To put it differently, if feminine "lack" is necessary to shore up the fiction of masculine wholeness, Finley demonstrates how that operation works. It is not merely that she becomes unclean and improper, which would only reassert the binary distinction through reversal, but rather she makes an audience see the process of this gendered construction that "works" in the social field only when it is not permitted to be seen.

Kaja Silverman points out that the subjectivity described by Freud and Lacan cannot be refuted when any cultural system presupposes something outside of or prior to it (1983:192). Finley's performance art is often described in such terms – she is "primal," or "primordial," or she evokes horror because she is an "unsocialized" woman (Carr 1986a, 1986b, 1990; Linn 1991). While I would argue that such descriptions of her do not do justice to her work, there is nonetheless a greater risk for such perceptions in performance art. In part this is due to a history of women's performance art that did posit some unmediated return to the body, to nature, or to the real. Perhaps one of the most striking examples would be Leslie Labowitz's retreat from the highly politicized, public, work of early pieces like *Three Weeks in May*, to the privatized ritual of *Sproutime*.[5] In addition, performance art does not allow for the perception of distance between the performer and her language and gestures, which the actor has automatically through the historical use of "character." Of course this model suggests that the character is a simulation and the actor is real, thus reinforcing the Platonic idealism of model and copy and securing an ontological subjectivity. Nonetheless, mimesis is not always naive realism, and the possibility for claiming

Figure 8.3 The Theory of Total Blame. (© Dona Ann McAdams)

mimesis by the female performance artist may be something feminists would not wish to relinquish. If the discourse of the family activates the paternal signifier and its complement, lack, it is nonetheless possible for the maternal signifier to deny this lack, hence undercutting the establishment and maintenance of the phallic signifier.

Finley makes a precarious, but I would argue, *necessary*, move by positioning herself within the nuclear family structure. Taking up any position necessitates a momentary arrest of meaning, and since meaning cannot be arrested without recourse to the transcendental signifier, a pause in the motility of endlessly deferred significations locates the subject in phallogocentrism. For women, this would imply repositioning themselves as lack. But is the only alternative hysteria? If in her performance art Finley might be understood as a witness to losses that survive in suffering, her body becoming a "theater for forgotten scenes," in *Blame* she gets mixed up in dirty things, and thus becomes more like the sister, or mother, to the hysteric – the sorceress. As Catherine Clément points out, both of these roles are disruptive to dominant social orders yet conservative at the same time, but for different reasons: the hysteric because she always becomes reenclosed within the family circle; the sorceress because she escapes by disappearing. Michelet proposes, "one would like to know, but one will not know, what has become of the wretched woman" (in Cixous and Clément 1986:5). In Finley's case, we might hope that she not disappear into the iconic signifiers to which the photographs I described at the beginning of this essay refer. Even as she pauses momentarily to inhabit a position, we might watch to see if she resists the pressures that are surely confronting her to become more palatable. Finley follows upon a long tradition of the maledictory woman, the scold who habitually engages in abusive language. She was banned from performing in London by a law that forbids women to be onstage nude and speak at the same time (Coffey 1990). As we know, prohibitions always imply obligations. The female body with an active tongue is still, evidently, a violation. Until the mid-19th century the "brank," an instrument of torture forced into the mouth of the scolding woman, was employed. This device reasserts itself in contemporary efforts to silence the woman who takes on the phallus (*lingus*, Latin for "tongue," derived from *lingam*, Sanskrit for "phallus"), and noisily shouts out the contradictions in the master's discourse.

NOTES

1. The "Black Sheep" monolog was performed in *The Theory of Total Blame*, and *We Keep Our Victims Ready*. It is published in *Shock Treatment* (Finley 1990).

2. Whether it is "motherhood" as a unifying position for women or genetic disposition for gays and lesbians, essentializing strategies are easily coopted by conservatives to promote their agenda. Lillian Faderman, for example, points to the resurgence of "congenital theory," in the guise of essentialism, as a reaction to the recent vigor of conservatism (Faderman 1991). But the constructionist position also lends itself to appropriation. I am thinking here of the ways in which conservatives have picked up the rhetoric of sexual identity *as a choice* to argue *for* the prohibition of homosexuality. The solution is of course not to push for a rigid adherence to either position, but to continually problematize, and *historicize*, the essentialist/constructionist binary.

3. *The Theory of Total Blame* is unpublished. These descriptions are taken from the program cover which has drawings of the characters. The performance first took place at The Kitchen, New York City, December 1988. The production I saw was at the RAPP Art Center in June 1989.

4. Based on interviews with 15 "average" spectators, Schuler found that most of the male spectators could not even remember having heard the "Cut off Balls" monolog in *The Constant State of Desire*. I would say that Schuler observed some hysterical forgetting among the spectators, rather than evidence to support her claim that Finley relies too much on an understanding of feminist theory to reach mainstream audiences. Finley's inaccessibility attests to her ability to avert commodification, not to a willful obscurantism that dilutes her effectiveness.

5. For a discussion of these performances and commentary on Labowitz's movement from overt political work to the spiritualism of later pieces like *Sproutime*, see Roth (1983).

REFERENCES

Carr, C. (1986a) "The New Outlaw Art." *Village Voice*, 17 July:61.

——(1986b) "Unspeakable Practices, Unnatural Acts, the Taboo Art of Karen Finley." *Village Voice*, 24 June:17–19, 86.

——(1990) "The Sexual Politics of Censorship: War on Art." *Village Voice*, 5 June:25–30.

Case, Sue-Ellen (1989) "Towards a Butch–Femme Aesthetic." In *Making a Spectacle: Feminist Essays on Contemporary Women's Theatre*, edited by Lynda Hart, 282–299. Ann Arbor: University of Michigan Press.

Cixous, Hélène, and Catherine Clément (1986) *The Newly Born Woman*. Translated by Betsy Wing. Minneapolis: University of Minnesota Press.

Coffey, Michael (1990) "Karen Finley's Disembodied Texts from City Lights." *Trade News/Publishers Weekly*, 14 September:90–92.

Derrida, Jacques (1981) *Positions*. Translated by Alan Bass. Chicago: The University of Chicago Press.

Diamond, Elin (1989) "Mimesis, Mimicry, and the True-Real." *Modern Drama* 32, no. 1 (March):58–72.

Faderman, Lillian (1991) *Odd Girls and Twilight Lovers: A History of Lesbian Life in Twentieth-Century America*. New York: Columbia University Press.

Finley, Karen (1988) *The Constant State of Desire*. TDR 34, no. 2 (T117):139–151. Also in this sourcebook, 293–302.

———(1990) *Shock Treatment*. San Francisco: City Lights.

Foucault, Michel (1980) *The History of Sexuality: Volume 1*. Translated by Robert Hurley. New York: Random House.

Kristeva, Julia (1982) *Powers of Horror: An Essay on Abjection*. Translated by Leon S. Roudiez. New York: Columbia University Press.

Linn, Amy (1991) "Raising Hell: The Beauty and the Beastliness of Karen Finley." *Philadelphia Inquirer Magazine*, 7 April:16–20, 32, 36–37.

Robinson, Marc (1986) "Performance Strategies: Interviews with Ishmael Houston Jones, John Kelly, Karen Finley, and Richard Elovich." *Performing Arts Journal* 10, no. 3 (PAJ30):31–55.

Roth, Moira (1983) *The Amazing Decade: Women and Performance Art in America 1970–1980*. Los Angeles: Astro Arts.

Schuler, Catherine (1990) "Spectator Response and Comprehension: The Problem of Karen Finley's *Constant State of Desire*." *TDR* 34, no. 1 (T125):131–145.

Silverman, Kaja (1983) *The Subject of Semiotics*. Oxford: Oxford University Press.

9

BRECHTIAN THEORY/FEMINIST THEORY

Toward a Gestic Feminist Criticism

Elin Diamond

This essay begins and ends with a short text on pointing.

> In the 1930s, Gertrude Stein and Alice Toklas, on their American lecture tour, were driving in the country in Western Massachusetts. Toklas pointed out a batch of clouds. Stein replied, "Fresh eggs." Toklas insisted that Stein look at the clouds. Stein replied again, "Fresh eggs." Then Toklas asked, "Are you making symbolic language?" "No," Stein answered, "I'm reading the signs. I love to read the signs."
>
> (Stimpson 1986:7)

One might devote an essay merely to unpacking this statement for its historical, discursive, and sexual resonances. Let me just say that Toklas' irritation seems justified. She is pointing to clouds; they have an ontological, referential status *as* clouds, but Stein playfully crosses ontology with textuality, object with symbol, referent with sign. Acting the self-conscious spectator, Stein produces a reading and says that *that* is more pleasurable than any Massachusetts clouds. I am concerned with how we point to and read signs in the theatre, and by "we" I mean feminist critics and theorists and also students of Brecht's theatre theory – an unlikely group, but then this is part of my argument. I would suggest that feminist theory and Brechtian theory need to be read intertextually, for among the effects of such a reading are a recovery of the radical potential of the Brechtian critique and a discovery, for feminist theory, of the specificity of theatre.[1]

At the outset I should say that like Gertrude Stein's clouds, feminist theory and Brechtian theory are moving, changing discourses, open to multiple readings. The umbrella term "feminist theory" covers feminist film theory, feminist literary theory, psychoanalytic feminist theory, socialist feminist theory, black feminist theory, lesbian feminist theory, cross-cultural feminist theory – many of which combine under different rubrics with different topoi, different political inflections. Yet perhaps all theories that call themselves "feminist" share a goal: the passionate analysis of gender in material social relations and in discursive and representational structures, especially theatre and film, which involve scopic pleasures and the body. Brecht's theatre theory, written over a 30-year period, constantly reformulates its concepts but it, too, has consistent themes: attention to the dialectical and contradictory forces within social relations, principally the agon of class conflict in its changing historical forms; commitment to alienation techniques and nonmimetic disunity in theatrical signification; "literarization" of the theatre space to produce a spectator/reader who is not interpellated into ideology but is pleasurably engaged in observation and analysis.

Now feminists in film studies have been quick to appropriate elements of Brecht's critique of the theatre apparatus.[2] In summer 1974, the British film journal *Screen* published a Brecht issue whose stated purpose was a consideration of Brecht's theoretical texts and the possibility of a revolutionary cinema. In autumn 1975, Laura Mulvey published her influential essay "Visual Pleasure and Narrative Cinema" in which, employing psychoanalysis "as a political weapon," she argues that Hollywood film conventions construct a specifically male viewing position by aligning or suturing the male's gaze to that of the fictional hero, and by inviting him thereby both to identify narcissistically with that hero and to fetishize the female (turning her into an object of sexual stimulation) (1975:6). In rejecting this dominant cinematic tradition, Mulvey powerfully invokes Brechtian concepts:

> The first blow against the monolithic accumulation of traditional film conventions . . . is to free the look of the camera into its materiality in time and space and the look of the audience into dialectics, passionate detachment.
>
> (1975:18)

Demystifying representation, showing how and when the object of pleasure is made, releasing the spectator from imaginary and illusory identifications – these are crucial elements in Brecht's theoretical project. Yet we feminists in drama and theatre studies have attended more to the critique of the gaze than to the Brechtian intervention that signals a way of dismantling the gaze. Feminist film theorists, fellow-traveling with psychoanalysis and semiotics, have given us a lot to think about, but we, through Brechtian theory, have something to give them: a female body in representation that resists fetishization and a viable position for the female spectator.

In this essay, then, I have two purposes. One, an intertextual reading of key topoi of feminist theory: gender critique and sexual difference;

questions of authority in women's writing and women's history; spectatorship and the body – with key topoi in Brechtian theory: *Verfremdungseffekt*, the "not, but," historicization, and *Gestus*. Two, emerging from this intertexting, a proposal for a theatre-specific feminist criticism. I call it "gestic criticism" and close the essay with a brief example (my second text on pointing).

Some quick qualifications and clarifications: I realize that feminists in drama studies might greet this coupling with some bemusement. Brecht exhibits a typical Marxian blindness toward gender relations,and except for some interesting excursions into male erotic violence, he created conventionally gendered plays and too many saintly mothers (one is too many). Moreover, the postmodern critique of Brecht by Heiner Müller-ites should not be ignored, particularly the rejection of the Brechtian "fable" which Müller describes as a "closed form" that the audience accepts as a "package, a commodity" (Weber 1980:121). This essay brackets both Brecht's plays and their retrograde (and unBrechtian) stagings in the German Democratic Republic and the West over the last three decades. My interest lies in the potentiality of Brecht's theory for feminism, and, as I mentioned above, a possible re-radicalization of his theory through feminism. In current literary theory, especially from the English Left, Brecht's concepts have become weapons in campaigns against mimetic linearity (see Dollimore 1984), bourgeois naturalism (see Barker 1984), and, in a fine reading by Terry Eagleton (1986), on the side of deconstructive rhetoric. Even Toril Moi (Oxford-based Norwegian), in her notorious *Sexual/Textual Politics*, parses the feminisms by enlisting Brecht's debate with Lukacs on the question of socialist realism to challenge Anglo-American critics of Virginia Woolf (1985:17). Strange bedfellows perhaps, but the point I wish to make is that these critics have understood that Brechtian theory in all its gaps and inconsistencies is not literary criticism, but rather a theorizing of the workings of an apparatus of representation with enormous formal and political resonance. I think we should be long past the point of accepting Martin Esslin's view that Brecht's theories "were merely rationalizations of intuition, taste, and imagination" (1971:146), or Eric Bentley's view that the theory is a didactic distraction from Brecht's true art (1981:46ff). Herbert Blau has the best if not the last word on theory-versus-practice debates: "Theater is theory, or a shadow of it.... In the act of seeing, there is already theory" (1982:1).

GENDER, VERFREMDUNGSEFFEKT

The cornerstone of Brecht's theory is the Verfremdungseffekt, the technique of defamiliarizing a word, an idea, a gesture so as to enable the spectator to see or hear it afresh: "a representation that alienates is one which allows us to recognize its subject, but at the same time makes it seem unfamiliar" (Brecht 1964:192); "the A-effect consists of turning an object from something ordinary and immediately accessible into something peculiar, striking, and unexpected" (1964:143). In performance the actor "alienates" rather than impersonates her character; she "quotes" or demonstrates the character's behavior instead of identifying with it. Brecht theorizes that if the performer remains outside the character's feelings, the audience may also, thereby remaining free to analyze and form opinions about the play's "fable." Verfremdungseffekt also challenges the mimetic property of acting that semioticians call iconicity, the fact that the performer's body conventionally resembles the object (or character) to which it refers. This is why gender critique in the theatre can be so powerful.

Gender refers to the words, gestures, appearances, ideas, and behavior that dominant culture understands as indices of feminine or masculine identity. When spectators "see' gender they are seeing (and reproducing) the cultural signs of gender, and by implication, the gender ideology of a culture. Gender in fact provides a perfect illustration of ideology at work since "feminine" or "masculine" behavior usually appears to be a "natural" – and thus fixed and unalterable – extension of biological sex. Feminist practice that seeks to expose or mock the strictures of gender usually uses some version of the Brechtian A-effect. That is, by alienating (not simply rejecting) iconicity, by foregrounding the expectation of resemblance the ideology of gender is exposed and thrown back to the spectator.[3] In Caryl Churchill's play *Cloud Nine*, cross-dressing, in which the male body can be seen in feminine clothes, provides A-effects for a gender critique of the familial and sexual roles in Victorian colonial society. In lesbian performances at New York's WOW Cafe – I'm thinking of Holly Hughes' *Lady Dick* and Split Britches' *Upwardly Mobile Home* – and in the broadly satirical monologs of Italy's Franca Rame, gender is exposed as a sexual costume, a sign of a role, not evidence of identity. Recalling such performances should remind us of the rigorous self-consciousness that goes into even the most playful gender-bending. A-effects are not easy to produce, but the payoffs can be stunning. When gender is "alienated" or foregrounded, the spectator is enabled to see a sign system *as* a sign system – the appearance, words, gestures, ideas, attitudes, etc., that comprise the gender lexicon become so many illusionistic trappings to be put on or shed at will. Understanding gender as ideology – as a system of beliefs and behavior mapped across the bodies of females and males, which reinforces a social status quo – is to appreciate the continued timeliness of Verfremdungseffekt, the purpose of which is to denaturalize and defamiliarize what ideology makes seem normal, acceptable, inescapable.

SEXUAL DIFFERENCE, THE "NOT, BUT"

Gender critique in artistic and discursive practices is often and wrongly confused with another topos in feminist theory: sexual difference. I would propose that "sexual difference" be understood not as a synonym for gender oppositions but as a possible reference to differences within sexuality. I take my cue here partly from the poststructuralist privileging of "difference" across all representational systems, particularly language. Derridean deconstruction posits the disturbance of the signifier within the linguistic sign or word; the seemingly stable word is inhabited by a signifier that bears the trace of another signifier and another, so that contained within the meaning of any given word is the trace of the word it is not. Thus the word is always different from itself, or, as Barbara Johnson patiently teases out its connotations, "difference" refers not to what distinguishes one identity from another – "it is not a difference between ... independent units ... but a difference within" (1980:4). Texts, she argues, are not different from other texts but different from themselves. Deconstruction thus wreaks havoc on identity, with its connotations of wholeness and coherence: if an identity is always different from itself it can no longer *be* an identity. Sexual *difference*, then, might be seen to destabilize the bipolar oppositions that constitute gender identity.

Psychoanalysis offers other cues. Despite the normative tone of his gender distinctions, Freud also makes clear that the drives and desires that constitute sexuality do not add up to a stable identity:

> [W]e are accustomed to say that every human being displays both male and female instinctual impulses, needs and attributes; but though anatomy, it is true, can point out the characteristic of maleness and femaleness, psychology cannot. For psychology the contrast between the sexes fades away into one between activity and passivity, in which we far too readily identify activity with maleness and passivity with femaleness, a view which is by no means universally confirmed.
>
> (in Watney 1986:16)

In fact the Freudian account of the diverse identifications and effects of childhood sexuality undermines the idea of a stable-gendered subject. To paraphrase Gayle Rubin, women and men are certainly different, but gender coercively translates the nuanced differences within sexuality into a structure of opposition; male vs. female, masculine vs. feminine, etc. (see 1978:179). In my reading of Rubin, the "sex/gender system," the trace of the difference of sexuality is kept alive within the sterile opposition of gender. I am suggesting that sexual difference is where we imagine, where we theorize; gender is where we live, our social address, although most of us, with an effort, are trying to leave home. Let me put it another way: no feminist can ignore the social and political battlefield of gender, but no feminist can ignore the fact that the language of the battlefield is a system based on difference whose traces contain our most powerful desires.

Keeping differences in view instead of conforming to stable representations of identity, and *linking those differences to a practical politics* are key to Brecht's theory of the "not, but," a feature of alienated acting that I read intertextually with the sex/gender system.

> When [an actor] appears on stage, besides what he actually is doing he will at all essential points discover, specify, imply what he is not doing; that is he will act in such a way that the alternative emerges as clearly as possible, that his acting allows the other possibilities to be inferred and only represents one of the possible variants.... Whatever he doesn't do must be contained and conserved in what he does.
>
> (Brecht 1964:137)

Each action must contain the trace of the action it represses, thus the meaning of each action contains difference. The audience is invited to look beyond representation – beyond what is authoritatively put in view – to the possibilities of as yet unarticulated actions or judgments. Brecht's early plays, particularly *In the Jungle of Cities*, thematize the "not, but": "I'm never anything more than half," says Mary Garga, who doesn't have the pleasure of joining the men in what Brecht called "the idealist dialectic" of the play or "the pure joy of fighting." Contemporary feminist plays by Michelene Wandor, Caryl Churchill, and Adrienne Kennedy also thematize the "not, but" in their sex/gender referents, but it would be interesting to query sex/gender nuances in *Measure for Measure*, *The Master Builder*, and *No Man's Land* to name only three.

The Brechtian "not, but" is the theatrical and theoretical analog to the subversiveness of sexual difference, because it allows us to imagine the deconstruction of gender – and all other – representations. Such deconstructions dramatize, at least at the level of theory, the infinite play of difference that Derrida calls *écriture* – the superfluity of signification that places meaning beyond capture within the covers of the play or the hours of performance. This is not to deny Brecht's wish for an instructive, analytical theatre; on the contrary, it invites the participatory play of the spectator, and the possibility for which Brecht most devoutly wished, that signification (the production of meaning) continue beyond play's end, congealing into choice and action after the spectator leaves the theatre.

HISTORY, HISTORICIZATION

The sex/gender system requires contextualization. The understanding of women's material conditions in history and the problematics of uncovering "women's history" are topoi in feminist theory that Brecht's theory of historicization greatly informs. Of course there must be limits to this discussion: Brecht was not writing history, but as a student devoted to the Marxist "classics" Brecht understood social relations, particularly class relations, as part of a moving dialectic. The crux of "historicization" is change: through A-effects spectators observe the potential movement in class relations, discover the limitations and strengths of their own perceptions, and begin to change their lives. There is a double movement in Brechtian historicization of preserving the "distinguishing marks" of the past and acknowledging, even foregrounding, the audience's present perspective (Brecht 1964:190). When Brecht says that spectators should become historians, he refers both to the spectator's detachment, her "critical" position, *and* to the fact that she is writing her own history even as she absorbs messages from the stage. Historicization is, then, *a way of seeing* and the enemy of recuperation and appropriation. One cannot historicize and colonize the Other or, as Luce Irigaray would have it, "reduce all others to the economy of the same" (1985:76). Brecht considered bourgeois illusionism insidious because it is guilty of precisely that:

> When our theatres perform plays of other periods they like to annihilate distance, fill in the gap, gloss over the differences. But what comes in our delight in comparisons, in distance, in dissimilarity – which is at the same time a delight in what is close and proper to ourselves?
>
> (Brecht 1964:276)

In historicized performance, gaps are not to be filled in, seams and contradictions show in all their roughness, and therein lies one aspect of spectatorial pleasure – when our differences *from* the past and *within* the present are palpable, graspable, applicable. Plays aspiring to realistically depict the present require the same historicization. Realism disgusted Brecht not only because it dissimulates its conventions but because it is hegemonic: by copying the surface details of the world it offers the illusion of lived experience, even as it marks off only one version of that experience.[4] This is perhaps why the most innovative women playwrights refuse the seamless narrative of conflicting egos in classic realism. Consider Adrienne Kennedy's *Funnyhouse of a Negro* or *The*

Owl Answers which lurch and reach through memory/fantasy staking the real in obsessional repetition and in fragmented characters who embrace and speak from their difference. Kennedy rejects the Brechtian fable – narrative progress is meaningless in her worlds – and instead dramatizes gaps and contradictions as, precisely, the black woman's experience of history. Brechtian historicization challenges the presumed ideological neutrality of any historical reflection. Rather it assumes, and promotes, what historians are now claiming: that reader/spectators of "facts" and "events" will, like Gertrude Stein reading the clouds, translate what is inchoate into signs (and stories), a move that produces not "truth," but mastery and pleasure.

SPECTATOR, BODY, HISTORICIZATION

Historicization in fact puts on the table the issue of spectatorship and the performer's body. According to Brecht, one way that the actor alienates or distances the audience from the character is to suggest the historicity of the character in contrast to the actor's own present-time self-awareness on stage. The actor must not lose herself in the character but rather *demonstrate* the character as a function of particular socio-historical relations, a conduit of particular choices. As Timothy Wiles puts it, actor and audience, both in present time, "look back on" the historical character as she fumbles through choices and judgments (1980:72). This does not, however, endow the actor with superiority, for as Wiles later points out this present-time actor is also fragmented: "Brecht separates the historical man who acts from the aesthetic function of the actor" (1980:85). The historical subject *plays* an actor presumed to have superior knowledge in relation to an ignorant character from the past, but the subject herself remains as divided and uncertain as the spectators to whom the play is addressed. This performer-subject neither disappears into a representation of the character *nor* into a representation of the actor; each remains processual, historical, incomplete. And the spectator? Aware of three temporalities within a single stage figure the spectator cannot read one without the other; her/his gaze is constantly split; her/his "*vouloir-voir*" (Pavis 1982:88) – the wanting to see and know all without any obstacle – is deflected into the dialectic of which the divided performer is only a part. Moreover, in reading a complex ever-changing text, spectators are "pulled out of [their] fixity" (Heath 1974:112); they become part of – indeed they produce – the dialectical comparisons and contributions that the text enacts.

The special characteristics of Brechtian reception emerge in relation to analogous processes in film theory. In psychoanalytic film theory, the film-text and the viewing-state are set in motion by unconscious fantasy.[5]

In the darkened room, in immobile seats, the spectator enters what Jean-Louis Baudry calls a "state of artificial regression" (1980:56), the womblike effects of film viewing which confuse boundaries and send the subject back to earlier states of psychic development, particularly the Lacanian mirror phase in which the infant, lacking controlled motor development, sees is image in a mirror or in its caretaker's eyes as a coherent whole. Misrecognizing himself (the male infant is specifically at issue here) as a complete, autonomous other, he spends the rest of his life unconsciously seeking an imaginary ideal – and discovers him, so the theory goes, at the movies.

Now the differences between the Brechtian spectator and the cinematic spectator are obvious. The last thing Brecht wants is a spectator in a "state of artificial regression," in thrall to his imaginary ideal. Brechtian theory formulates (and reformulates) a spectatorial state that breaks the suturing of imaginary identifications and keeps the spectator independent. Much influenced by Brecht, Patrice Pavis' semiotics of the mise-en-scène rests almost entirely on the spectator: ". . . the mise-en-scène is not entirely an indication of the intentionality of the director, but a structuring by the spectator of materials presented . . . whose linking is dependent on the perceiving subject" (Pavis 1982:138). In film theory the subject position is constructed ready-made for the spectator, only his capacity to regress is assumed. In Brechtian theory the subject's capacity to regress is suppressed. Film semiotics posits a spectator who is given the illusion that he creates the film; theatre semiotics posits a spectator whose active reception constantly revises the spectacle's meanings.

But Pavis is too much of a postmodernist to theorize a spectator with total authority. He deconstructs the spectatorial position by locating its difference within: "What we need," he says, "is a theory of 'reception desire'" – a theory that, without positing a spectator "in a state of artificial regression," accounts for the spectator's unconscious desire and thereby opens the door to pleasurable identification with stage figures (Pavis 1982:158).

What does Brecht contribute to "reception desire"? Although he talks a lot about pleasure, it is the pleasure of cognition, of capturing meaning; Brecht does not apparently release the body, either onstage or in the audience. The actor's body is subsumed in the dialectical narrative of social relations; the spectator's body is given over to rational inquiry (unless there's pleasure to be had with the Brechtian cigar). And Brecht exhibits the blindness typical of all Marxist theorists regarding sex/gender configurations. Feminist theory, however, insists on the presence of the gendered body, on the sex/gender system, and on the problematics of desire.

It is at this point – at the point of conceptualizing an unfetishized female performer and a female spectator – that an intertextual reading of Brechtian and feminist theories works productively. If feminist theory sees the body as culturally mapped and gendered, Brechtian historicization insists that this body is not a fixed essence but a site of struggle and change. If feminist theory is concerned with the multiple and complex signs of a woman's life: her color, her age, her desires, her politics – what I want to call her *historicity*[6] – Brechtian theory gives us a way to put that historicity on view – in the theatre. In its conventional iconicity, theatre laminates body to character, but the body in historicization stands visibly and palpably separate from the "role" of the actor as well as the role of the character; it is always insufficient and open. I want to be clear about this important point: the body, particularly the female body, by virtue of entering the stage space, enters representation – it is not just *there*, a live, unmediated presence, but rather (1) a signifying element in a dramatic fiction; (2) a part of a theatrical sign system whose conventions of gesturing, voicing, and impersonating are referents for both performer and audience; and (3) a sign in a system governed by a particular apparatus, usually owned and operated by men for the pleasure of a viewing public whose major wage earners are male.

Yet with all these qualifications, Brechtian theory imagines a polyvalence to the body's representation, for the performer's body is also *historicized*, loaded with its own history and that of the character, and these histories ruffle the smooth edges of the image, of representation. In my hybrid construction – based in feminist and Brechtian theory – the female performer, unlike her filmic counterpart, connotes not "to-be-looked-at-ness" (Mulvey 1975:11) – the perfect fetish – but rather "looking-at-being-looked-at-ness" or even just looking-ness. This Brechtian-feminist body is paradoxically available for *both* analysis and identification, paradoxically within representation while refusing its fixity.

SPECTATOR, AUTHOR, GESTUS

The explosive (and elusive) synthesis of alienation, historicization, and the "not, but" is the Brechtian Gestus: a gesture, a word, an action, a tableau by which, separately or in series, the social attitudes encoded in the playtext become visible to the spectator. A gest becomes *social* when it "allows conclusions to be drawn about social circumstances" (Brecht 1964:105). A famous social gest is Helene Weigel's snapping shut her leather money bag after each selling transaction in *Mother Courage*, thereby underscoring the contradictions between profiteering and survival – for Brecht the social reality of war. This gest has become something of a reification, but Brecht always emphasized complexity:

> [The] expressions of a gest are usually highly complicated and contra-
> dictory, so that they cannot be rendered by any single word and the actor
> must take care that in giving his image the necessary emphasis he does not
> lose anything, but emphasizes the entire complex.
>
> (1964:198)

The gestic moment in a sense explains the play, but it also exceeds the play, opening it to the social and discursive ideologies that inform its production. Brecht writes that the scene of the social gest "should be played as a piece of history" (1964:86) and Pavis elaborates: Gestus makes visible (alienates) "the class behind the individual, the critique behind the naive object, the commentary behind the affirmation.... [It] gives us the key to the relationship between the play being performed and the public...." (1982:42). If we read feminist concerns back into this discussion, the social gest signifies a moment of theoretical insight into sex/gender complexities, not only in the play's "fable," but in the culture which the play, at the moment of reception, is dialogically reflecting and shaping.

But this moment of visibility or insight is the very moment that complicates the viewing process. Because the Gestus is effected by an historical actor/subject, what the spectator sees is not a mere miming of social relationship, but a *reading* of it, an interpretation by an historical subject who supplements (rather than disappears into) the production of meaning. As noted earlier, the historical subject playing an actor, playing a character, splits the gaze of the spectator, who, as a reader of a complex sign system, cannot consume or reduce the object of her vision to a monolithic projection of the self. In fact, Gestus undermines the stability of the spectatorial "self," for in the act of looking the spectator engages with her own temporality. She, too, becomes historicized – in motion and at risk, but also free to compare the actor/character's signs to "what is close and proper to [herself]" – her material conditions, her politics, her skin, her desires. Sitting not in the dark, but in the Brechtian semilit smoker's theatre, the spectator still has the possibility of pleasurable identification. This is effected not through imaginary projection onto an ideal but through a triangular structure of actor/subject–character–spectator. Looking at the character, the spectator is constantly inter-cepted by the actor/subject, and the latter, heeding no fourth wall, is theoretically free to look back. The difference, then, between this triangle and the familiar oedipal one is that no one side signifies authority, knowledge, or the law. Brechtian theatre depends on a structure of representation, on exposing and making visible, but what appears even in the Gestus can only be provisional, indeterminate, nonauthoritative.[7]

This feminist rereading of Gestus makes room, at least theoretically, for a viewing position for the female spectator. Because the semiosis of Gestus involves the gendered bodies of spectator, actor/subject, and character, all working together but *never harmoniously*, there can be no fetishization and no end to signification. In this Brechtian-feminist paradigm, the spectator's look is freed into "dialectics, passionate detachment" (Mulvey 1975:18). She might borrow Gertrude Stein's line, and give equal emphasis to each word: "I love to read the signs."

If Gestus invites us to think about the performer and the spectator in their historical and sexual specificity, it also asks us to consider the author's inscription. "The author's attitude to the public, that of the era represented and of the time in which the play is performed, the collective style of acting of the characters, etc., are a few of the parameters of the basic *Gestus*" (Pavis 1982:42). In the case of women writers and particularly of women dramatists, the erasure from history has been so nearly complete that the feminist critic feels compelled to make some attempt at recovery – and here Brechtian theory, fellow-traveling with feminist theory, suggests a critical practice – gestic feminist criticism – that would contextualize *and* reclaim the author.

A gestic feminist criticism would "alienate" or foreground those moments in a play-text in which social attitudes about gender could be made visible. It would highlight sex/gender configurations as they conceal or disrupt a coercive or patriarchal idealogy. It would refuse to appropriate and naturalize male or female dramatists, but rather focus on historical material constraints in the production of images. It would attempt to engage dialectically with, rather than master, the play-text. And in generating meanings, it would recover (specifically gestic) moments in which the historical actor, the character, the spectator, *and* the author enter representation, however provisionally.

GESTIC FEMINIST CRITICISM, APHRA BEHN

In the brief space remaining, it is impossible to flesh out this critical schema, but I want to draw attention to a gestic moment that Aphra Behn has provided – in the prolog of her first play, produced in 1670. A middle-class woman with prestigious connections but no supporting family, a former spy and recent inmate in debtor's prison, Behn had her first play produced for the Duke's company, originally patented to William Davenant, and very much committed to the Davenant style of movable scenes, machines, spectacular tableaux, songs, and dances. The Restoration theatre was fully "culinary" in its desire to lure and entertain the public exclusively for private profit. It was also, from the giver of the royal patent to the patentees and playwrights, upper class and male.[8]

The audience, historians are finally telling us, was more varied – and contradictory – than was previously believed. Professional men and respectable women and their maids went regularly to the theatre, as did noisy unattached rakes, prostitutes, and members of royal entourage. There had been women writers – the Duchess of Newcastle, Katherine Phillipps, and Frances Boothby each had a play produced. But when Behn's *The Forced Marriage, or The Jealous Bridegroom* opened in December 1670, it was a novelty and no one knew whether she would have staying power. The female performer, having arrived on the professional stage only 10 years earlier, though she was paid a lower salary than her male colleagues, had already proved her staying power; in décolletage, in breeches, in "undress," the actress represented an important financial lure and provocation, especially to male spectators.

Conventionally, the Restoration prolog describes the state of literary production, complains about the lowly status of poetry, berates the audience for its stupidity, disparages the whores, condemns the factions of noisy fops, refers to any current political turmoil, introduces and/or playfully positions the author, and, in a vague way, describes the play.

In the prolog to her first play, Behn takes note of the factions in the audience and genders them. She writes lines for a performer (gender unclear, but I would guess male) who enjoins the males in the audience to be leery of "spies" – by implication whores whom the author has planted "to hold you in wanton Compliment / That so you may not censure what she'as writ, / Which done, they face you down 'twas full of Wit" (Behn 1915:286).

I come now, at last, to my second short text on pointing.

Within moments the stage directions read "*Enter an Actress*," who "*pointing to the ladies*" asks, "Can any see that glorious Sight and say / A Woman shall not Victor prove today?" In that pointing gesture, the actress sets up a triangular structure – between historical performer, the role she is destined to play, and the female spectators in the audience. She also mentions "A Woman," a potential victor, and that seems to have a referent: the writer Aphra Behn (although it could be one of the females in the play). In that shared look, actor-subject, character, spectator, and author are momentarily joined, and for perhaps the first time on the English stage all four positions are filled by women. But not for long. In casting a closer eye at the female spectators, the actress soon differentiates, and in specifically sexual terms. Insisting, ironically perhaps, that "There's not a Vizard in our whole Cabal" she condemns the lower-class whores, the Pickeroons, "that scour for prey," but ends by promising total female "sacrifice" to "pleasure you" (Behn 1915:286).

Whom that "you" now designates has become fully undecidable. In the sexual slang of the day, actress meant whore, authoress was soon to mean whore, and both were commodities in a pleasure market whose major consumers were male. Still, before conventional representation resumes, the signifying space is dominated by the interlocking look of women. I would call the actress's pointing, and the entire prolog, a Gestus, a moment when the sex/gender system, theatre politics, and social history cathect and become visible. For the feminist critic and theorist this Gestus marks a first step toward recovering a woman playwright in her sexual, historical, and theatrical specificity. It also marks a site, in the text, of indeterminacy, of multiple meanings – a pleasure moment for reading the clouds.

NOTES

1. An earlier version of this paper was presented at the American Theater in Higher Education (ATHE) Conference in Chicago, August 1987.
2. I am grateful to Barton Byg, whose excellent paper, "Brecht on the Margins: Film and Feminist Theory" provided many useful insights.
3. Without discussing gender per se, Brecht refers briefly to this phenomenon in the "Short Organum," no. 59: ". . . it is also good for the actors when they see their characters copied or portrayed in another form. If the part is played by somebody of the opposite sex the sex of the character will be more clearly brought out . . ." (Brecht 1964:197).
4. Brecht elaborates in various ways on this point:

    > The individual whose innermost being is thus driven into the open then of course comes to stand for Man with a capital M. Everyone (including the spectator) is then carried away by the momentum of the events portrayed, so that in a performance of *Oedipus* one has for all practical purposes an auditorium full of little Oedipuses, an auditorium full of Emperor Joneses for a performance of *The Emperor Jones*.
    >
    > (in "On the Use of Music in an Epic Theatre," Brecht 1964:87)

    Also:

    > The bourgeois theatre emphasized the timelessness of its objects. Its representation of people is bound by the alleged "eternally human." Its story is arranged in such a way as to create "universal" situations that allow Man with a capital M to express himself: man of every period and every colour.
    >
    > (in "Alienation Effects in Chinese Acting," Brecht 1964:97)

5. I was very much helped by the extensive summary/analysis of psychoanalytic film theory in Sandy Flitterman-Lewis' "Psychoanalysis in Film and Television" (1987) which I read in manuscript form.
6. I use "historicity" not "history" as the latter term suggests a narrative from which feminists have sought to problematize. In film studies see de Lauretis (1984); in fiction see Brewer (1984); in drama and theatre see Diamond (1985).
7. This is fully played out in Brecht's attitude toward textual authority. As is well known, he revised constantly and cared little about definitive or authoritative versions of his plays.
8. One of Behn's biographers, Maureen Duffy, provides this context:

Of the fifteen living dramatists who had had two or more plays produced since the theatres reopened in 1660, two were earls, one a duke, one was to be a titular baron, four were knights. . . . In 1671 [most of the new writers] were of the gentry or nobility, and almost all had university or Inns of Court educations. Compared with such a company Aphra Behn's pretensions must have seemed even more extravagant.

(1977:103–104)

REFERENCES

Barker, Francis (1984) *The Tremulous Private Body: Essays on Subjection*. London: Methuen.

Baudry, Jean-Louis (1980) "The Apparatus: Metapsychological Approaches to the Impression of Reality." In *Apparatus*, edited by Theresa Hak Kyung, 41–62. New York: Tanam Press.

Behn, Aphra (1915) *The Forced Marriage, or The Jealous Bridegroom*. In *The Works of Aphra Behn*, vol. 3, edited by Montague Summers, 285–381. London: Heinemann.

Bentley, Eric (1981) *The Brecht Commentaries*. London: Methuen.

Blau, Herbert (1982) *Take Up the Bodies: Theater at the Vanishing Point*. Urbana: University of Illinois Press.

Brecht, Bertolt (1964) *Brecht on Theatre*, edited by John Willet. New York: Hill and Wang.

Brewer, Mária Minich (1984) "A Loosening of Tongues: From Narrative Economy to Women Writing." *MLN* 9, no. 5 (December):1141–1161.

Byg, Barton (1986) "Brecht on the Margins: Film and Feminist Theory." Paper presented at the annual convention of the Modern Language Association, New York, December.

Diamond, Elin (1985) "Refusing the Romanticism of Identity: Narrative Interventions in Churchill, Benmussa, Duras." *Theatre Journal* 37, no. 3 (October):273–286.

Dollimore, Jonathan (1984) *Radical Tragedy: Religion, Ideology and Power in the Drama of Shakespeare and His Contemporaries*. Chicago: University of Chicago Press.

Duffy, Mauren (1977) *The Passionate Shepardess: Aphra Behn (1640–89)*. London: Jonathan Cape.

Eagleton, Terry (1986) "Brecht and Rhetoric." In *Against the Grain: Essays 1975–1985*, 167–172. London: Verso.

Esslin, Martin (1971) *Brecht: The Man and His Work*. New York: W.W. Norton.

Flitterman-Lewis, Sandy (1987) "Psychoanalysis in Film and Television." In *Channels of Discourse: Television and Contemporary Criticism*, edited by Robert C. Allen, 170–210. Chapel Hill: University of North Carolina Press.

Heath, Stephen (1974) "Lessons from Brecht." *Screen* 15, no. 2 (summer):103–127.

Irigaray, Luce (1985) "The Power of Discourse and the Subordination of the Feminine." In *This Sex Which Is Not One*, translated by Catherine Porter with Carolyn Burke, 68–85. Ithaca, NY: Cornell University Press.

Johnson, Barbara (1980) *The Critical Difference: Essays in the Contemporary Rhetoric of Reading*. Baltimore, MD: Johns Hopkins University Press.

de Lauretis, Teresa (1984) *Alice Doesn't: Feminism, Semiotics, Cinema*. Bloomington: University of Indiana Press.

Moi, Toril (1985) *Sexual/Textual Politics: Feminist Literary Theory*. London: Methuen.

Mulvey, Laura (1975) "Visual Pleasure and Narrative Cinema." *Screen* 16, no. 3 (autumn):6–18.

Pavis, Patrice (1982) *Language of the Stage: Essays in the Semiology of the Theatre*. New York: Performing Arts Journal Publications.

Rubin, Gayle (1978) "The Traffic in Women: Notes on the 'Political Economy' of Sex." In *Toward an Anthropology of Women*, edited by Rayna Reiter, 157–210. New York: Monthly Review Press.

Stimpson, Catherine R. (1986) "Stein and the Transposition of Gender." In *The Poetics of Gender*, edited by Nancy K. Miller, 1–18. New York: Columbia University Press.

Watney, Simon (1986) "The Banality of Gender." In *Sexual Difference*, edited by Robert Young, 13–21. London: The Oxford Literary Review.

Weber, Carl (1980) "Brecht in Eclipse?" *The Drama Review* 24, no. 1 (T85):114–124.

Wiles, Timothy J. (1980) *The Theater Event: Modern Theories of Performance*. Chicago: The University of Chicago Press.

10

READING PAST THE HETEROSEXUAL IMPERATIVE

Dress Suits to Hire

Kate Davy

> Lesbians should be mistresses of discrepancies, knowing that resistance lies in the change of context.
>
> (*Joan Nestle 1984:236*)

When Holly Hughes, Peggy Shaw, and Lois Weaver embarked on the collaboration that resulted in *Dress Suits to Hire*, all three artists had a history of creating work to be performed in the WOW Cafe, a lesbian theatre space in Manhattan's East Village.[1] An unmistakable specificity is evident in pieces performed at WOW – the address is clearly lesbian. Freely borrowing from popular culture forms, WOW artists produce pieces based on scenarios from familiar, recognizable entertainment genres. In this work, they construct subcultural, under-the-text imagery, metaphors, and conventions derived from lesbian culture. Making work for this context assumes a certain coherence of exchange between performance and spectators that cannot be presumed in other arenas. Meanings shift radically when a site-specific work is taken out of its production context.

From its inception, *Dress Suits* was made to be performed at P.S. 122, an East Village venue for new, or nonmainstream, theatre, dance, music, and performance art.[2] Hughes, Shaw, and Weaver understood that the tacit assumptions operant when making work specifically for WOW and its audience – assumptions that inform the nature and shape of the work – could not be taken for granted outside WOW turf. Working toward performance in a sociologically (if not artistically) mainstream, predominantly heterosexual space influenced the narrative and performative strategies developed for *Dress Suits* in an attempt to resist dominant culture readings of the piece. While the objective remained the same as that of WOW productions, *Dress Suits* marks a significant departure from the style and some of the strategies that distinguish WOW theatre work.

A basic tenet of reception theory is that a production and its audience are not separate. A performance text intersects with individual audience members who, in turn, intersect with it – producing meaning in terms of their own relationships with discourses and practices in society. Meanings do not reside exclusively in the work of art, nor solely in individual readings. Moreover, the context in which a work and its audience are positioned materially influences reception. For instance, under certain conditions a work that attempts to subvert dominant culture's system of representation can instead be assimilated into it, thereby reinforcing, rather than disrupting, its codes.

The WOW Cafe is a context that presumes a lesbian worldview. In this context, WOW artists create a theatre *for* lesbians, a theatre that responds to lesbian subjectivity. *Dress Suits* attempts to maintain this stance in a context that presumes a heterosexual worldview. Hughes, Shaw, and Weaver devised strategies of resistance for this context that manifest a fierce struggle to thwart the assimilation of their discourse. My purpose in this essay is to examine the dimensions of this struggle and, through my reading of the work, indicate some of the wider implications for lesbian performance in particular and feminist performance in general.

When misreadings of lesbian work occur even within WOW space – as they did in WOW's spring 1988 production of Lisa Kron's *Paradykes Lost* – the difficulty of resisting an appropriation by the spectator into dominant, heterosexual cultural readings is apparent. Two critics reviewing the performance eschewed the play's lesbian perspective by imposing a heterosexual worldview on the work and reading the performance through this worldview, thereby misinterpreting a crucial dimension of the piece.

A closer look at the response to *Paradykes Lost* informs the project of *Dress Suits*. Set in the parlor of an English manor during the 1920s, *Paradykes Lost* loosely follows a conventional murder mystery formula. Among the cast are a detective, an ingenue, a couple, a butler, and an assortment of eccentric singles. All the characters have women's names, all are explicitly identified as lesbian in the dialogue, and all the roles were played by women. Yet in her review for *The New York Native* – a gay newspaper – Amy L. Eddings writes about "the all-woman cast who play male characters and refer to each other as 'she'" (1988:29). This represents a fundamental misreading of a butch/femme dynamic that is the MO of this detective spoof, as well as the modus operandi of most WOW work. The cast of *Paradykes* most definitely did not play male characters – they refer to each other as "she" because they play lesbian characters.

Writing for the *Village Voice*, Robert Massa also read *Paradykes* as drag performance: "As in men's camp, the characters refer to each other as 'she' regardless of gender ..." (1988:97). Although WOW productions are similar to male camp performances and Theatre of the Ridiculous in their farcical style, there are important differences. Male drag emphasizes the illusionistic qualities of impersonation. The actor attempts to simulate that which he is not, the "other." Instead of foregrounding dominant culture's fiercely polarized gender roles, men's camp assumes them and plays them out. Like much of men's camp, WOW artists use scenarios from popular performance forms as sources for their narratives, but WOW performers do not adopt the heterosexual imperative operant in these scenarios. They do not impersonate women and men in heterosexual couplings. Ironically, male camps tends to reinscribe, rather than undermine, the dominant culture paradigms it appropriates for its farce and means to parody.

Men – both gay and straight – are the intended audience for male camp, while the projected spectator in WOW productions is lesbian – a subject who, as defined by Monique Witting, stands outside dominant culture categories as not-man, not-woman.[3] WOW performances efface a heterosexual address by constructing a spectator who is neither man nor woman but lesbian – a subject defined in terms of sexual similarity. Same-sexuality is the model and organizing principle from which WOW artists work.

Massa goes on in his review to describe a dimension of his own position as spectator – "As a gay man, I feel less left out at WOW than at straight burlesque" – and then singles out one performance in *Paradykes* to critique: "Kate Stafford as the detective manages to suggest Cary Grant without caricature. Even I swooned" (1988:97). Could there be any clearer evidence of the role desire plays in reception? Here, a gay man appropriates a lesbian character by reading her performance as "in drag," then swoons over the male character he constructs. Unfortunately, in appropriating the character, Massa deprived himself of the radical experience of the play.

Given such misappropriations, it is useful to examine how butch/femme as a system of representation in lesbian theatre differs from drag performance. The iconography and dynamics of butch/femme culture present in WOW productions is not, as it is often described, about cross-dressing. Wearing the gender of the "other" sex, in dominant culture terms, is not the point. Nor is it about drag in the sense of simulation. No attempt is made to hide the lesbian beneath a mask of male or female gender identity. To fool the audience, even momentarily, is not the objective. In their essay "The Misunderstanding: Toward a More Precise Sexual Vocabulary," Esther Newton and Shirley Walton wrote:

The terms "butch" and "femme" refer to gay erotic identities, derived historically from dominant gender categories but now distinct. Thus "butch" is a gay erotic identity in which symbols from the male gender category play a significant part, and "femme" is the complementary gay identity, drawing on feminine gender symbols.

(1984:245)

As a dimension of erotic identity, butch/femme is about sexuality and its myriad nuances. It is also about gender in that it appropriates gender in its social articulation and representational construction, but not as it functions in material social relations in dominant cultural terms.[4] In butch/femme iconography, attributes which in dominant culture are associated with strict gender roles are not sex-class specific. Worn by lesbians, these attributes have meanings for lesbians in a same-sex, lesbian culture that do not necessarily symbolize conformity to rules of gender behavior and the oppositional dynamics of polarized gender roles.

Femme and butch constructions exist outside of these paradigms and foreground the problem of confusing sexuality with gender. When sexuality and gender are mistakenly conflated and collapsed into one "sex/gender" concept and assumed to be social facts according to a binary opposition (one sex/gender being male; the other sex/gender being not-male), the effect is to construe sex and gender as the same phenomenon. Moreover, it is to construe sex and gender as "natural" – a law of nature enforced by a law of culture. Compulsory heterosexuality. Sexuality and gender are discrete, albeit linked, phenomena in what Gayle Rubin has described as the sex/gender system (1978). Butch/femme as a social dynamic in lesbian culture is a manifestation of the separation of sexuality from polarized gender constructs and imperative heterosexuality.[5]

Each WOW artist mines the material, social terrain of butch/femme culture somewhat differently in her theatre work. In *Paradykes Lost*, Lisa Kron's use of butch/femme iconography must be largely overlooked in order to read her production in heterosexual terms. For instance, although Kate Stafford's detective "costume" was butch, her makeup and hair were femme in style. The stance and deportment of another butch character in *Paradykes* echoed the femme. When dominant culture notions of man and woman are "present" it is *not* because they are presented as such – they are read into the performance.

The title *Paradykes Lost* is rich in canonical connotation. It critiques the absence of lesbian work in the canons of theatre and dramatic literature. Ironically, a lesbian perspective is (re)found, recuperated, and given a voice in productions like *Paradykes*, only to be obfuscated in heterosexual readings of the work. The dykes are lost once again.

For the makers of *Dress Suits*, then, the project is to insist that the lesbian represent herself on her own terms, through strategies that thwart rather than facilitate the propensity to read her signs and symbols from a heterosexual perspective.

Dress Suits to Hire is set in a cramped storefront room of a cheesy New York clothing rental store where two women live and where clearly no one ever comes to rent anything. Before the performance begins, the audience can see the set. It is constructivist in style – its back and side walls comprised of empty frames that delineate two large windows and a door. Another empty frame is positioned downstage. It faces front, suggesting a window through which the audience can look into the private space of the room. Positioned in this vertical plane it echoes both the illusionary fourth wall of frontal staging, and the proscenium "opening" of theatrical space – the theatre's keyhole through which the voyeuristic gaze of the spectator is engaged.

Because the stage embodies the "to-be-looked-at" dimension of the theatrical apparatus – the site of the spectacle, the artificial, the histrionic, the site of deceit, conceit, and disguise – it is sometimes linked metaphorically with "the feminine." Of course, ultimately, "woman" – woman as sign, as the collective essence of femininity – is conflated with spectacle itself, *woman as spectacle*, woman as object of the spectatorial gaze. This gaze, the looking itself, is male. As E. Ann Kaplan explains in her book *Women and Film*, "The gaze is not necessarily male (literally), but to own and activate the gaze, given our language and the structure of the unconscious, is to be in the 'masculine' position" (1983:30).

In their collaboration on *Dress Suits to Hire*, Hughes, Shaw, and Weaver created a production in which this configuration – one that constitutes the gaze as masculine and locates both the site and recipient of the gaze as feminine – is played out with a vengeance and a twist. The apparatus is made aware of itself – woman looks back. And she is femme.

As the lights come up at the beginning of the play, two performers sit across a small table looking into each other's eyes. Their bodies are covered with identical floor-length boudoir robes made from sturdy fabric that hangs from them in a way that hides their bodies. Deeluxe (played by Shaw) sings a song quietly to herself as she pulls nylon stockings onto each leg, fastens them to garters, and puts high-heeled shoes on her feet. The song is a list of things she is going to do for and to her body – "Gonna buy myself a diamond ring / Gonna stuff my nose with cocaine" – which she sings as she dons the clothing and accessories that are the trappings of femininity. She pulls on long, black evening gloves and, still singing, crosses to the downstage window. Just as she starts to look out the window at the audience, she is attacked, mid-song, by her own right hand which – like a separate, possessed being – grabs her throat and strangles her. She staggers backward and dies noisily center stage.

As Wittig suggests, lesbian as a category may sidestep dominant constructions and classifications of woman and man in the economy of the sex/gender system, but the lesbian performer nonetheless confronts the complex significative workings of the female body as sign the moment she sets foot on stage. From the outset, Shaw and Weaver, in their identical, body-concealing garb, begin the arduous process of interrupting the dynamics of signification that in dominant culture conflate women exclusively with the body.

In theatre, as in the rest of culture, woman as speaking subjects are missing from representation. In their place, "woman" appears as a construction that signifies a (feminine) essence intrinsic to all women. This construction is anathema to women as historical beings and social subjects because it reduces them to "nature," "mother," and, ultimately, the object of (male) desire. The absence of women as speaking subjects in representation is central to what feminist scholars have described as the crisis in representation. For practitioners who work in forms that have a visual dimension, the central issue is how to image the female body without engendering "woman."

Feminist filmmakers and theorists have accomplished much in the project of dismantling "woman"; from identifying and articulating the male gaze and the ways in which the female body is placed in the service of that gaze through operations of voyeurism and fetishism,[6] to manipulating the narrative and cinematic mechanisms that produce meaning in film through strategies that subvert or disrupt the cinematic apparatus. While it is not possible to adequately describe here the many important ways feminist filmmakers work, a brief description of a crucial dimension of Yvonne Rainer's film *The Man Who Envied Women* (1985) serves the purpose of this discussion by demonstrating a significant approach to grappling with the problematic of imaging the female body.

Working against the dynamics of the male gaze, Rainer constructs the female protagonist in her film by means of a voice-over. The spectator hears the protagonist but never sees her, for Rainer refuses to embody her voice in a single, coherent image of a woman's body. Rainer removes the object of the cinematic fetish (the fetishized female body) from the screen, thwarting the operations of voyeurism. This strategy produces a kind of "radical absence" that echoes the nature of filmic representation itself. For, unlike theatre, film by definition is marked by absences – the objects the camera "sees" are not in fact present at the moment of screening.[7]

Since some of the mechanisms operant in cinema are similar to those at work in live performance, feminist theatre scholars and practitioners have turned to film theory and practice for insight and direction. Although this research continues to be enormously fruitful, there are obvious limitations. In theatre, for example, the mechanisms of voyeurism, fetishism, and scopophilia (pleasure in looking) work in analogous ways to film, but not in the same ways. Feminist filmmakers work both with and against the (inter)mediating "eye" of the camera which, together with editing, create the illusion of point of view, temporal continuity, and in general what Stephen Heath terms "narrative space" (1986). If Mary Ann Doane (1982) is right when she suggests that the absence of the live body in filmed images makes it possible to fetishize that body (precisely because of the extreme distance from the image/object this absence engenders and permits),[8] then the very presence of the performing body in live, three-dimensional, theatrical space suggests a venue for undermining the mechanisms that contribute the fetishism in representational systems that have a visual dimension.

Indeed the conditions of the theatre – the very *presentness* of the theatrical apparatus, and the *immediacy* of theatrical representation – are key to the subversion of "woman" within *Dress Suits*. Just as Rainer takes filmic absence to its logical extreme in her film, Hughes, Shaw, and Weaver seize the theatre as an 'arena of presence," overconstructing the performative dimensions of their piece, to produce a kind of "radical presence." By overconstructing the body in *Dress Suits*, the operations of theatrical representation are overdetermined, foregrounded, and made visible, thereby undermining, paradoxically, the construction of *woman as body*.

A number of devices are employed repeatedly and cumulatively in *Dress Suits* to undercut the illusory dimension of theatre and insist on the material presence of the body. Opening the performance with Shaw dressing on stage, literally putting on femininity, foregrounds gender as "man-made." Wearing the reference marks of femininity under her robe – referents that inscribe the body as female and, conversely, the female as body – Deeluxe sings the body's pleasures before killing it off. Significantly, the script's first stage direction states that the body is "dead for the rest of the play."

After Deeluxe collapses, the audience hears the high-pitched yapping of a small dog. Michigan (Weaver), with the dog on her lap, has been seated with her back to the corpselike Deeluxe, who lies between her and the audience. The dog – a battery-operated toy – rouses Michigan. (Significantly, it is the mechanical dog that bears a woman's name,

"Linda" – the characters do not.) Michigan turns, sees Deeluxe, and begins frantically to search for a telephone. She pulls out a pink, plastic receiver, puts it to her ear and says, "Hello? Ninth Precinct?" The cord on the receiver has been cut and the rest of the telephone apparatus is missing. As in *Lady Dick*, Hughes' 1985 production with WOW, a character calls on the "authorities" for help.[9] The obviously cut cord signals that this attempt "to get outside" is futile. The action of the performance literally and figuratively remains within the confines of this small room, circumscribed by the nature of theatrical representation. The challenge is to find a way out from within, to articulate another kind of author(ity), one inside the discourse of *Dress Suits*, but outside the Law.

Michigan's monolog that follows is a kind of micro-articulation mapping the terms of the rest of the performance. In her phone conversation, Michigan refers only to "the body," emphasizing that the murder she calls to report is not the death of Deeluxe. This distinction between the speaking subject and the body is further complicated when Michigan speaks of her desire. In answer to questions from the Ninth Precinct officer (as a matter of course, or better, as a matter of gender, we presume the officer on the other end of the line is male), Michigan smiles seductively and says slowly and suggestively, "Yes there certainly is a body. Did I discover it? Many years ago.... I lay down on the bed and discovered the body.... And after that first time I would discover the body again and again." She suggests a distinction between the (dead) body and the lesbian body that is the object of her desire. A repeated and insistent articulation of lesbian desire within the piece positions it outside heterosexuality both as a social institution and representational model, by realigning what Jill Dolan describes as the "dynamics of desire" between performance and its spectators. Dolan writes, "desire is not necessarily a fixed, male-owned commodity, but can be exchanged, with much different meaning, between women. When the locus of desire changes, the demonstration of sexuality and gender roles also changes" (1987:173). *Dress Suits* breaks the "heterosexual contract" that Teresa de Lauretis identifies as "the very site in which the social relations of gender and thus gender ideology are reproduced in everyday life" (1987:17).

Of course the heterosexual model in representation is not dismantled simply and unproblematically, especially outside a lesbian performance context. In *Dress Suits* a narrative/performative strategy addresses the dilemma in the form of "Little Peter" – an entity that resides in the right hand of Deeluxe. Although the spectator doesn't learn his name until later in the piece, "Little Peter" as a performative "figure of speech" is identified almost immediately. Michigan doesn't report a murder to the Ninth Precinct, she says, "There's a man in here.... He lives with us. More with her than with me. Me, this man, and the body." The hand that

Figure 10.1 Linda yaps in Michigan's lap as Deeluxe lies dead with Little Peter still at her throat. (© Dona Ann McAdams)

strangles the body represents the male economy that "the body" was constructed to serve. If "the body" signifies women as trade, commodity, and use value in the sexual marketplace, and "woman" in the representational marketplace, then it is significant that the murdering hand is an extension of that body for it belongs to the male economy that inscribes and appropriates it.

The not-so-subtle phallic signifier, Little Peter, is the force that repeatedly attempts to contain what de Lauretis calls the "trauma of gender – the potential disruption of the social fabric and of white male privilege ..." (1987:21). That he resides in Deeluxe acknowledges poignantly the great complexity of imagining a different order while immersed in the current sociosymbolic order.

During the opening monolog-cum-monodrama, Michigan "redecorates." She performs a seemingly senseless series of actions over the ostensibly dead body. She covers the waist with a small table, for instance, and then removes it; she spreads the arms out away from the body and then moves them back – all the while relating in explicit language the history of her lesbian erotic desire, identifying herself as an "animal" ("Being a girl is just a phase I'm going through"). It's as though she performs some transformative ritual designed to (re)articulate and transform this dead body, resurrect it, into the lesbian body.

In grappling with the problematic of the body, this opening monolog also establishes exhibitionism both as subject matter and an identifying dimension of theatre itself. Shaw and Weaver are performers who present performers that move from one showbiz "turn" to another, using recognizable bits – the stand-up-comic routine, the song-and-dance number – that foreground the theatrical nature of live performance as well as the voyeur/exhibitionist relationship it engenders. Michigan says to Deeluxe's murderous right hand: "I suppose you know what this will mean. There will be no show. She will be unable to do the show. You're not going to like this.... She probably won't be able to perform anymore!"

Hundreds of narratives, from *Antigone* to *'Night Mother* and *Fatal Attraction*, end with the physical death of a woman, or her psychological death, or, as in (romantic) comedy, her recuperation through marriage. *Dress Suits* inverts narrative closure by beginning the play with a death, the momentous event that is usually the target of narrative suspense, the resolution of processes of expectation. Hughes' play also undercuts those narratives that begin with a murder which propels the action toward an eventual resolution – 10 minutes into *Dress Suits* the body is resurrected.

As befits her name, Deeluxe is resurrected "in spectacle." Pulling herself up from the floor, she "over sings" (forcefully and very dramatically) the song "*Amato Mio*" from *Gilda*, a Rita Hayworth film. At the same time, she pulls a large, gold, gaudy accordion fan up behind her. It is as tall as she is and frames her still-robed body, *à la* Cecil B. de Mille. Michigan hands her a bouquet of tulips attached to an electric cord. As Deeluxe strikes a final pose against the fan, the tulips light up. Deeluxe is "in spectacle" – decorated, lit-up like a Christmas tree – a performance within a performance.

It is significant that in this micro-extravaganza musical number – one that refers visually to the genre of Hollywood spectacle – Deeluxe is posed against the fan still wearing a shapeless robe. The curvaceous female body, conventionally associated with this Hollywood image, is hidden. Hence, an image that invites a fetishistic response is deconstructed by "displaying" a hidden body. Throughout *Dress Suits*, iconic expectations are repeatedly thwarted by images that are consistently skewed: there is always something wrong with the "picture."

Resurrected, Deeluxe grabs a piggybank and threatens to leave home. While it seems as though this scene is one she's enacted many times before, like everything in the play, it's unclear. Nothing in *Dress Suits* is stable, not the time in which the action takes place, not the characters, not the actions. Even dialects and idioms shift in style from lofty theatrical monolog to lesbian bar-culture slang to underworld gun moll to Midwestern twang. The linguistic, behavioral, and gestural signs indicative of a core character from which all else is merely a departure, are repeatedly subverted. Michigan and Deeluxe change clothes and personas frequently.

Although smacking of vaudeville and burlesque in its humor and presentational style, the ambiance of *Dress Suits* is definitely not an upbeat, playful one of "let's make a show" for each other. Instead, there is a seemingly random, fragmented exploration of the dark side of sexuality. The atmosphere is heavy, private, subterranean. The spectator can feel the weight and import of a private symbol system without necessarily being able to decipher, decode, or complete it. Gone is the butch/femme play that is a hallmark of WOW productions, but that threatens to reinforce rather than subvert gender polarizations. Gone, too, are conventional narratives (like those based on romance novel formulas, or television sitcoms) that can be parodied in lesbian performance contexts. Instead, throughout *Dress Suits'* roughly 75 minutes, there are continuous shifts narratively and visually as the artists attempt to create, moment-to-moment, points of identification with the potential for engaging their subjectivity as lesbians, as women, as girls, as femme, as butch, as femme fatale. And as "animal," nonhumans (the cat, palomino, werewolf) who transgress the boundaries of the body and conventional femininity.

These points of identification are continuously, almost breathlessly, constructed and then dissolved and are not to be confused with a single, coherent "point of identification" related to some unproblematic notion of identity with which all well-meaning spectators can identify. Manipulating the operations of identification through an articulation of many different and rapidly changing points of view creates a continuously shifting subject field. Spectators are invited to repeatedly (re)engage with shifting subject positions, intermittently activating certain kinds of subjectivity. Narrative episodes in *Dress Suits* interrupt narrative coherence – the "flowing with" narrative that ostensibly comes "naturally" but is in fact manufactured by the processes and organizing principles of narrative itself (see de Lauretis 1984).

Within *Dress Suits'* shifting subject field, power relations are repeatedly redistributed. Both women in "Dress Suits" are "suited" with femme iconography, so that when one emerges as more powerful than the other, the action is played out in the context of sameness – same-sex partner, same erotic identity. If power is understood as distributed according to "difference," then, again, the "picture" is out of kilter. The "difference" is in erotic role, which is not fixed – power positionings change, slide back and forth, throughout the performance. Power is exchanged between the two performers.

The underlying assumption is that power and sexual desire are deeply connected. Power is not denied women in *Dress Suits*. Lesbian theatre artists refuse to agree that power belongs solely to male constructs. But because power dynamics and gender identity are fiercely linked in dominant discourses (in positionings that in heterosexual culture are seemingly inextricably grounded in the configuration "male/female," construed as active/passive, powerful/powerless, and prescribed according to gender) the butch/femme play that works so subversively in lesbian performance contexts is not employed in *Dress Suits*. Outside of lesbian venues, butch/femme can too easily be read as male/female. *Dress Suits* scrambles the signals, the processes of identification, when it "unhooks" power from polarized gender relations and heterosexual desire.

The butch, however, is not erased – she appears within the femme construct. Once Deeluxe removes her concealing robe, an iconographic process is begun whereby meaning is layered upon meaning, establishing an increasingly complex iconicity. When Deeluxe "disrobes," she is seen wearing a black, strapless, waist-length corset, black satin panties, and a black garter belt. Her back to the audience, Deeluxe faces Michigan who, as spectator, watches while Deeluxe dresses herself in a strapless, full-length, satin evening gown, gartered nylon stockings, heels, long black evening gloves, and dangling earrings. Deeluxe bends over, throws her mane of curly red hair forward, and brushes it. Standing, she throws her head back suggestively, and extends her arms to suggest she is displaying herself for Michigan.

She is in full masquerade, that is, she has *made a spectacle of herself.* She has, in Mary Russo's words, "put on femininity with a vengeance" (1986:224). But what prevents this flaunting of femininity from being recuperated back into "woman"? Shaw's demeanor, the performative quality of her work, is important in understanding how this problematic is worked out in the complexity of Deeluxe as an iconic sign. Michigan refers to Deeluxe as, "Half woman, half something weird. French, maybe. All cat." Shaw's masquerade hints at the butch, but she does not fully play it at this point in the performance.

Having presented herself for Weaver's attentive gaze, Shaw slowly turns to the audience and sinuously walks downstage to sing another Rita Hayworth song – "Put the Blame on Mame" from *Gilda* – in her own version as "Put the Blame on Me." The relationship between performer, character, and spectator that Elin Diamond delineates in her reading of Brecht (1988) is multiplied and problematized as Shaw performs Deeluxe performing Rita Hayworth performing still another character, Gilda. Shaw culls bits of gesture, stance, and attitude from Hayworth's performing style in *Gilda*, and then overstates and overplays them in her own performance, projecting an ironic, knowing attitude about what she is doing. It's as if she's winking at the audience, sharing a private understanding. The critique of objectification is clear. Shaw plays the fetishized object of the male gaze and at the same time critiques that position.

The articulation and circulation of the gaze is further complicated when Shaw looks back at the spectators and interacts with them directly. With Weaver positioned as "onstage spectator" watching her from behind while the audience watches her from the front, Shaw is caught in the fourth wall. In the P.S. 122 production and on tour in Milwaukee, Wisconsin, the audience seating section was so close to the performing area that spectators seated on the floor in front of the first row were literally at Shaw's feet. During the "Blame" song, she played the vamp, the femme fatale, transforming the theatre into an intimate cabaret, choosing individual women in the audience to address seductively – teasing them with the possibility of tossing out one of her gloves. Not only are the dynamics of same-sex desire absolutely clear in this sequence – the address lesbian – but the physical separation and psychological distance provided by the fourth wall of proscenium staging is breached.

The enormous influence on reception of this crucial dimension of distance was apparent in performances at the University of Michigan,

Ann Arbor, where the production circumstances were especially skewed. A physical distance of several yards separated the performing space from the audience seating sections, establishing a kind of Wagnerian "mystic gulf" that produced a certain "lesbian theatre under glass" aura. Because Shaw could not close the gap and indicate precisely the spectators she was addressing, it was not difficult to apply a dominant culture model, read from that perspective, and engage in fetishizing the image.[10]

Shaw plays the femme utterly in her "Blame" song so that when she shifts to the butch, during the play's one blatantly conventional seduction scene, her masquerade becomes so (over)loaded with seemingly contradictory meanings that it virtually "vibrates" and threatens to rupture. The scene ostensibly takes place at the pumps of a desert filling station. Weaver wears a white full slip that clings to her body, and pink high-heeled boots that zip to her ankles. Shaw ties a bandanna around her neck, puts a cowboy hat on her head, a toothpick in her mouth and, as the theme song from the film *A Man and a Woman* swells up, crosses the stage to Weaver, moving (according to a stage direction) "as much like a cowboy as you can in a strapless gown and heels." Weaver "comes on" to Shaw who plays the butch fully while still embedded visually in femme iconography.

Onstage, Shaw and Weaver are frequently described as "hot," and the stage in this seduction scene is exceedingly sexually charged. The femme and femme-cum-butch tease each other, seduce each other, until Shaw pulls Weaver to her in a long stage kiss – the music from *A Man and a Woman* swells again. Like the sentence "This is not a pipe," that Magritte scrawled in French under his careful drawing of a pipe, the soundtrack in this scene states, "This is *not* a man and a woman." Taken together, the elements of this scene conspire to skew the potential for gender polarization in butch/femme play by overdetermining femme iconography and inserting the butch into it – creating an especially ironic distance from the body, or masquerade.[11]

In her essay entitled "The Technology of Gender," de Lauretis argues persuasively for what she describes as "the movement in and out of gender as ideological representation." She writes,

[A] movement between the (represented) discursive space of the positions made available by hegemonic discourses and the space-off, the elsewhere, of those discourses: those other spaces both discursive and social that exist, since feminist practices have (re)constructed them, in the margins (or "between the lines," or "against the grain") of hegemonic discourses. ... These two kinds of spaces are neither in opposition to one another nor strung along a chain of signification, but they coexist concurrently and in contradiction. The movement between them, therefore, is not that of a dialectic, of integration, of a combinatory, or of *difference*, but is the tension of contradiction, multiplicity, and heteronomy.

(1987:26)

It is from this other space that *Dress Suits* attempts to exist in contradiction with dominant discourse. Especially (although not only) in the seduction scene, played out in terms of lesbian desire, a palpable tension between dominant discourse and lesbian discourse is created, and a voice emerges from under the masquerade: a voice-under that articulates a nonrecuperable discursive space. Little Peter, of course, reappears at the scene's conclusion, the ever just-around-the-corner phallic principle that, when threatened, surfaces. The two discursive spaces coexist, the tension of the female-body-in-contradiction delineates their respective positions.

The issue of objectification is repeatedly addressed directorially and narratively in scenes that foreground, throw into relief, the meaning-producing mechanisms of the theatrical apparatus. In what could be called "the stargazing scene," the performers look back through the proscenium opening, creating a kind of reversed voyeurism that – like Shaw's "Blame" number – addresses concretely the issue of the gaze. Michigan stargazes out the window through a prop that represents a telescope but is not one – it is an unusually long, phallic flashlight turned on the audience. Its beam of light metaphorically projects her gaze and literally traces it visually. Unlike the receptive nature and passive activity a telescope suggests – the gazer receiving images – a flashlight is aggressive, its beam is visible across space and its spot of light hits and reveals its target. In this scene, the target of the gaze is the audience, individual spectators are "spot-lighted." The distance separating performers from spectators is effaced as the "object" of fetishistic gazing assumes an active stance and looks back.

Deeluxe takes the flashlight from Michigan, looks out the window "through" it, and says to Michigan, "Hey! You can see right into my bedroom! You been looking at me! This is proof." Michigan responds, "I been more than looking. I been watching. That's looking with a reason." By virtue of their "looking with a reason," with lesbian desire, the gaze is reinscribed, detaching the scopophilic drive from its association, or sole alliance with masculinity.

Just as Michigan and Deeluxe, with a beam of light, take the gaze both literally and metaphorically into their own hands, Hughes, Shaw, and Weaver take the theatrical apparatus in hand and, through *Dress Suits to Hire*, make every dimension of it resonate with meaning for lesbians and women. The set, for example, suggests meanings anyone can read: the walls that separate public (male) from domestic (female)

Figure 10.2 Stargazing with a flashlight. (© Dona Ann McAdams)

space; the division between the outside world of "social reality" and the interior realm of subjectivity, and so forth. But the physical space, like nearly every other element of the production, also generates meanings that resonate in ways that bear significance especially for lesbians and women – a private experience in a public, gender-mixed and gender-inscribed, arena. When the characters perform a sweeping, *à la* 1940s-movie-musical dance number in the small space, they nearly smash into the walls and crash into the furniture. It is a very funny number ("hysterically" funny?) during which the room seems smaller, even more claustrophobic. Like the destroyed illusion of backdrop scenery painted in perspective when performers move too close to it, Shaw and Weaver appear too large to be contained by the space. Whether received at a conscious level or not, the experience of this dance number carries the potential for engendering a resonance for lesbians and women that describes the entire project of *Dress Suits to Hire*.

As if to punctuate finally and emphatically the artificiality and meaning-making nature of the theatrical apparatus, the production employs one of theatre's most unconvincing mechanisms – the "deus ex machina" ending. Deeluxe has killed Little Peter. In a hilarious struggle with herself, she strangles him, until her left hand holds nothing but a limp right hand. The two women then sit quietly across from each other, robed as they were at the beginning, when "out of nowhere" a letter falls from above into the room. Michigan picks the envelope up off the floor, looks at it and says, "It's for you." Deeluxe opens it and reads a letter from Little Peter in which he describes the future. It is a sober narrative on the uses to which men will put the tears of women. Deeluxe says, "So that's the future, huh?" Michigan responds, "Don't worry. We'll never see it." As the lights fade out, a certain residue, a certain resonance, hangs in the air.

In the theatre, artists like Holly Hughes, Peggy Shaw, and Lois Weaver have consistently pushed at the boundaries of a seemingly monolithic representational system in order to re(image)ine a subject position for lesbians and women. The ultimate aim is social change, but in order to achieve a different position in the social order, it is crucial to reconceptualize this position in the symbolic order.

What does it mean, then, when lesbian theatre is performed in venues outside of lesbian performance spaces? It doesn't necessarily mean assimilation into the mainstream, a virtually automatic appropriation by dominant culture. We need to be aware, however, that even when lesbian artists organize the narrative, visual, and symbolic dimensions of their work to address other lesbians, the theatre as a social technology that includes its spectators is still firmly embedded in the sociosymbolic systems and discourses of dominant culture. *Dress Suits* confronts this challenge and grapples with it.

When signals are crossed in every dimension, increased effort and attention are required on the part of spectators to "read" the performance, scanning and rescanning the production's visual and narrative fields. The additional effort prompted by this kind of performance attempts to dissolve the conventional filters through which spectators usually receive theatre – as a matter of custom, habit, and gender – to suggest new meanings, new ways of seeing, and foreground how those readings and meanings are produced. *Dress Suits to Hire* does not set out to reinvent the wheel, only to punctuate and deflate it long enough to create a space in which to imagine lesbians and women differently in the symbolic order.

The production's performance context influenced this project in ways that cannot be ignored. In Ann Arbor where *Dress Suits* was performed in a conventional theatre setting, in the legitimate (and legitimizing) institutional setting of a major university, the work's potential to subvert dominant ideology was seriously undermined. In Milwaukee, where *Dress Suits* was performed in an unconventional, marginal, "illegitimate" theatre space for audiences made up almost entirely of working- and middle-class lesbians,[12] the exchange of meaning between performance and spectators was arguably different. Still, the struggle to critique objectification and interrupt the processes by which theatrical representation inscribes and prescribes meaning was no less intense. Having experienced the production in several contexts, I could argue with conviction, if not without contradiction, both sides of an ongoing debate: the importance of *Dress Suits* as an instance of lesbian discourse outside of lesbian performance contexts, and the importance of segregating pieces like *Dress Suits* in spaces where lesbians and women are the only spectators.

By mainstream theatre standards, *Dress Suits to Hire* was successful. It received favorable reviews in New York's major newspapers, and Peggy Shaw won an Obie award for her performance of Deeluxe. The political implications of this success for lesbian theatre are more complex and difficult to measure. As I write, a group of WOW artists are making a full-length piece that will open at WOW. At least at this point in their improvisational rehearsal process, they intend to play heterosexual couples. How will such a piece differ from men's camp and Theatre of the Ridiculous? And, extrapolating further, what would it mean for the project of feminism if the next wave of lesbian performance were to enter the mainstream in drag?

NOTES

1. For an excellent introductory history of this performance venue see Solomon (1985), Davy (1985), and Dolan (1985), all published in an issue of *TDR* devoted to East Village performance.
2. *Dress Suits to Hire* was first produced at the May 1987 Veselka

Performance Festival at P.S. 122. In December 1987 it was presented by Split Britches at Women's Interart on W. 52nd Street where it played through February 1988.

3. See Witting (1981). Jill Dolan was the first critic to apply Witting's theoretical position to lesbian performance and articulate its implications for the exchange of meanings between performers and spectators (1984). See also Dolan (1988).

4. The distinction between gender as a social and representational construction and its role as a *system* of representation is a vital part of recent feminist debate. See de Lauretis (1987:1–30).

5. I am, admittedly, overstating the case here, relating a butch/femme performative strategy back to lesbian culture, that is, in the way it is played out by some, not all, lesbians. See de Lauretis (1988) for a different theoretical argument and far-reaching analysis of lesbian representation. She refers to an essay by Sue-Ellen Case entitled "Towards a Butch–Femme Aesthetic" in *Making a Spectacle: Feminist Essays on Contemporary Women's Theatre*, edited by Lynda Hart (Ann Arbor: University of Michigan Press, 1989:282–299).

6. Laura Mulvey's 1975 essay is so central to an understanding of how voyeurism, fetishism, and scopophilia (pleasure in looking) apply to cinema that nearly every theorist working from a feminist psychoanalytic perspective continues to refer to it, even though new work (including Mulvey's own) rethinks some of her initial positions. See also Mayne (1984) for an analysis of the structures of voyeurism in relation to women as filmmakers and film voyeurs.

7. For a different theoretical approach and in-depth analysis of Rainer's film, see Phelan (1988) and the chapter entitled "Strategies of Coherence: Narrative Cinema, Feminist Poetics, and Yvonne Rainer" in de Lauretis (1987:107–126). See also Silverman (1984) for an analysis of how filmic strategies, like the voice-over and intertitles, are employed to "denaturalize" the female voice.

8. Doane (1982) discusses, among other things, how distance from the body functions in representational forms, especially distance from the female body on the cinema screen.

9. For an analysis of how the spectator is constructed in Hughes' *Lady Dick* see Davy (1986).

10. In Ann Arbor all the dimensions of material context conspired to undermine *Dress Suits* as an act of resistance. Strategies designed to subvert dominant culture codes tended instead to emphasize them. The critique of objectification was erased and the production became another, albeit different, instance of objectification.

Feminist theatre scholars Sue-Ellen Case and Elin Diamond were invited by the university to respond to *Dress Suits* and lead a discussion with the audience. One of the issues that surfaced in the discussion following the first performance centered on assimilation: Is lesbian theatre's political import and impact neutralized when it is produced in a major university? Is it assimilated by virtue of its very acceptance in the academy – academe being the storehouse and (re)manufacturer of dominant ideologies and epistemologies? And what are the implications if lesbian performance is perceived as entertainment for predominantly straight audiences? Since some felt the university context radically reshaped the reception of *Dress Suits*, it was suggested that the piece be performed exclusively in lesbian or women-only performance spaces. *Dress Suits* was created by Hughes, Shaw, and Weaver as a way to move lesbian theatre out of the ghetto of lesbian performance spaces. The production circumstances in Ann Arbor made manifest the risks involved in that move.

11. For the original work on masquerade, see Riviere (1986) – her essay was first published in 1929.

12. The only publicity for *Dress Suits*' three performances in Milwaukee was a promotional mailing to approximately 1,700 names on the list of a local organization that produces women's music concerts, an annual Kate Clinton (a lesbian stand-up comedian) show, dances, and other events for the lesbian community. The piece was performed in a warehouse that had been converted into a makeshift theatre by a local performing group. Because this group was using the theatre part of the warehouse, *Dress Suits* was mounted in the large "lobby" area of the space – literally on the margins of an already marginal space.

REFERENCES

Davy, Kate (1985) "*The Heart of the Scorpion* at the WOW Cafe." *The Drama Review* 29, no. 1 (T105):52–56.

———(1986) "Constructing the Spectator: Reception, Context, and Address in Lesbian Performance." *Performing Arts Journal* 10, no. 2 (September/October):74–87.

Diamond, Elin (1988) "Brechtian Theory/Feminist Theory: Toward a Gestic Feminist Criticism." *The Drama Review* 32, no. 1 (T117):82–94. Also in this sourcebook, 120–135.

Doane, Mary Ann (1982) "Film and Masquerade: Theorizing the Female Spectator." *Screen* 23, no. 4 (September/October):74–87.

Dolan, Jill (1984) "Lesbian as Refuser, Lesbian as Creator: An Anti-Aesthetic." Paper delivered at the ATA conference. August, San Francisco, CA.

———(1985) "*Carmelita Tropicana Chats* at the Club Chandalier." *The Drama Review* 29, no. 1 (T105):26–33.

———(1987) "The Dynamics of Desire: Sexuality and Gender in Pornography and Performance." *Theatre Journal* 39, no. 2 (May):156–174.

———(1988) *The Feminist Spectator as Critic*. Ann Arbor: UMI Research Press.

Eddings, Amy L. (1988) "Comic Interludes." *The New York Native* 258 (28 March):29.

Heath, Stephen (1986) "Narrative Space." In *Narrative, Apparatus, Ideology*, edited by Philip Rosen, 379–420. New York: Columbia University Press.

Kaplan, E. Ann (1983) *Women and Film: Both Sides of the Camera*. New York: Methuen.

de Lauretis, Teresa (1984) "Desire in Narrative." In *Alice Doesn't: Feminism, Semiotics, Cinema*, 103–157. Bloomington: Indiana University Press.

———(1987) *Technologies of Gender: Essays on Theory, Film, and Fiction.* Bloomington: Indiana University Press.

———(1988) "Sexual Indifference and Lesbian Representation." *Theatre Journal* 40, no. 2 (May):155–177.

Massa, Robert (1988) "Sightlines." *Village Voice* 33, no. 12 (22 March):97.

Mayne, Judith (1984) "The Woman at the Keyhole: Women's Cinema and Feminist Criticism." In *Re-Vision: Essays in Feminist Film Criticism*, edited by Mary Ann Doane, Patricia Mellencamp, and Linda Williams, 49–66. Los Angeles: American Film Institute, University Publications of America.

Mulvey, Laura (1975) "Visual Pleasure and Narrative Cinema." *Screen* 16, no. 3 (autumn):6–18.

Nestle, Joan (1984) "The Fem Question." In *Pleasure and Danger: Exploring Female Sexuality*, edited by Carole S. Vance, 232–241. Boston: Routledge & Kegan Paul.

Newton, Esther, and Shirley Walton (1984) "The Misunderstanding: Toward a More Precise Sexual Vocabulary." In *Pleasure and Danger: Exploring Female Sexuality*, edited by Carole S. Vance, 242–250. Boston: Routledge & Kegan Paul.

Phelan, Peggy (1988) "Feminist Theory, Poststructuralism, and Performance." *The Drama Review* 32, no. 1 (T117):107–127. Also in this sourcebook, 157–182.

Riviere, Joan (1986) "Womanliness as a Masquerade." In *Formations of Fantasy*, edited by Victor Burgin, James Donald, and Cora Kaplan, 35–44. London: Methuen.

Rubin, Gayle (1978) "The Traffic in Women: Notes on the 'Political Economy' of Sex." In *Toward an Anthropology of Women*, edited by Rayna Reiter, 157–210. New York: Monthly Review Press.

Russo, Mary (1986) "Female Grotesques: Carnival and Theory." In *Feminist Studies: Critical Studies*, edited by Teresa de Lauretis, 213–229. Bloomington: Indiana University Press.

Silverman, Kaja (1984) "Dis-Embodying the Female Voice." In *Re-Vision: Essays in Feminist Film Criticism*, edited by Mary Ann Doane, Patricia Mellencamp, and Linda Williams, 131–149. Los Angeles: American Film Institute, University Publications of America.

Solomon, Alisa (1985) "The WOW Cafe." *The Drama Review* 29, no. 1 (T105):92–101. Also in this sourcebook, 42–51.

Witting, Monique (1981) "One is Not Born a Woman." *Feminist Issues* (winter):47–54.

11

FEMINIST THEORY, POSTSTRUCTURALISM, AND PERFORMANCE

Peggy Phelan

When a man is in the midst of his hubbub, in the midst of the breakers of his plots and plans, he there sees perhaps calm, enchanting things glide past him, for whose happiness and retirement he longs – *they are women*. He almost thinks that there with the woman dwells his better self; that in these calm places even the loudest breakers become still as death and life itself a dream of life.

(Friedrich Nietzsche in Derrida 1978:45)

There is no such thing as the essence of woman because woman averts, she is averted of herself. Out of the depths, endless and unfathomable, she engulfs and distorts all vestiges of essentiality, of identity, of property.

(Jacques Derrida 1978:51)

Life in this society being, at best, at utter bore and no aspect of society being at all relevant to women, there remains to civic-minded, responsible, thrill-seeking females only to overthrow the government, eliminate the money system, institute complete automation and destroy the male sex.

(Valerie Solanis in Morris 1979:166)

I

Between the romanticism of Nietzsche and the "civic-minded" feminist revolution of Morris/Solanis, Derrida's formulation of the "antiessential" essentiality of woman casts a curiously shaped net. If Derrida is right to say that "she engulfs and distorts all vestiges of ... identity," what then does this "she" (re)present in performance? A shadow where "identity" should/ought to be? Is the representation of woman's presence in fact a catalog of negation and absence – the perfect expression of Derrida's idea of language-as-absence? Are her performances a "hubbub" in which the "loudest breakers become still as death"? Or is Derrida's claim just another example of a man defining "the problem of woman"? In what ways does Derrida speak to feminism, if at all? Or to put it another way, what do feminist theory and poststructuralism have to say to one another?

It is a wearying and often maddening task to reconcile the contradictory ideological underpinnings of poststructuralism and feminism; and those who hold Grand Conspiracy Worldviews might note the conservative savvy involved in letting both movements share the same historical limelight. Poststructuralism and feminism each check the other's most radical appeal. For just as feminism declares that the gender of a particular artist serves a crucial function in her/his signifying practice, poststructuralism declares that the author is dead, that the notion of an individual subject is extremely problematical, and that all signifying practices are "traces" of Language's grand circulation. For the poststructuralist, "Previous Texts" function in the same way individual artist's biographies do for the Anglo-American feminist critic. History for the poststructuralist takes the place psychology, as distinct from psychoanalysis, holds for the Anglo-American feminist. And even now, in the spring of 1987, New Historicism waits in the wings, eagerly anticipating its chance to claim the center stage of Critical Discourse (see Pechter 1987).

These were (and are) the contradictions that have dominated my thinking for the past six years. When Richard Schechner invited me to attend the September 1986 International School for Theatre Anthropology (ISTA) Congress entitled "The Female Role as Represented on the Stage in Various Cultures," I anticipated an international moan and groan about the difficult paradoxes inherent in "representation" in general, and a kind of multilingual opera about the different politics of representing "the female role" cross-culturally. More wrong I could not have been.

The congress, hosted and organized by Eugenio Barba, was not at all concerned with the politics of representation. Issues of cultural hegemony, as well as issues of gender and sexual dominance/submission, were ignored: Barba explicitly stated in the program notes that the congress was not interested in the "psychology" of the performer – by implication, he was not interested in the psychological/political consequences of the performers' roles.[1] Although the reasons Barba chose not to pursue these issues are extremely important as an indication of where the European "third theatre" is (and is not) locating itself, it is unfair to criticize the conference for not doing what it never intended to do. The focus of the conference was on what Barba calls "the actor's energy." Barba believes that a study of the use of the actor's energy on a "'biological' level ... permits us to make an intercultural examination of the various theatrical traditions, not as historically determined systems but as [physiological] technique." Energy exists at a visible and an invisible level; Barba is interested in the "invisible" energy which emerges on (and in) the "pre-expressive level." Interestingly enough, Barba's pre-expressive level (see Barba 1986a:135–156) is strikingly similar to what psychoanalytically inclined feminists call the "pre-oedipal stage." In both ideas, there is a kind of Nietzschean romanticism, an ache for one's "best self" which can be seen only by continually turning back, by a continual turn away from the hubbub of competing meanings. (Nietzsche: "The most essential question of any text is its *hinterfrage* [back-question].")

In the effort to reclaim and isolate both the "pre-expressive" and the "pre-oedipal," a similar hope to understand the construction of meaning (literal and symbolic) is at work. Pre-expressive energy, for Barba, "refers to something intimate, something which pulses in immobility and silence, a retained power which flows in time without spreading through space" (1986b). For Laura Mulvey: "The pre-Oedipal, rather than an alternative or opposite state to the post-Oedipal, is in *transition* to articulated language: its gestures, signs, and symbols have meaning but do not transcend into the full sense of language" (Mulvey 1986:10). Just as Barba wants to isolate that intimate and immobile silence which underlines the energy one sees and hears, Mulvey wants to isolate the language of "gesture, sign, and symbol" which is not yet attached to a fully expressive language. In both projects, that which precedes "full sense" – or full expression – is important because it is in the pre-formed gesture/sound that one can perhaps find a way to rejuvenate and manipulate the rigid coding of performed expression and spoken language.

In order to make this clear, let me propose a distinction between "reading" (constructing a narrative in a full language) and "seeing" (a chaotic observation which does not fit into a narrative – either the movement narrative or the narrative of a sentence). At the pre-expressive level and the pre-oedipal level, "seeing" is dominant because full narratives have not yet been formed and therefore "reading" is impossible. Both the pre-expressive state and the pre-oedipal period posit a recoverable phase in which differentiation, opposition, and dualism are not yet operative. Hence, for Barba, the pre-expressive level is of interest as a site for the study of "pure" energy, and as a tool to develop in an actor's training; hence the pre-oedipal is of interest to those who want with Mulvey to upset and undermine the psychological/philosophical narrative of difference and opposition – particularly as it relates to gender, "power-knowledge," and erotic desire.

Barba's investigations of the actor's energy were based upon various cross-cultural performances of the female role. The Eastern dance forms represented at the congress – Balinese dance-drama, Indian *kathakali* and *odissi*, Japanese *kabuki*, and Chinese opera – proved to be the most disturbingly interesting. These Eastern theatrical roles are essentially mythic and, as Roland Barthes has remarked, myth "organizes a world which is without contradiction because it is without depth, a world wide open and wallowing in the evident, it establishes a blissful clarity: things appear to mean something by themselves" (1972:143). Such classical female roles played by men or women do not, by definition and design, penetrate the "identity" of any female; they are surface representations whose appeal exists precisely *as* surface. "Reading" them depends not on plausibility or coherence but rather upon immediate recognition of the comic artifice *and* reverent idealization of the form which organizes the image the dancer projects. But the substance and style of these dances are perhaps not the most interesting thing about them: for Barba it was the crucial discipline of the training; for a group of Western participants (primarily from the US and Canada) it was the contradictory portraits these dances created, not of femaleness per se, but of the social/political imaginations which they serve and express.

I'd like to discuss these issues in terms of one dancer: an 11-year-old boy named Gautam, the gotipua performer. Admittedly, this discussion wrenches the dance from its context. I am not trying here to analyze the intricacies of gotipua, but rather trying to isolate the terms of address operative between the spectator and the performer.

Gautam's hot pink costume and elaborate makeup (lips painted berry red, face painted with flowers) are conventional tropes of seduction. As a child, Gautam's ability to look nonmale was perhaps the most literally convincing of all the performers. While several women performers played the male role, Gautam's youth and his silence pointed out another implicit aspect of the "power-knowledge" system operative in the role division of classical dance. A child can play the part of an adult female, but not of an adult male. Or as Schechner recently put it, "woman equals girl but man does not equal boy" (1987).

On a more complicated level, however, the excess and "surplus" encoded within Gautam's surface femininity reminds the spectator of the absence of the female (the lack) rather than of her presence. The choreography of gotipua is punctuated by a series of tableaux in which the dancer rests squarely in front of the spectator and smiles seductively. He gazes boldly at the spectator and holds his smile. The directness of his seductive appeal is disarming, and it is that directness which paradoxically illuminates the way in which the dance is addressed to the male spectator. No one forgets that the dancer is male; the invocation of the nonmale is controlled by the security of the performer's male body. As a substitution for the female in the sphere of visual desire, Gautam's dance questions the function of erotic substitutions – what Freud calls

Figure 11.1 Gautam is an 11-year-old boy and a gotipua performer. He dances here in hot pink, his lips berry red, at the 1986 ISTA Congress in Denmark. (© Torbin Huss)

fetishes – in the incitement of desire which all performance exploits. The fetishized "female" image so perfectly encoded in Gautam's costume, makeup, and movement works not to bring the female into the spectacle of exchange between spectator and performer but to leave her emphatically outside. In place of the female, a fetishized image is displayed which substitutes for her and makes her actual presence unnecessary.

Freud's analysis of fetishism elucidated the ways in which all fetishes function as a phallic substitute, a reassuring projection of male narcissistic fantasy. The fantasy generated by Gautam's performance is the fantasy of exchange *between* men *about* women. In other words, "the female role" turns out to be another reinforcement of the primacy of desire between men for men/boys (the homoerotic), and the inequitable power relationship between the spectator and the performer (the young boy flatters the male spectator's physical and visual prowess). In short, the fetishized female image reinforces rather than subverts the structure of the patriarchal unconscious.

Much of this reading of Gautam's dance is indebted to a Western feminist discourse, a discourse not addressed or summoned by the dance itself. I'm treating the dance not as a series of movements but as a Western visual representation. My reading is obviously indebted to feminist rereadings of Freud, a revisionary project which has had the most important consequences for the criticism of film. Feminist film criticism has been the discourse most attentive to the relationship between the position of the spectator and the construction of "gendered texts." Employing psychoanalysis as a method, feminist film critics have outlined the complex relationships between visual pleasure, the conventions of camera work in Hollywood film, and the structure of the patriarchal unconscious in order to uncover the inscription of desire in narrative and avant-garde film. Central to the first generation of this project has been an analysis of the male gaze. If a feminist critical analysis of gender issues in performance is going to be written, however, it must begin not with an analysis of the male gaze, but rather with a reexamination of the economy of exchange between the performer and the spectator in performance.[2]

Yvonne Rainer's *The Man Who Envied Women* (1985), perhaps the best filmic treatment of this new economy of exchange, is acutely conscious of the problem of performance for women. Moreover, Rainer's film extends a challenge to the second generation of feminist film theorists: feminist film theory and practice must construct a way out of the frames of visual pleasure and pursue a different investigation of desire, narrative, and filmic pleasure. In live performance, the provocative and troubling work of Angelika Festa represents a different treatment of the economy of exchange between the spectator and performer, and it too is motivated by a feminist analysis of and frustration with the limitations of visual pleasure. In different ways the work of Rainer and Festa advance our critical understanding of women and representation and begin to expand the possibilities of female presence within the conventions of representation.

II

The Man Who Envied Women is the most recent expression of Rainer's long and extraordinarily intense concentration on issues of representation in both film and performance. The film's attention to the relationship between spectacle and spectator is informed by her work as a dancer and choreographer. *Trio A* (1968), perhaps Rainer's most famous piece of choreography, anticipates the exploration of the relationship between performer and spectator in *The Man Who Envied Women*. In *Trio A*, the dancer's "gaze was averted or the head was engaged in movement" (Rainer 1974:69), so that the customary visual exchange between performer and observer was denied. However, while the dance did not look at the spectator, the spectator could of course look at the dancer (perhaps even with a more uninhibited voyeurism), and the dancer, presumably, would still be aware of that gaze. While aware of "the narcissistic–voyeuristic duality of doer and looker" (Rainer 1974:238), Rainer was unable in *Trio A* to completely escape it. It is ironic, retrospectively, that Rainer's initial meditation on the psychological (and political) aspects of visual representation was framed by the medium of dance, since the form itself demands a present-body, a commanding belief in the manipulative possibilities of space, and an "authentic" (and ideal) movement signature to connote Presence. Narcissistic red-herrings are endemic to a form in which subjectivity and objectivity are located in the physical body – as a dancer, one's own body; as a choreographer, the bodies one author/izes to move. In this sense (admittedly counter-intuitive), dance is too literal, too claustrophobic a medium to pursue the kind of hypothesis about the interrelationship between representational subjectivity and objectivity to which Rainer's line of thinking inevitably leads. By moving to film Rainer gained a much-needed distance and a philosophically more reliable perspective from which to choreograph the ongoing dance of "seduction, ambivalence, attraction and withdrawal" between spectators and performers (Rainer 1989).

In *The Man Who Envied Women* Rainer takes some of the insights of feminist film theory to their logical conclusion: if the male gaze is an integral structure of cinematic desire (so integral that it is inscribed by everything from camera position to narrative structure), what happens when the (usual) object of that gaze, the heroine, is denied a visual presence within the film? Trisha, the central female character of the film, is not imaged.[3] Rainer seems to have taken Teresa de Lauretis' appeal to feminist filmmakers to create "another (object of) vision and the conditions of visibility for a different social subject" (1984:68) very much to heart. But while Trisha's visual image is "averted," her presence is still registered within the film. And it is this aspect of "presence" that suggests a form of analysis other than visual pleasure for the construction of desire and identification. By moving away from the importance of the image, Rainer creates a soundtrack which is dense, witty, and immensely pleasurable. Continuing the use of off-screen commentators central to her previous film *Journeys from Berlin/1971* (1979), Rainer extends the theoretical work on sound undertaken by Mary Ann Doane (1980) and Kaja Silverman (1984), both part of the second generation of feminist film theorists. In particular, Rainer's disruption of sound/image unity extends Silverman's contention that such a disruption of the signifying practices for representing the female body "reveal[s] the degree to which the [female voice] has been used to talk about and regulate" the female body (Silverman 1984:147).

If filmic presence is registered not through a (visible) body but through a voice, an invisible but audible consciousness, what pressure does this form of identification exert on psychoanalytic categories themselves? Voyeurism, scopophilia, and fetishism are all psycho/sexual paradigms activated by the eye, by seeing. Since the entire Freudian system is itself built on the crucial ability to *see* sexual difference ("the critical difference" centering around the ability/inability to see that the boy "has" a penis and the girl "lacks" visible genitalia), the subsequent developmental story psychoanalysis narrates is also dependent upon the fascination/repulsion of seeing sexual difference. Rainer's refusal to activate this (visual) source of cinematic pleasure, consequently (almost) desexualizes the process of identification and projection which the spectator has come to expect.

I say "almost" because while Trisha is visually absent from the film and thus blocks this form of identification, another woman, Jackie Raynal, activates the sexual/visual process of identification in an amazing scene shot in a narrow hallway. This scene, which occurs late in the film, is shot as a classic seduction sequence *except* it is impossible to know who "controls" the seduction: Jack Deller, the male protagonist and central visual presence of the film, or Jackie Raynal, his former lover who appears only in this scene.[4] In about a 20-minute editing tour de force, Rainer juxtaposes the visual narrative of seduction – two bodies in various layers of clothing move toward and away from each other, embrace and then disentangle themselves from the embrace – with other narratives which make that seduction alternately comical, bitter, absurd, necessary, delightful, euphoric, and ridiculous. These juxtapositions include cuts to (and from) the Manhattan City Council's vote against artist housing, film clips from Max Ophüls' *Caught* (1949), and an oedipal romp from a dream whose main characters are Jack, Trisha, Trisha's mother, and a one-eyed cat. These juxtapositions occur in the midst of a harrowing and hilarious rhetorical contest between Jack and

Figure 11.2 Melody London, Jackie Raynal, and William Raymond (Jack) in the hallway seduction scene from Yvonne Rainer's *The Man Who Envied Women*. Note Rainer's psychological doubling: the spectator (London), the mirror, the dualist seduction. (Photo from the film *The Man Who Envied Women*, directed by Yvonne Rainer)

Jackie; he quotes Foucault's *Discipline and Punish* (1977) and she responds with Morris' "The Pirate's Fiancee" (1979). The soundtrack here is extremely dense, making the images subservient. As Jackie moves in on Jack she gets to utter questions like: "What is happening when women must work so hard in distinguishing the penis and the phallus?" Jack's reply is a Foucauldian proposition about power-knowledge which sets up Rainer's elaborate pun on the (lack of) difference between the penis, the phallus, and the penal system.

The pleasure of this seduction comes not only from the playfulness of the verbal and political connections Rainer's deeply associative mind keeps turning up, but from the reflexive stance she takes toward her own use of film. By cutting back and forth to *Caught* (it occurs three times in this sequence), Rainer at once acknowledges the tradition of filmic seduction she is working to undercut as well as its hold on the spectator's imagination. Most avant-garde film works so hard to thwart narrative structure that the rigidity of the exclusion paradoxically increases the spectator's desire for its presence. Rainer here shows the convention (the *Caught* clip ends with James Mason and Barbara Bel Geddes dancing), and then "rewrites" it. It's as if one of Harold Bloom's young poets invites the precursor poet into the poem and says: "Hey watch this everybody." Rainer's customary way of dealing with anxiety – and not only anxiety of influence – is to overpower the spectator/auditor with details, elaborations, and a kind of boldly acknowledged attempt to fake it.[5]

Despite all the cuts and the rhetorical embellishment, the hallway scene is still a pleasurable *seduction*. Neither Foucault's assertive pronouncements nor Morris' dizzying speculations can distract anyone too long from the inevitability of Jack and Jackie's embrace. The elaborate rhetorical disguise does not completely cover the banality of their desire for each other; nor does it let us escape ours for them. But the disguise does make our desire for them funny and wry. Rainer's embellished and stylized distance from her characters, a distance measured by the elaborate editing and cutting in this sequence, makes the seduction we see almost diametrically opposed to the conventions of seduction operative in Ophüls' *Caught*. By refusing to let either Jack or Jackie be exclusively "the aggressor" or "the pursued," Rainer also robs the spectator of these familiar points of view from which to "identify." Jack and Jackie's tangled and shifting rhetoric highlights the psychological knots Rainer is creating for the spectator. By the time Trisha breaks in with her revisionary dream of The Family Romance we can only be relieved to see that Trisha and Trisha's mother not only have the same lover (Jack – of course) but that they also "have" the same body

Figure 11.3 Jack and Jackie's dual seduction is juxtaposed with an oedipal romp from a dream in which Trisha is both mother and lover. (Photo from *The Man Who Envied Women*, directed by Yvonne Rainer)

Figure 11.4 Jack's sessions with his psychiatrist occur while clips from Hollywood and avant-garde films play beside his head – Rainer's literal application of the connection between psychoanalytic and cinematic projection. (Photo from *The Man Who Envied Women*, directed by Yvonne Rainer)

(Rainer's own). Just as "He" gets to play both father and lover in Trisha's oedipal trauma, so Trisha (here played by Rainer behind a paper mask) gets to play both lover and mother (played by Rainer half-behind a door). The narrative doubling of the dream is precisely the kind of psychological doubling Rainer hopes to incite in her spectator. This impulse in Rainer's work comes not so much from an effort to increase "audience participation" or from some liberal sense of aesthetic democracy, but from the more radical hope that a continually shifting point of view might transform the means by which we know and perceive one another. Since such knowledge and perception is imbued with a postpsychoanalytic consciousness, the transformation of this consciousness will be derived from an engagement with the informing metaphors of psychoanalysis.

In *The Man Who Envied Women* the connection between psychoanalysis and cinema is foregrounded primarily through Jack's sessions with his psychiatrist.[6] These sessions occur along with clips from Hollywood and avant-garde films playing on a screen next to his head. In part because of Trisha's visual absence, but more importantly because of his role as patient-confessor, Jack is in what is usually associated with a "female" role. Jack's implicit "femaleness" (as patient and as film performer) is set against his obsessive ruminations on his "macho" sexual and intellectual conquests of women.[7] (These confessions come from the letters and diaries of Raymond Chandler.) Admitting that he is "not an average man," Jack goes on to boast that "there's nothing predatory in me ... I have never seduced a virgin nor intruded upon a valid marriage." The excessive weight he gives to these sexual experiences compromises his assertions of self-possession. But, more importantly, it is the overlaying of Trisha's narrative and her invisibility which reverse the power relationship between the seen and the unseen, the speaker and the listener, and potentially the spectator and the performer. Insofar as Trisha remains unexposed, she is in the position to "hear" (and thus judge) Jack's confessions. In this sense she is a *spectator* of her own film, almost more than she is the subject/object which motivates it. Rainer thus reverses the traditional conventions of filmic identification: instead of assuming that audiences exist in order to "identify with" characters, Rainer creates in Trisha a character who assumes that she might identify with the audience. When she interrupts one of Jack's long speeches about how thoroughly he knows women in order to supply the predictive subtext, "This is where he says, 'A man is nothing without a woman,'" Trisha is like a spectator who has "seen it all before."

As a response to classical film's ignorance of the female spectator, Trisha's voice-over implicitly and explicitly addresses that female spectator. The terms of address however are radically different from the ones to which we are accustomed. Rather than initiating spectator identification motivated by visual/psychological envy and fantasy (integral to what Mulvey has termed the "cult of the female star" [1975:15]), the spectator's identification with Trisha is motivated by a wry empathy in which a sense of equality between the spectator and the film performer suddenly seems possible. Alternately pensive and comic, Trisha modulates the aural and visual rhythms of the film. By remaining invisible, her presence within the narrative of the film is always somewhere "outside" its frame. As such it possesses a peculiarly powerful pull on the spectator's imagination: it keeps pushing one toward a de Lauretian consideration of "the conditions of visibility for a different social subject" (1984:68). Such conditions imply that since social subjects inhabit both the position of the spectator and the position of the performer, filmic representation (and psychoanalysis) ought to allow them/us this dualism also. Within the film, that dualism is most successfully articulated by the disruption of the unity between the image of Trisha's body and the sound of her voice.

Much of *The Man Who Envied Women* rigorously critiques the representational conventions which have disfigured the figure(s) of women. These two tendencies in the film allow Rainer to admit and indulge her fascination with Theory, even while underlining the reasons she finds its politics flabby in all the wrong places, its charms duplicitous, and its appeal suspicious. (In this sense, Rainer might be seen as an antitheoretical theorist.) The persistent question raised by *The Man Who Envied Women* is: If the constant qualifications necessary for presenting an averted women are so numerous that these qualifications effectively abolish her visual presence, how can she be re-presented? In the gaping hole opened up by this question and Trisha's visible absence, her disembodied voice resonates with a new metaphysics of filmic presence.

Rainer is too susceptible to the charms of melodrama (and too smart a filmmaker) to create a film in which the only interesting character is the one nobody can see. Rainer complicates the relationship between subjectivity and objectivity with her visually present characters as well as with Trisha. Rainer's characters are distinguished by their hyperbolic attraction to self-disclosure. Jack's sessions are framed by Rainer in such a way as to make the notion of a filmic "secret" or "intimate confession" completely oxymoronic. His inaugural speech to the doctor is interrupted by the title "Screen Tests," and he reads much of Chandler's text as if he is auditioning for a Godard film. In the middle of psychoanalytic sessions in which self-possession is defined exclusively in terms of sexual conquest, Jack's endless monologs about his relationships with women

Figure 11.5 Yvonne Rainer in *The Man Who Envied Women*. How can an "averted" woman be re-presented? Sideways? (Photo from *The Man Who Envied Women*, directed by Yvonne Rainer)

bespeak only his own thralldom with the courtship attendant upon self-seduction.

> There are women who are inaccessible, and I can tell that in five minutes. I always could. There are women who could be had tomorrow night but not tonight. That I know also. . . . I don't know whether it is a talent or a curse, but I always know.

Even more than The Patient's formidable chatter to the shifting (and shifty) Psychiatrists in *Journeys from Berlin/1971*, the insulation of Jack's confessions make the doctor completely dispensable. Fittingly, in the place where we would expect to see a calm, bespectacled analyst, Rainer's camera reveals instead an unruly film audience mimetically repeating the violence and mayhem visibly projected in a grisly sequence from *Night of the Living Dead*. The only audience able to hear Jack's "soul searching" is a filmic one. By continually reminding us that we are watching a film in which our own position is neatly accounted for, Rainer forces us to invent another position – one *outside* the frames she offers to put us in.

By not allowing the spectator to "see" Trisha, Rainer breaks down the conventions of filmic "reading." Rather than locating her film in either the pre-expressive or pre-oedipal spheres, Rainer suggests that these spheres are themselves indications of the post-expressive and post-oedipal imagination; an imagination addicted to turning back (to endlessly reexamining the hinterfrage) for inspiration about how to move forward.[8] Rainer's own turning back to *Caught* takes place in the context of her active construction of a new seduction. A seduction which presents the spectator with images of Jackie in both a lamé dress and in a gray, mechanic's jumpsuit (she appears in the jumpsuit after a jump-cut); a seduction in which Jack's body assumes stances that are at once menacing and endearingly awkward. (He leans against the wall the way teenage boys lean against their cars – half a claim to bravado, all to keep from swooning with fear.) But the soundtrack throughout this sequence is what anchors the seduction. It is as if the earnestness of the effort to be abstract, enunciated by Jack and Jackie's quotations from Foucault and Morris, temporarily disengages the film from its dependency upon character, body, and image. For Rainer, it is precisely film's thralldom with these staples of narrative which will continue to make the enunciation of a visual pleasure for the female spectator extremely difficult to achieve. In the hallway scene, the spectator is awash in words rather than images, and the eroticism of the words comes in part from being unable to pin them to one character, one image. The soundtrack does not substitute for the image track so much as it overpowers it. The entire question of fetishism and erotic substitution is played out not on the body of the performer – as in Gautam's dance – but on the body of the film. *The Man Who Envied Women* creates a dichotomy between sound and image in which the female voice becomes an intimate barometer of female presence. As Silverman astutely points out, the male voice-over in film is always embodied in the discourse of Authority and omniscience, while the female voice-over remains dis-embodied (see 1984:131–149). Less optimistic than Silverman about the liberating features of such dis-embodiment, I want to emphasize that this form of female presence is contingent upon the absence of her image and therefore comes dangerously close to fetishizing the female voice.

III

Whereas Rainer's film often seems to be "all talk," Angelika Festa's performance work seems to be, like Gautam's, "all image." Her work, however, is radically different from classical dance. It literally and directly illustrates the first sentence of the Derrida quotation with which I began this essay. Accepting the idea of women's aversion, Festa is more puzzled by Derrida's second statement: "Out of the depths, endless and unfathomable, she engulfs and distorts all vestiges of essentiality, of identity, of property." Festa creates performance pieces in which she appears in order to disappear. Her appearance is always extraordinary: she suspends herself from poles; she sits fully dressed in well-excavated graves, attended by a fish; she stands still on the crowded corner of 8th and Broadway in downtown New York, wearing a red rabbit suit and holding two loaves of bread; she holds a white bowl of fruit and stands by the side of a country road, wearing a mirror mask and a black, vaguely antiquarian dress, her hands and feet painted white. The more dramatic the appearance, the more disturbing the disappearance. As performance contingent upon disappearance, Festa's work is allied with much postmodern performance art in that its primary interest comes from the discourse it promotes after the fact, rather than from the immediacy of the image it creates when it is "presented."[9]

In her performance entitled – appropriately – *Untitled Dance with Fish and Others* at the Experimental Intermedia Foundation in New York, Festa hung suspended from a pole for 24 hours. The performance took place between noon on Saturday 30 May 1987, and noon on Sunday the 31st. The pole was positioned between two wooden supports at a 45-degree angle and Festa hung suspended from it, her body wrapped to the pole with white sheets, her face and weight leaning toward the floor. Her eyes were covered with silver tape. About two-and-a-half feet from the bottom of the pole was a small, black cushion which supported her bare feet. Her feet in turn were projected onto a screen behind her and to the left. The projection enlarged them so much that they seemed to be as big as the rest of Festa's body. On a video monitor in front of Festa and to the left, a videotape loop of the embryogeny of a fish played continuously. Finally, on a smaller monitor facing Festa, a time-lapsed

Figure 11.6 Angelika Festa on the side of a road in Banff, Canada. This performance, "You Are Obsessive, Eat Something," lasted three weeks. (Photo by Claudine Ascher)

video documenting the dance (re)played and re(in)flected the entire performance.

The images of death, birth, and resurrection were visually overlaid, illustrating Festa's point that they are philosophically (and mythologically) inseparable. The work was primarily a spectacle of pain; while I do not wish to minimize this aspect of the performance, I will begin by discussing some of the extravagant paraphernalia which frames *Untitled*. The performance seeks to display the lack of difference between some of Western metaphysics' tacit oppositions – birth and death, time and space, spectacle and secret. By suspending herself from a pole, itself suspended between two poles (two polarities), Festa's performances suggest that it is only within the space *between* oppositions that "a woman" can be represented. Such representation is, therefore and necessarily, extremely up-in-the-air, almost impossible to map or lay claim to. It is in a space in which there is no ground, a space in which (bare)feet cannot touch the ground.

The iconography of the performance is self-contradictory: each position is undermined by a succeeding one. Festa's wrapped body conjures images of dead mummies and full cocoons. Reading the image one can say something like: the fecundity of the central image is an image of History-as-Death (the mummy) and Future-as-Unborn (the cocoon). The 24-hour performance defines the Present (Festa's body) as that which continually suspends and thus prohibits the intrusive return of that death and the appealing possibility of that birth. The Present is that which can tolerate neither death nor birth but can only exist because of these two "originary" acts. Both are required for the Present to be present, for it to exist in the suspended animation between the Past and the Future. But this truism is undercut by another part of the performance, thus forcing endless redefinition of the Nietzschean "hubbub" which constitutes any Present. The fish tape stops at precisely the moment the fish breaks out of the embryo; then the loop begins again. The tape thus revises the definition of History offered by the central image (History-as-Death). History is figured by the tape as an endless embryogeny whose import is not in the breaking out of – the ubiquitous claim to historical "transformation" – but rather in the continual repetition of the cycle of that mutation which produces birth. ("Be fruitful and multiply" is wittily made literal by the repeated projection of the tape loop.)

The third image then undercuts the first two. The projected images of Festa's feet seem to be a half-ironic, half-devout allusion to the history of representations of the bloody feet of the crucified Christ. On the one hand (one foot?), the projections are like photographic "details" of Mannerist paintings and on the other they seem to "ground" the

Figure 11.7 In her 1987 performance, *Untitled Dance with Fish and Others*, at the Experimental Intermedia Foundation in New York, Festa hung suspended from a pole for 24 hours. (Photo by Hubert Hohn)

performance; because of their size they seem to demand more of the spectator's attention. The spatial arrangement of the room – Festa in the middle, the feet-screen behind her to the left, the fish tape in front of her also to the left, and the time-lapsed mini-monitor raised directly in front of her – forces the spectator constantly to look *away from* Festa's suspended body. In order to look at the projected feet, one has to look "beyond" Festa; in order to look at the fish embryo or at the video monitor recording the performance itself, the spectator has to turn away from her. That these projected images seem to be consumable while the central image – Festa herself – is, as it were, a "blind" image, suggests that it is only through the second-order of representation that we see anything. The "endless and unfathomable" spectacle of Festa's body (and particularly her eyes) are "averted," denying the spectator the ability to exchange – to see, and thus to seize.

While this brief outline of the *Untitled* piece sketches the parameters of the issues raised by this performance, it obscures the somewhat wittier aspect of Festa's work. In a perverse way, *Untitled* is an elaborate pun on the notion of women's strength. The "labor" of the performance alludes to the labor of the delivery room – and the white sheets and red headdress are puns on the colors of the birthing process – the white light in the center of pain and the red blood which tears open that light.[10] The projected feet wryly raise the issue of the fetishized female body – the part (erotically) substituted for the whole – which the performance "as

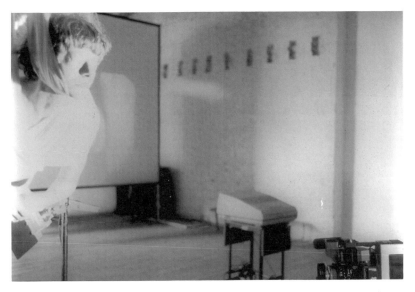

Figure 11.8 Images of Festa's feet were projected behind and to the left of her body. A videotape of fish embryogeny ran continuously at another spot and in front of her ran a video monitor of the entire performance. (Photo by Hubert

a whole" seeks to confront. As I tried to find a way to read this suspended and yet completely controlled and confined body, images of other women "tied up" flooded my eyes. Images as absurdly comic as the damsel Nell tied to the railroad ties waiting for Dudley Do-Right to beat the clock and save her and images as harrowing as the traditional burning of martyrs and witches coexist with more common images of women tied to white hospital beds in the name of "curing hysteria," force-feeding anorexia, or tending to the various medical conditions by which women have been painfully dominated and with which we continue to be perversely enthralled. The "wit" here is admittedly macabre. The austere minimalism of this piece (which is performed in complete silence), actually incites the spectator to make lists of this type. The lists become dizzyingly similar until it's almost impossible to distinguish between Nell screaming on the railroad tracks and the hysteric screaming in the hospital. The riddle is as much about figuring out how they became separated as about how Festa puts them back together.

In all of these images there is a peculiar sense in which their drama hinges absolutely on the sense of seeing oneself and of being seen as "Other." The anorexic obsessed by the image of a slender self; Nell, the epitome of cross-cutting, neck-wrenching melodrama; the martyr and witch whose public hanging/burning is dramatized as a lesson in moral certitude either by the victim-martyr herself or by her executioners, are each defined in terms of what they are not: healthy, heroic, or legitimately powerful. That these terms are themselves slippery, radically subjective, and historically malleable emphasizes the importance of maintaining a fluid and relative ocular perspective. These images reenact the subjective perception which defines The Fall, assigning it a significance more profound than expulsion from "fertile ground" – the usual interpretation of significant loss. Emphasizing the importance of perceptual transformation rather than the loss of property, Festa's work implicitly underlines the clause "The eyes of both of them were opened" (Genesis 3:7) as the most compelling consequence detailed in this narrative of origin.

The belief that perception can be made endlessly new is, of course, one of the fundamental drives of all visual arts. But in most theatre the opposition between watching and doing is broken down; the distinction becomes ethically immaterial.[11] Festa, whose eyes are covered with tape throughout the performance, questions the traditional complicity of this visual exchange. Her eyes are completely "averted" and the more I, as a spectator, try to see her, the more I realize that "seeing her" requires that I be seen. Unlike Rainer's film in which the (female) protagonist cannot be seen, here the (female) protagonist cannot see. In the absence of that customary visual exchange, the spectator can only see her own desire to be seen. The satisfaction of desire in this spectacle is perpetually thwarted; the spectator has to play both parts of the performative exchange and become the spectator of *her own performance* in the face of Festa's aversion. In this sense, Festa's work operates on the other side of the same continuum as Rainer's – where Trisha becomes a kind of spectator, Festa's spectator becomes a kind of performer.

But while Festa successfully eliminates the ethical complicity between watching and doing associated with most theatre, she does not create an ethically neutral performance. Festa's body is a public spectacle displayed in a completely private (in the sense of enclosed) manner. She becomes a kind of sacrificial object entirely vulnerable to the spectator's gaze. As I watched Festa's exhaustion and pain, I felt cannibalistic, awful, guilty, sick. But after a while another more complicated response emerged: there is something almost obscenely arrogant in Festa's invitation to this display. (An arrogance manifest in the imitative aspect of her allusions to Christ's crucifixion/resurrection and latently present in the endurance she demands of both her spectator and herself.) This arrogance, which she freely acknowledges and makes blatantly obvious, in some senses cancels my cannibalism. And while all this addition and subtraction is going on in my accountant eyes, I begin to realize that this, too, is superficial. The performance resides not at all in the sums and differences of our difficult relationships to it, but somewhere else – somewhere in the reckoning itself. Yet this thought does not evoke an easy sense of equality or democracy – though that is part of her intention. I feel instead the terribly oppressive physical, psychic, and visual cost of this exchange. If Festa's work can be seen as a hypothesis about the possibility of human communication, it is an uncompromising one. There is no meeting place here which can escape the imposing shadow of those (bloody) feet: if History is figured in the tape loop as a repetitious birth cycle, the Future is figured as an unrelenting cycle of death. Where e. e. cummings writes, "We can never be born enough" (1972:461), Festa counters, "We can never die sufficiently enough." And yet this sense of the ubiquitousness of death and dying is not completely oppressive (though at times it comes close) because the performance simultaneously insists on potential resurrection. By making death multiple and repetitious Festa also makes it less absolute – less sacred – less the exclusive province of the gods.

My hesitation about this aspect of Festa's work stems not from the latent romance of death (that's common enough), but rather from her apparent belief (or perhaps "faith" is a better word) that this suspension/surrender of her own ego can be accomplished in a performance. It is this belief/faith which makes Festa's work so extravagantly literal. (And as seen in the discussion of Rainer's dance career, this literalization may be why Festa refers to her work as dance.) Festa's piece is contingent upon the possibility of creating a narrative which reverses the narrative direction of The Fall; beginning with the postlapsarian second-order of Representation, Festa's *Untitled Dance with Fish and Others* attempts to give birth – through an intense process of physical and mental labor – to a direct and unmediated Presentation-of-Presence. That this Presence is registered through the body of a woman *in pain* is the one concession Festa makes to the pervasiveness (and the persuasiveness) of postlapsarian Perception and Being. Enormously and stunningly ambitious, Festa's performances leave both the spectator and the performer so exhausted that one cannot help but wonder if the pleasure of presence and plenitude is worth having if this is the only way to achieve it.

In the spectacle of endurance, discipline, and semimadness that this work evokes, an inversion of the characteristic paradigms of performative exchange occurs. In the spectacle of fatigue, endurance, and depletion, Festa asks the spectator to undergo first a movement parallel to her narrative and then an opposite movement. The spectator's second "performance" is a movement of accretion, excess, and the recognition of the plenitude of one's physical freedom in contrast to the confinement and pain of the performer's displayed body.

That displayed body is opposite from the image figured in Gautam's dance. While Gautam creates a male/nonmale dichotomy and enacts a form created by and addressed to men, Festa's work examines the female body's relationship to dichotomy by literally suspending herself between two poles. While Gautam's performances are pleasurable "entertainments," Festa's are painful accounts of the psychic and physical costs of such pleasure for the (usually bound and confined) woman.

IV

> [T]he agency of domination does not reside in the one who speaks (for it is he who is constrained), but in the one who listens and says nothing; not in the one who knows and answers, but in the one who questions and is not supposed to know.
>
> (Michel Foucault 1978:64)

Foucault is describing the power-knowledge fulcrum which sustains the Roman Catholic confessional, but as with most of Foucault's work it resonates in other areas as well. As a description of the power relationships operative in many forms of performance Foucault's observation suggests the degree to which the silent spectator dominates and controls the exchange. As Dustin Hoffman made so clear in *Tootsie*, the performer is always in the feminine position in relation to power. That is, women and performers, more often than not, are "scripted" to "sell" or "confess" something to someone who is in the position to buy or forgive. Traditional theatre evokes desire based upon and stimulated by this inequality between performer and spectator – and by the (potential) domination of the silent spectator. This works both ways: "the silent spectator desires to be dominated by (to submit to) the performance and the performer's presence, while at the same time maintaining the distance of dominant judge" (Schneider 1987). That this model of desire is apparently so compatible with (traditional accounts of) "male" desire is no accident.[12] But more interestingly, this account of desire between speaker/performer and listener/spectator also suggests how these positions are dependent upon visibility and a coherent point of view. A visible and easily locatable point of view provides the spectator with a stable point upon which to turn on the machinery of projection, identification, and (inevitable) objectification. Performers and their critics must begin to redesign and confound this stable set of assumptions about the positions of theatrical exchange.

Rainer and Festa, in very different ways, are involved in this project. The obvious question raised by both women's work is the extent to which their interest in visual or psychic aversion signals an interest in refusing to participate in an economy of exchange at all. By virtue of having spectators they do, I think, accept at least the initial dualism necessary to all exchange. Rainer has repeatedly stressed that her film is not a manifesto or a "solution" to the representational puzzle of the female character, and Festa's performances are so profoundly "solo" that her work can't pretend to solve the problem of women's representation. *The Man Who Envied Women* and *Untitled Dance with Fish and Others* are retreative works which, like Gautam's dance, raise the specter of the absent women. But unlike Gautam's performance, this work addresses the female spectator; it does not speak about men (although in Rainer's film she and Trisha sometimes speak *through* men), it speaks rather about the loss and grief attendant upon the recognition of the chasm between presence and re-presentation.

While I want to emphasize that I do not think that the radically different projects begun by *The Man Who Envied Women* or *Untitled Dance with Fish and Others* are "solutions" in any sense, I cannot help but notice that my response to both Festa's and Rainer's work involves a sigh of deep relief. By taking the notion that women are not visible within the dominant narratives of history and the contemporary customs of performance literally, Rainer and Festa prompt new considerations about the central "absence" integral to the representation of women in patriarchy. Part of the function of women's absence is to perpetuate and maintain the presence of male desire as desire – as unsatisfied quest. Since the female body and the female character cannot be "staged" or "seen" within representational mediums without challenging the hegemony of male desire, might it be effective politically and aesthetically to deny representing the female body (imagistically, psychically) in order to bring about a new form of representation itself? (I'm thinking only half-jokingly of the sex strike in *Lysistrata*: no sex till the war ends.) In Rainer's film, the absence of Trisha's visual image accentuates the presence constituted by her voice. Circumventing the assumed unity between image and sound, Rainer's film postulates a different order of filmic presence and avoids the oppressive habits of spectator identification activated by visual pleasure. Festa's performance work underlines the suspension of the female body between the polarities of presence and absence, and suggests that "the woman" exists *between* these categories of analysis.

Redesigning the relationship between self and other, subject and object, sound and image, man and woman, spectator and performer, is enormously difficult. But perhaps more difficult still is withdrawing from representation altogether. I am not advocating that kind of retreat or hoping for that kind of silence (since that is the position language assigns to women with such ease). The task, in other words, is to make counterfeit the currency of our representational economy – not by refusing to participate in it at all, but rather by making work in which the cost of women's perpetual "aversion" is clearly measured. Such forms of accounting might begin to interfere with the structure of male desire which infects and informs all forms of representation.

NOTES

1. Despite Barba's reiteration of his antipsychologism, his insistence that each performer tell the story of her/his "first day of training" has more than a little in common with psychoanalysis' interest in the "primal scene," the "originary cause," and "earliest memories." "The first days of [the performer's] work leave an indelible imprint," Barba notes in the congress program (1986b).
2. For a full discussion of "the male gaze" see Kaplan (1983) and Mulvey (1975). For a discussion of the construction of the spectator in cinema see de Lauretis (1984). For an excellent analysis of the relationship between mainstream and avant-garde cinema's treatment of the female character see Claire Johnston (1973). While this work is crucial for an initial understanding of representation, it cannot fully account for the difficult tensions inherent in *live* performance.
3. Although a slow-motion film clip of Trisha Brown's (who reads the part of the off-screen "Trisha") performance of *Water Motor* is inserted within one of Jack's psychoanalytic sessions, the clip serves to indicate the state of Jack's grief, and not the narrative presence of the off-screen Trisha.
4. I should say appears *visually* only in this scene. Her voice is heard on the telephone earlier, when she makes the date with Jack to meet at the party.
5. In *The Man Who Envied Women* this habit consistently shows up in Trisha's speeches. Whenever she is about to make some completely damning (but probably accurate) statement about the relationships between men and women she "fakes" her authority and half-hopes she'll be wrong. Some of her best lines include these prefaces to incisive speeches: "OK, here we go; I can't avoid this any longer. It's one theory, OK?"; or, "And how about this (I mean someone has to do this dirty work, right?) – I shall be bold . . .'; or, "Sometimes, fresh from reading Frederic Jameson or Russell Jacoby, I could play his [Jack's] game at equal cross-purposes." The anxiety comes from wanting not to believe the clarity of her own argument.
6. For a detailed discussion of the connection between psychoanalysis and cinema in *The Man Who Envied Women*, see Phelan (1986).
7. As the film goes on it becomes increasingly difficult to separate the sexual and the intellectual.
8. A woman's (Trisha's) "back" is seen once early on in the film when she is collecting things from the apartment she had been sharing with Jack. The question raised by this back is what the film keeps turning over.
9. Schechner wrote that this aspect of performative "aftermath" – the documentation, discussion, and discourse effected by performance – is increasingly as important as the experience of the performance itself (see 1985:16–21).
10. Festa actually began the *Untitled* performance wearing a white rabbit headdress, which is lighter and cooler than the red; she has on other occasions worn the red one. The themes of "red" and "white" are constant preoccupations of her work. The temperature during *Untitled* (in the 90s)

was intense enough that she was eventually persuaded to abandon the white headdress.

11. This is one of the reasons "shock" is such a limited aesthetic for theatre. It is hard to be shocked by one's own behavior/desire, although easy to be shocked by someone else's.

12. In fact it may account for the intense male homoeroticism of so much of theatrical history.

REFERENCES

Barba, Eugenio (1986a) *Beyond the Floating Islands*. New York: PAJ Publications.

———(1986b) "The Female Role as Represented on the Stage in Various Cultures." In the ISTA Program, compiled and edited by Richard Fowler. Holstebro, Denmark.

Barthes, Roland (1972) *Mythologies*. Translated by Annette Lavers. New York: Hill and Wang.

cummings, e. e. (1972) *Complete Poems: 1913–1962*. New York: Harcourt Brace Jovanovich, Inc.

Derrida, Jacques (1978) *Spurs/Nietzsche's Styles*. Translated by Barbara Harlow. Chicago: University of Chicago Press.

Doane, Mary Ann (1980) "The Voice in Cinema: The Articulation of Body and Space." *Yale French Studies* 60:33–50.

Foucault, Michel (1977) *Discipline and Punish*. Translated by Alan Sheridan. New York: Pantheon Books.

———(1978) *The History of Sexuality*, vol. I. Translated by Robert Hurley. New York: Pantheon Books.

Johnston, Claire (1973) "Women's Cinema as Counter-Cinema." In *Notes on Women's Cinema* edited by Claire Johnston. London: Society for Education in Film and Television. Reprinted in *Movies and Methods: An Anthology*, edited by Bill Nichols, 208–213. Berkeley and Los Angeles: University of California Press (1976).

Kaplan, E. Ann (1983) *Women and Film: Both Sides of the Camera*. New York: Methuen.

de Lauretis, Teresa (1984) *Alice Doesn't: Feminism, Semiotics, Cinema*. Bloomington: Indiana University Press.

Morris, Meaghan (1979) "The Pirate's Fiancée." In *Michel Foucault: Power, Truth, Strategy*, edited by Meaghan Morris and Paul Patton, 148–168. Sydney, Australia: Ferral Publications.

Mulvey, Laura (1975) "Visual Pleasure and Narrative Cinema." *Screen* 16, no. 3 (autumn):6–18.

———(1986) "Changes." Paper presented at New York University Humanities

Institute Colloquium on Sex and Gender, fall.

Pechter, Edward (1987) "The New Historicism and Its Discontents: Politicizing Renaissance Drama." *PMLA* 102, no. 3 (May):292–303.

Phelan, Peggy (1986) "Spatial Envy: Yvonne Rainer's *The Man Who Envied Women*." *Motion Picture* 1, no. 3 (summer):1–19.

Rainer, Yvonne (1974) *Work: 1961–1973*. New York: New York University Press.

———(1989) *The Films of Yvonne Rainer*. Bloomington: Indiana University Press.

Schechner, Richard (1985) "Points of Contact Between Anthropological and Theatrical Thought." In *Between Theatre and Anthropology*, 3–34. Philadelphia: University of Pennsylvania Press.

———(1987) Personal communication.

Schneider, Rebecca (1987) Personal communication.

Silverman, Kaja (1984) "Dis-Embodying the Female Voice." In *Re-Vision*, edited by Mary Ann Doane, Patricia Mellencamp, and Linda Williams, 131–149. Los Angeles: American Film Institute: University Publications of America.

PART III Interviews

12

ANNA DEAVERE SMITH

The Word Becomes You

An Interview by Carol Martin

Anna Deavere Smith's *Fires in the Mirror: Crown Heights, Brooklyn and Other Identities* is a series of portraits of people enmeshed in the Crown Heights riots where Jews and blacks were so violently pitted against one another, in Brooklyn, August 1991. The riots were provoked when Gavin Cato, a black child, was hit and killed by a Lubavitch rebbe's motorcade. By the end of that day Yankel Rosenbaum, a young Jewish scholar from Australia, was murdered in retaliation. The piece was first performed at the Public Theatre in the late spring and summer of 1992, with Christopher Ashley as director. *Fires in the Mirror* was then mediated for television broadcast by PBS's "American Playhouse," directed by George C. Wolfe. The TV adaptation first aired in April 1993.

In the stage version Smith performed barefoot in a white shirt and black pants. Sitting in an armchair, or at a desk, donning a yarmulke, or a cap of African kente cloth, or a spangled sweater, Smith brought her 29 subjects to the stage to speak *their own* lines. That there were unresolvable contradictions in the multiple versions of truth Smith portrayed did not diminish the conviction of each character that what they said was true.

Smith's apparently hypernaturalistic mimesis – in which she replicates not only the words of different individuals but their bodily style as well – is deceiving. Derived from a method more documentary than "artistic" in the usual sense, Smith's performance can easily be understood as a feat of technical virtuosity. Brilliantly portrayed characters, however, are not enough to generate the enormous critical success of a work about a very turbulent set of events. The authority of one group over another, of one individual over others, is undermined by the presence of Smith as the person through whom so many voices travel. Smith gives these people the chance to speak as if to each other – in much the same way a "spirit doctor" brings ancestors or other spirits in contact with the living – in the presence of the community of the audience. It is this fictional and yet actual convergence of presences that give Smith's work its power. Angela Davis, Ntozake Shange, Letty Cottin Pogrebin, Rabbi Shea Hecht, Reverend Al Sharpton, and others, known and unknown, speak together. They speak together across race, history, theory, and differences in their own words through Smith's conjuring performative language. Their "presence" and words mark the absence and silence of the two people around whom the drama revolves, Gavin Cato and Yankel Rosenbaum.

Fires in the Mirror is part of a series of performances titled *On the Road: A Search for American Character*. Smith began working on this series in 1979 by walking up to people on the street and saying "I know an actor who looks like you. If you'll give me an hour of your time, I'll invite you to see yourself performed" (1992:18). Early in her work Smith's focus shifted from individuals to groups of individuals at gatherings, conferences, or as members of a community. Some of the work has been commissioned and performed for specific conferences, while other pieces were developed for theatre audiences. Often the title of the work reveals the theme: *Building Bridges Not Walls* (1985); *Gender Bending: On the Road Princeton University* (1989); *On Black Identity and Black Theatre* (1990); *From the Outside Looking in* (1990). Smith's desire is to "capture the personality of a place by attempting to embody its varied population and varied points of view in one person – myself" (Smith 1992:18).

I spoke with Smith in August 1992 after seeing *Fires in the Mirror* at the Public Theatre.

MARTIN: How did you become interested in Crown Heights?

SMITH: George Wolfe had asked me to participate in a festival of performance artists called "New Voices of Color" last December [1991 at the Public Theatre]. The thought of coming to New York and doing *On the Road* was pretty overwhelming.

Then, on August 19th Crown Heights happened. I put it in the back of my mind. When I went to the Bunting Institute at Harvard in September I still didn't know if the festival was going to happen. It wasn't until the day Anita Hill began to testify that I got a call from the theatre formally inviting me to the festival. I didn't have a commission so there was no money to build anything big. I thought I would do a show that I'd already done before and just put a couple of things about New York in it. I asked the Public Theatre for four days in a hotel and a round-trip air ticket. In those four days I had to get everything. I only performed it twice but it went very well so they decided to think of it for a run.

What was personally compelling about Crown Heights was that it was a community with very graphic differences. Everyone wears their beliefs on their bodies – their costumes. You can't pass. Crown Heights is no melting pot and I really respect that.

MARTIN: You were already dealing with issues of race, identity, and difference.

SMITH: Yes.

MARTIN: So Crown Heights was really a graphic way for you to. . . .

SMITH: Explore.

MARTIN: How did you make your contacts?

SMITH: I usually get a few contacts from the newspaper and then try to make my way into any institution, to somebody in authority. In this case, I went to various people in the mayor's office and asked them for ideas for people to interview. People lead to more people. Eventually, I know very specifically what kind of people I want to meet so I know what kind of person to try to find.

MARTIN: Did people in the community get to know your presence?

SMITH: I wasn't there long enough. I did all the interviews in about eight days.

MARTIN: The two anonymous young black men were very interesting and very important. How did you find them?

SMITH: That was lucky. There were few women in the piece. In the "Crown Heights" section there was only one. One of my goals when I came back to New York in the spring was to do a few more interviews with women. I found one young woman who was a friend of Henry Rice. I went to interview her. She runs – it's so sad – a center in the Ebbets Field apartment houses, but it's just an empty dark room with a few chairs. A radio was playing in the background. It's no place for her [Kim] to be making activities.

I went to interview Kim around eight o'clock at night and two boys were just sitting there. They inched their way into the interview. I didn't invite them in. They just, you know, invited themselves. The second one, the "bad boy," really did not even come into the group. The one who talked about justice was "Anonymous #1." He came right into Kim's interview and sat down with his friend. His friend said nothing the entire time but the "bad boy" [Anonymous #2] just lurked in the dark corner watching. When we discussed Limerick Nelson, the 16-year-old accused of killing Yankel Rosenbaum, the

On the Road series
Anna Deavere Smith

1982   *On the Road, New York City*
A Clear Space, New York, NY.
1983   *A Birthday Party* and *Aunt Julia's Shoes* (original poems and *On the Road* material)
Ward Nasse Gallery, New York, NY.
1984   *Charlayne Hunter Gault*
Ward Nasse Gallery, New York, NY.
1985   *Building Bridges Not Walls*
National Conference of Women and the Law, New York, NY.
1986   *On the Road, ACT*
Summer Training Congress, American Conservatory Theatre, San Francisco, CA.
1988   *Voices of Bay Area Women*
Phoenix Theatre, San Francisco, CA.
1988   *Chlorophyll Post-Modernism and the Mother Goddess: A Convers/Ation*
Hahn Cosmopolitan Theatre, San Diego, CA.
1989   *Gender Bending: On the Road Princeton University*
Princeton University, Princeton, NJ.
1990   *Gender Bending: On the Road University of Pennsylvania*
University of Pennsylvania, Philadelphia, PA.
1990   *On Black Identity and Black Theatre*
Crossroads Theatre Company, New Brunswick, NJ.
1990   *From the Outside Looking in*
Eureka Theatre, San Francisco, CA.
1991   *Fragments*
Conference on Intercultural Performance, Bellagio, Italy.
1991   *Identities Mirrors and Distortions I*
Calistoga Arts Festival, Calistoga, CA.
1991   *Identities Mirrors and Distortions II*
Bay Area Playwrights Festival, San Francisco, CA.
1991   *Identities Mirrors and Distortions III*
Global Communities Conference, Stanford University, Stanford, CA.
1991   *Identities Mirrors and Distortions IV*
Festival of New Voices, Joseph Papp Public Theatre, New York, NY.
1992   *Dream* (a workshop)
Crossroads Theatre Company, New Brunswick, NJ.
1992   *Fires in the Mirror: Crown Heights, Brooklyn and Other Identities*
Joseph Papp Public Theatre, New York, NY.
1993   *Twilight: Los Angeles, 1992*
Mark Taper Forum, Los Angeles, CA.

"bad boy" started talking. None of these kids believe that Limerick did it. They told me they know who it is but they won't tell. So then he [the "bad boy"] spoke up. I loved what he said and I just loved how he talked.

MARTIN: There is a sense in the performance that when you interview blacks they acknowledge you as a member of their community. There's no sense, however, when you're interviewing the Jews that they looked at you as a member of the black community.

SMITH: Could you tell me a little bit more?

MARTIN: There is the use of pronouns like "us" and "we." There is the guy in the restaurant scene who comments about rape of black women and people ending up like you [light-skinned]. There's a sense of inclusion.

SMITH: I actually tried to heighten the sense of inclusion for everybody by using the pronouns "us" and "we" in relation to everybody. I address the text like a poem. I work on "us" and "we" whenever anybody, regardless of race, says them. I don't want to confront the audience or make them feel that it's you and me. My experience of the interviews I included was that there was an "us" before I left. People's will to communicate came forward even with Roz, the Jewish woman at the end. She acknowledges me. She says, "I wish you could have been here. I would have showed you the *New York Times*."

It's a fact that Muslim [Conrad Mohammed] calls me "sister." I think everybody else calls me by name.

MARTIN: You are easily included when you're speaking to the members of the black community in Crown Heights. At the same time, there's also an openness in the interviews with the Lubavitchers.

SMITH: I think that has to do with how the Lubavitchers are. It doesn't have to do with me or with any stranger. Obviously, there are clear lines. But they are taught, as I understand it, that the expression of feelings is superior in some ways to the intellect. It doesn't have to do with me. It has to do with the fact that the Lubavitchers will come forward with what they feel. That's how they are with each other. They forget that not everybody is like that.

My experience in academia is the antithesis. I've realized people in academic circles aren't really talking to me. They're trying to figure out if I'm smart or not. I'm not so stupid that I don't know I'm being sized up. It's so sad!

MARTIN: You're involved with feminism. How does feminism shape your work? How does feminism really inform the end product?

Figure 12.1 In the latest segment of her *On the Road* series, *Twilight: Los Angeles, 1992*, Smith interviewed nearly 200 people, including Katie Miller, a bookkeeper and accountant (performed here). The premiere performance was at the Mark Taper Forum, Los Angeles, in May 1993. (Photo by Jay Thompson)

SMITH: I don't know because I don't understand the intellectual part of feminism. Feminism ... this is tricky ... I hope you don't mind if I have to think here.

MARTIN: I could tell you some of my reactions. One of the things about *Fires in the Mirror* that most moved me was the lack of closure. You didn't attempt to resolve the complications and contradictions of these conversations. There was a continual presentation of diverse people with all their faults and insights. You didn't shy away from some of the qualities of Al Sharpton, for example. The same is true of the characteristics of some of the Jews. At certain moments your portrayal was close enough to caricature to make spectators uncomfortable – close to but not really caricature.

In displaying ethnicity in a slightly magnified way you underscored the humanity of the people you interviewed. Instead of trying to make a cohesive picture, you revealed different landscapes of emotions and histories. I connect this approach to feminist ideas about open-ended narratives, about the refusal of ultimate authority – even though there's an authority operating.

SMITH: I think you're right. But the honest truth would be that I've always been like this. Since I was a girl my creative life has been about trying to find a way of being me in my work. I felt very oppressed by the formal structures of theatre, the first one being the role of an acting teacher in a classroom. When I became the acting teacher, there was this expectation that I was going to be this authority who resolved everything and came up with the answers.

The through-line always made me feel bad in teaching, reading, and trying to write plays. It was something inherently I, Anna, was trying to express. Period. If anything opened me intellectually it was when I was trying to write about acting in order to find out why I had trouble with the Stanislavsky technique. I came across a graph of the objectives of the Stanislavsky technique. Super objective. Little objective. It was straight lines with arrows. Quite soon after that I was reading a book about African philosophical systems and saw a picture of a wheel that had all these little spokes with arrows pointing towards the center. I knew then that I wanted to try to find a way of thinking or a structure that was more like that.

As you know, the black church is not only about speaking to one God. The whole thing is supposed to be an occasion to evoke a spirit. This was one of the things that led me to thinking in more circular ways and resisting the through-line.

MARTIN: You don't really understand feminism?

SMITH: It's not that I don't understand feminism. I try to understand things but I'm also an empathetic and intuitive person.

Why don't you offer some words and I'll see if I feel like they fit. I understand that feminism is ... is about us, finding our place and finding our language.

MARTIN: Yes, but it's also given women a means to read texts, life, power relations, and interactions. Feminism is implicated in ways of seeing, believing, and feeling as well as intellectual life. Intellectual life is divorced from other senses. The lack of closure in *Fires in the Mirror* worked so well because it kept expanding the complexities of the communities and giving us an opportunity to acknowledge that truth, in both the divine and mundane sense, is difficult to discern. Acknowledging this difficulty is a humbling experience that also contains the possibility of acknowledging difference.

Your performing style, not the obvious – that you play both men and women – but the way that you present and characterize people through language and at the same time remain present as Anna also seems informed by feminist ideas. You're not invisible nor do you step aside in a Brechtian way and comment on those you are presenting.

You're visible and yet so are all those other people. This palimpsest creates a density and authority in individual characters and, at the same time, calls into question the absoluteness of our differences.

Sometimes we see you obliquely when someone refers to the process of being interviewed. You've formed this difficult material in a very emotional and human way. It must take some struggle, to get to that place, to make those decisions.

SMITH: My grandfather told me that if you say a word often enough, it becomes you. I was very interested before I developed this project in how manipulating words has a spiritual power.

I can learn to know who somebody is, not from what they tell me, but from *how* they tell me. This will make an impression on my body and eventually on my psyche. Not that I would understand it but I would feel it. My goal would be to – these kinds of words are funny and probably, in print they sound even worse – become possessed, so to speak, of the person. I don't set out to do anything as intellectual as what you're talking about.

MARTIN: My observations are from the outside.

SMITH: I know that this is there. I've emphasized to my students that acting is becoming the other. To acknowledge the other you have to acknowledge yourself.

It's not psychological realism. I don't want to own the character and endow the character with my own experience. It's the opposite of that. What has to exist in order to try to allow the other to be is separation between the actor's self and the other.

What I'm ultimately interested in is the struggle. The struggle that the speaker has when he or she speaks to me, the struggle that he or she has to sift through language to come through. Somewhere I'm probably also leaving myself room as a performer to struggle and come through. Richard Schechner talks about this much better than I when he talks about "not me" and "not not me."

MARTIN: Yes, but in the case of *Fires in the Mirror* we know several of the people from the media. There is the media image of people like the Lubavitchers and Al Sharpton. Familiar representatives of different communities are brought onstage through you and this is somehow less fictional than documentary footage or journalistic accounts of the same people.

How did you decide to give Carmel Cato the last word? I thought it was right and emotionally difficult at the end of the piece.

SMITH: In December, he did not have the last word. The Crown Heights section ended with him, but I had more stuff. JoAnne [Akalaitis] said "When the father speaks the show is over."

When I left that interview, I knew that I'd met a remarkable man. I have never heard anybody journey in a language across so many realms of experience. From the facts of a personal experience, to his own belief system and his own sensitivity – his power – to the circumstances of his birth. When I first developed *On the Road*, and was leaning how to do this, I would ask people for an hour interview and I would talk to them. I'd tell them we could talk about anything. I was looking specifically not for what they said but for these places where they would struggle with language and come through. I talked to a linguist about it and she gave me three questions I could ask that would guarantee this would happen.

MARTIN: What were the questions?

SMITH: One of them was: What were the circumstances of your birth? So I end this show with how I began my own exploration. He [Carmel Cato] answers that question. I didn't ask him. I didn't ask him.

MARTIN: You didn't ask him!

SMITH: No! He just said it. I interviewed him on the street at night. We were standing on the street and this man was talking about knowing his kid was going to die before he dies. Then he says he's a man, a special person. I thought he was going to say, "I'm a man, a black man." But he said "I was born with my foot" [feet first]. The very beginning of my project was that question so, in a way, for me, it would have to be the end.

MARTIN: You've spoken about integration being a nostalgic idea. Where are we now? There's no operative paradigm – not multicultural or intercultural. What do you think about us now?

SMITH: I'm very excited because I think we're going to find something better. I think a lot of people feel very betrayed by integration because it didn't work.

MARTIN: Did people really try it?

SMITH: Some people gave their lives, some people died for it. Died. I would never say that people didn't try. It's only going to be a few people who are willing to sacrifice their lives for the experiment.

There are people who are willing to change the course of their lives for the experiment. At Bellagio [a 1991 conference on intercultural performance[1]] there was this language about negotiating boundaries and difference that I hadn't heard before. I've been wondering how to find the tools for thinking about difference as a very active negotiation rather than an image of all of us holding hands. There are too many contradictions, problems, and lies in American society about the melting pot. You're invited to jump into the hot stew but you're not wanted. That's the case for black people, even with seemingly well-meaning, well-minded people who would benefit from my presence and the presence of others like me. We're not wanted.

It's going to be hard.

Motion is what I'm interested in right now. People who talk about motion, who use the word "move." In my show I've become interested in which characters can move in the space and which ones can't.

Angela [Davis] walks. Richard Green walks. Sharpton moves his chair. Whatever we think about Sharpton's limitations, he's in motion.

You know, we normally think of passing as something that you do. You pass up, right? If you're a light-skinned black, you pass up. You never pass down. Guillermo Gómez-Peña talks about passing as going back and forth between borders. This is very exciting to me. It brings back images of the underground railroad. . . .

MARTIN: Seems impossible. I taught public speaking at City College [City University of New York] at 138th Street for a year. My experience there was very different. Just taking the subway was a demonstration of inequities. The white and Asian students got off at Columbia, the rest of us got off two stops later and walked through a park of drug dealers. In that situation, I was a minority among minorities [a white person among mostly black and Hispanic students] in a very heated atmosphere. It was during the time of the clash between Leonard Jeffries and Michael Levin.[2] I had to bridge the gap being a white woman speaking to a class of 25 mostly black and Hispanic men.

SMITH: Oh my God!

MARTIN: I could never pass in any sense of the word. I had to be who I was or they would surely feel I was disingenuous. I had to allow them to see my vulnerability. The class was a public speaking class and one of the required speeches was a commemorative speech. Many of these young men used this as an opportunity to talk about their lives and the people who inspired them and helped them to survive – mothers, uncles, clergy. A few even cried during their speeches. There was always this silence after each of them spoke. I knew they were witnessing one another in ways they never had before. Many of them found a way to talk about the reality of their lives to one another and to me. They were able to be supportive *and* critical of one another's work. The dynamic was about each of us being who we were, not about passing. I was teaching them about how to use language to present themselves – a calculated performance of self that would help them gain entry. Ultimately, I wasn't wanted. The Speech Department wanted me and so did my students but there was a feeling on campus that only black and Hispanic professors belonged there. Anyway. . . .

SMITH: In terms of passing up and passing down, it's probably harder for a white person to pass in, if we think of the social structure as black on the bottom and white on the top. There's less structure for you to pass than for those black males. For them there is a structure. They could go to jail on the way but there is a structure. It may be corrupt but there are steps for going up. Very few and mysterious steps but they are there.

It's just like in speech. It's easier to make a rising inflection and it's much harder to do a downward build because you have to work with gravity a different way.

MARTIN: What we are talking about is a concern with language and what language reveals and. . . .

SMITH: That was the birth of the project 10 years ago.

MARTIN: Language?

SMITH: My major fascination in the world.

MARTIN: You do quote Shakespeare a lot.

SMITH: If it hadn't been for Shakespeare, I wouldn't be where I am because it was my Shakespeare teacher who got to me. In the first class we had to take any 14 lines of Shakespeare and say it over and over again to see what happened. So I picked, of all things, Queen Margaret in *Richard III*:

> From forth the kennel of thy womb hath crept
> A hellhound that doth hunt us all to death.
> That dog that had his teeth before his eyes
> To worry lambs and lap their gentle blood,
> That foul defacer of God's handiwork,
> That excellent grand tyrant of the earth
> That reigns in galled eyes of weeping souls,
> Thy womb let loose to chase us to our graves.
>
> (*Richard III* 4.4.47–54)

Right? I knew nothing; it was my first acting class ever and I had some kind of a transcendental experience. I was terrified, I was mystified. For the next three years, as I trained seriously, I never had an experience like that again. Ever. I kept wanting to have it so I kept exploring what language was.

I remembered what my grandfather told me because it's one of those experiences that is so peculiar you have try to explain it to somebody. What happened to me? Was I crazy? What was it? It sounds really interesting but nobody can name it, so it's your quest.

MARTIN: No more psychological realism?

SMITH: The opposite. Psychological realism is about – this is a real oversimplification of Stanislavsky – saying: here's Leonard Jeffries.

Figure 12.2 The Rodney King story as told by Smith as Angela King, aunt of Rodney King. From the Mark Taper Forum, Los Angeles, May 1993 production of *Twilight: Los Angeles, 1992.* (Photo by Jay Thompson)

Figure 12.3 The Rodney King story as told by Smith as Judith Tur, ground reporter for the Los Angeles News Service. From the Mark Taper Forum, Los Angeles, May 1993 production of *Twilight: Los Angeles, 1992.* (Photo by Jay Thompson)

You have to play Leonard Jeffries now. Let's look at Leonard. Let's look at his circumstances. Let's look at your circumstances? How are you two alike? How can you draw from your own experience? Contrary to that, I say this is what Leonard Jeffries said. Don't even write it down. Put on your headphones, repeat what he said. That's all. That's it.

MARTIN: And what happens as you repeat what he said?

SMITH: When dealing with somebody as powerful as Leonard Jeffries with such a fascination with details, I almost didn't have to memorize him. He made a psychic impression, it just went, FOOM! You and I could talk at great length or go into a studio and work on Leonard Jeffries. We'd have a good time figuring out his psychological realities, we'd get a blast, right?

MARTIN: Maybe.

SMITH: That's not the point. The point is simply to repeat it until I begin to feel it and what I begin to feel is his song and that helps me remember more about his body. For example, I remembered he sat up but it wasn't until well into rehearsal that my body began to remember, not me, my body began to remember. He had a way of lifting his soft palate or something. I can't see it because it's happening inside. But the way it played itself out in early performances is that I would yawn, you know, 'cause he yawned at a sort of inappropriate moment [yawns]. I've realized now what is going on. My body begins to do the things that he probably must do inside while he's speaking. I begin to feel that I'm becoming more like him.

MARTIN: What you're saying in *Fires in the Mirror* is that differences between people are very complicated and maybe unresolvable as well as interesting and wonderful. When you perform, however, you give over to each person in a very deep way and become them.

SMITH: In spite of myself. Many of the characters have chiselled away at the gate that's between them and Anna. That's the part that's very fascinating, challenging, difficult, painful. Psychological technique is built on metaphors for a reason. I believe it's quite organic. You listen to some of the characters and you begin to identify with them. Because I'm saying the stuff over and over again every night, part of me is becoming them through repetition – by doing the performance of themselves that they do.

I become the "them" that they present to the world. For all of us, the performance of ourselves has very much to do with the self of ourselves. That's what we're articulating in language and in flesh – something we feel inside as we develop an identity.

These words are knocking at my door and they're saying, "parts of Anna, come out."

MARTIN: Where is the spectator in all this?

SMITH: I don't know. I'm just talking about my process. I hope that the words are knocking at their door too.

MARTIN: How much did you edit the interviews? You may have an hour of material but you obviously can't give each person an hour of time.

SMITH: I try to find a section that I don't have to interrupt. The performance is much more difficult if I've created chaos in their frame of thought. I'd rather have a section in which their psychological through-line is reflected in language. Everybody does it. I just wait. I think the longest section is seven minutes.

MARTIN: What were the other two questions that the linguist advised you to ask?

SMITH: Have you ever come close to death? and, Have you ever been accused of something that you didn't do?

MARTIN: Did you use those in any interview?

SMITH: That was way back when I was inventing this in the early 1980s. Now I'm working with events. I'm just trying to get the story.

MARTIN: The deaths of Gavin Cato and Yankel Rosenbaum created an event but in a certain sense they're not the subject of your piece.

SMITH: That's the real reason I ended with Mr. Cato. Around Thanksgiving I read an article in the *Voice* called "Toilet Diplomacy." It was all about the big figures in the [Crown Heights] story. I didn't know why I was so sad and over a series of days I realized I was so sad because the more I read, the more Gavin Cato's name was disappearing.

Only the first rabbi in my show refers to Angela Cato [Gavin's sister, who was also struck by the car]. That the father's first line is, "In the meanwhile" – in the meanwhile, 90 minutes ago, we started talking. In the meanwhile, Angela was on the ground and she was trying to move. This little girl was in a body cast for months. The neighbors were still concerned about Gavin. I thought it would be powerful to have the audience forget about Gavin. I'm sure many people leave the theatre and still don't know anything about Angela. She's only mentioned twice.

There's a way in which the larger powers obliterate the smaller powers even when those smaller powers are the very reason for our gathering. It's like parents giving their kid a birthday party and getting drunk.

MARTIN: Is there such a thing as an American character, as the subtitle of *On the Road* suggests?

SMITH: I'm looking for it. I think different people are shaping it. I suppose what I should do is try to collaborate with David Hammonds [an installation artist], or somebody like that.

Figure 12.4 An anonymous Hollywood Talent Agent admits that "maybe – not maybe but, uh – the system plays unequally" to Smith, and emphasizes his confusion during her performance of *Twilight: Los Angeles, 1992* at the Mark Taper Forum, May 1993. (Photo by Jay Thompson)

MARTIN: In the US there was the myth of the American character formed on the frontier. This myth was destroyed by industrialization, massive immigration at the beginning of this century, and the resulting urbanization. Now the question seems to be what experience constitutes being an American?

Are we specialists in diversity? When one goes to Europe it's apparent that there's very little conversation or language about diversity, about difference – even where there needs to be.

SMITH: We could be specialists. That's what's exciting. We could become specialists if we could get up off of our hate and our elitism. Some of the people who have the best equipment for helping to do this are such snobs and the system makes people who have the ability into snobs.

I know from interviewing people who are experts that they have a lot of armor. I guess they have to get it to survive. Some of the people who have a real facility for language get very snobby about the very language they own. To talk about passing again – I think we need to pass language back and forth across borders.

There is great resistance to including less articulated ideas. All this does is force words on us that have nothing to do with our experience. I know I don't have the language to argue with the people who have the key and have the privilege.

MARTIN: Having the language is one thing. Having the presence of mind or the ability to keep one's emotional nerve is also necessary. One has to be able to say, "Hey, wait a second, this is not quite right or what it should be."

SMITH: This is why the "bad boy" is so fascinating. When he talked to me I knew he did not have very many words. I knew he wasn't telling the complete truth because he knows, he thinks he knows, who killed Yankel Rosenbaum. He performed for me, looked me straight in the eye with very kind eyes – talking to me as though I were stupid. Not like condescending stupid, not like that. More like "this sister doesn't understand so I'm going to help the sister get it." He wasn't arrogant but more like the kindest person talking to Sophia [Martin's 5-year-old daughter]. I loved that. I am the sister who don't get it and he was nice enough to tell me the way it was. With his repetition of words he sang it to me. That's what's compelling.

MARTIN: What about his final line: "That's between me and my creator."

SMITH: He's saying: "I have to have my dignity. I know who did it and I'm not telling you." He doesn't appropriate his own culture.

Anonymous Boy #2

from Anna Deavere Smith's *Fires in the Mirror: Crown Heights, Brooklyn and Other Identities*

BAD BOY

(The same recreation room as Anonymous Boy #1. He is wearing a black jacket over his clothes. He has a gold tooth. He has some dreadlocks, and a very odd shaped multicolored hat. He is soft spoken, and has a direct gaze. He seems to be very patient with his explanation.)
That sixteen year old
didn't murder that Jew
For one thing
He played baseball
Right?
He was a athalete
Right?
A bad boy
does
bad things
is
does bad things
only a bad boy could stabbed a man
somebody who
does those type a things
A atha lete
sees people
is interested in
stretchin
excercisin
goin to his football games
or his baseball games
He's not interested
in stabbin
people
so
it's not on his mind
to stab
to just jump into somethin
that he has no idea about
and kill a man
Somebody who's groomed in badness
or did badness before
stabbed the man
Because I used to be a atha lete
and I used to be a bad boy
and when I was a atha lete
I was a atha lete

all I thought about was atha lete
I'm not gonna jeoparsize my athleticism
or my career to do the things
that bad people do
And when I became a bad boy
I'm not a atha lete no more
I'm a bad boy
and I'm groomin myself in things that is bad
you understand so
He's a athalete
he's not a bad boy
It's a big difference
Like
mostly the black youth in Crown Heights have two things to do
either DJ or a bad boy right
You either
DJ be a MC
rapper
or Jamaican rapper
ragamuffin
or you be a bad boy
you sell drugs and rob people
What do you do
I sell drugs
what do you do I rap
That's how it is in Crown Heights
I been living in Crown Heights most a my life
I know for a fact that that youth
didn't kill that that that that Jew
that's between me and my creator

NOTES

1. Under the auspices of the Rockefeller Foundation, Richard Schechner, working with a steering committee that included Peggy Phelan, Jean Franco, Folabo Ajayi, Judith Mitoma, and Tomas Ybarra-Frausto, convened a conference on "intercultural performance" that met at the Bellagio Conference Center from 17 to 22 February 1991 – at the height of the Gulf War. Participants in the conference included Eugenio Barba, Barbara Kirshenblatt-Gimblett, Guillermo Gómez-Peña, Sanjukta Panigrahi, Trinh T. Minh-ha, William Sun, Gayatri Chakravorty Spivak, Michael Taussig, Yamaguchi Masao, Drew Taylor, and Smith.

2. A heated black/white, Jewish/black conflict roiled New York's City University in the early 1990s. Professor Leonard Jeffries made a public speech disparaging Jews and accusing Jews of controlling and manipulating the media; Professor Michael Levin voiced the opinion that blacks were not mentally the equal of whites. After a particularly inflammatory speech in Albany (July 1991), Jeffries was replaced as chair of the Black Studies

Department. He sued, claiming his First Amendment rights were denied him. In May 1993, he won his case in federal court.

REFERENCE

Smith, Anna Deavere (1992) *Playbill* 92, no. 7:18. Program for *Fires in the Mirror: Crown Heights, Brooklyn and Other Identities*.

13

ROBBIE McCAULEY

Obsessing in Public

An Interview by Vivian Patraka

"IS WE FREE YET?"

Family Stories and Serial Collaborations

PATRAKA: Candy stores figure in two of your performance pieces – the candy store where a white store owner in a black neighborhood falsely accuses you of shoplifting, and the candy store deep in a white neighborhood that you walk into to buy strawberry gum. It made me think about the way you encase history in childhood events.[1]

McCAULEY: The store was a magical place for me as a kid, where you go in and buy things, especially sweet things. I have store references in a lot of pieces. I hadn't thought of it as a category, except that I know it's the place where events that had to do with white people happened. It was that other world. The incidents that I talk about are the troublesome ones, but the other side of that store thing was the magic of the things up on the shelves. There's one story I have about Mr. Reddick's store in Columbus, Georgia. He couldn't read and write and my sister and I considered him "trash." But he had the store, and we felt connected to that. My grandmother would send us with a note and my sister and I had to read it to him. I even taught his daughter Martha Fay how to read, but when we got to be 10, we didn't play together anymore.

PATRAKA: Suddenly you had to behave in a particular way.

McCAULEY: That store had to do with class and caste issues in a working-class neighborhood in the South – the segregation was more internal than external. White people simply lived on the *other side* of the street and the store was right there and we knew we had "more class" than they did, but there were certain boundaries you didn't cross that had to do with white as privilege, caste.

PATRAKA: For a child, buying candy would be a way to move into the public arena. There's a powerful place in your performing, after you've been accused of stealing and have come home, where you're crying and pushing out the pain of that story. . . . When do you move your body most in performance?

McCAULEY: The lighter moments are when I move most, when I'm trying to release and dance it out. The part that you mention about the pain and hurt over these incidents. I don't like to do, I have to go through those. I wish I were a dancer and could dance on the pain. But I feel more like a clown than a tragedian. Like that song I perform, "The Oppressor Tango," with the line "The oppressor is smarter than we thought," a funny song with a tragic element to it that is the moment of release after the gas station story. Dancing "The Oppressor Tango" means to look oppression in the face and dance. And doing that is movement: to face the oppressive elements, to understand and move through them *is* change. It's where an artist is useful because the audience can share that kind of release.

PATRAKA: Lisa Kennedy [1990] described the 1990 version of *Sally's Rape* performed at BACA [New York, NY] as an exorcism. Does that really fit with what you were just describing?

McCAULEY: That's too easy. It's fine if it's an exorcism for an audience member, but I see it more as an opening for movement, as creating a kind of groundwork for dialogue. The idea of releasing for its own sake means that you then don't move anywhere. I prefer when people say, "You made me think; I disagreed with you, but I was moved to think."

PATRAKA: Being moved to think is different from a traditional kind of catharsis where the experience is over.

McCAULEY: Yes. I think the mind and the body have to work together in order to create the movement of political theatre. When I say movement, I mean going from something blocked and unclear to something open and clearer so that we can move to change things. That's what my art is about. It's not political in the sense that right after the show we're going to march to the capital. But it is something for a regular audience to *use*, rather than simply having an evening in the theatre.

PATRAKA: Something for the audience to use to start thinking about particular issues that have somehow become unspeakable, invisible?

McCAULEY: Yes. To help them to think and speak about those things that are blocked. It's more for individuals within communities than for a mass movement kind of thing. People are going to react in different ways, but I hope they don't go backwards. I like the concept of speaking the unspeakable.

PATRAKA: I write about the Holocaust, and sometimes I write about sexual abuse to women and children, and I always have a problem with storing that content on my body. There's a disco and a blues club in Toledo and I do go dance, but it's difficult to get it off once you've moved into the weight of that kind of pain.

McCAULEY: That's part of what I'm addressing, the idea that the oppression stays on you unless you dialogue about it. Dancing is, of course, a way to speak, but not if there's no dialogue, not if nothing comes back. I could go on just rapping and singing by myself in a show, but I try to open it so that the audience is involved if by no more than eating with me or, as in *Sally's Rape* [1991], by giving them moments to talk. I know it's very controlled, but it still allows me to create an event for the audience to come into around this oppression. I also want them to identify with me. I don't want to scream and yell at the oppressor. I consider the audience as with me, I'm not against the audience, so "they" are always those who are not in the room. Even if they are in the room, I want them for the moment to identify with me. One of the good jokes about *Sally's Rape* is that Jeannie Hutchins and I had a long talk about whether or not she was playing "the stupid white girl." And it's not that, it's the two of us enjoying the dialogue about my stuff. But it's not one of those equal time things, not like "this is about the white view and the black view," but that we're joined in it being my view, my personal view, so it's not even all black people.

PATRAKA: And part of what *Sally's Rape* is about is making people in the audience who are carrying that history – who don't feel like they are – making them aware of what they are carrying with them.

McCAULEY: I'm carrying shame, and many others are carrying guilt. And those two are distortions of information and of the material that we are living with. When the material of our past turns into shame and guilt, we stop talking about it, and it gets bigger and bigger and more distorted.

PATRAKA: And one of the things you say is that guilt is really a covering emotion for pain.

McCAULEY: And shame is a real feeling but it's often mixed up with blame. It's like any rape victim who walks around feeling like she's at fault and is therefore ashamed.

PATRAKA: There seems to me to be two kinds of invisibility. There's white people not seeing black people, making them invisible, but there's also the room of white men who are invisible to themselves because they are the norm. So part of the power of whiteness is its invisibility.

McCAULEY: You know, there have always been more non-white people in the world. Except that now this fact is more visible because we are smarter about the demographics. And that brings up the question what are *we* going to do about it? One thing I like about Julie Dash's film *Daughters of the Dust* [1991], is that she tells a story and we're all in it, all have our parts in it and can therefore see ourselves. When the story is told this way, the blame and guilt and responsibility are all part of it. Otherwise, if we've behaved as separate parts disconnected from each other, we don't get the connections between us that lead to the ability to change things that aren't working.

PATRAKA: I recently saw an autobiographical and political performance piece and there was almost a kind of nostalgia because of the absence of references to contemporary events, something beautiful in the piece that almost closed it off. In your pieces you have a number of key, what I might call "signature stories," that belong to your life and history, and that you move around, recycle, from one piece to another. But the larger context isn't the narrative of that personal history, it is the political perspective that you have on that personal history, on events that are happening in the past and events that are shaped by them now. It's your vision, and the stories are part of it, but the stories aren't the narrative that you're creating. Does that make sense?

McCAULEY: Put that in the interview. Because people are always asking me about stories, and I say I'm not a storyteller, although I understand the worth of stories. But I'm not interested in telling the old stories. I think the worth of them is pleasure, nostalgia, and connection and those are good things. Again, what I liked about Julie Dash's work was that it was not a period piece, it was set at a time, used a time and gave us information about that time. History of the past is simply folklore. History has to be connected to the realities of the present.

PATRAKA: I'm reminded of a question that runs insistently through so much of your work, "Is we free yet?," and how you push audiences to think about it in terms of understanding its implications in 1992.

McCAULEY: Yes. And if I do any of this work again, I want to find a way to move the audience to have to say, "Is we free? Massa, is we free?"

PATRAKA: And one of the things that your work makes clear continually is that history is a text that changes all the time, that you're the interpreter of it, and that you're arranging it in a number of different ways from music, to slides, to voice, and to the multiple voices I especially love in *Indian Blood* [1987], where you have a number of different personae on video. We need to emphasize that difference in your work between the larger story you're telling and the individual very powerful stories, such as your father and the car and the gas station, and the time that your grandfather's car breaks down, and the Uncle Buck stories.

McCAULEY: I recently heard another black woman tell a gas station story, a travel story with her family. So these *are* signature stories, but they're also stories that have the universality of the father driving the car with the family in it. And it's also a black family story. One thing that most black people of that era recognize is that we had to drive at night, because if you drove in the day you were too visible and could get in trouble. There was something so dangerous about my father walking out there being bold in the daytime.

PATRAKA: I remember when I was a kid growing up in East New York, and we'd be driving through black neighborhoods, and my mother would say, "Lock your doors." And that's real hard-wired, that "lock your doors."

McCAULEY: It's that bit of message and its effect I try to get to when I'm working with or on white people in these community histories that I'm doing. To get you to find the racism in your lives. Most of the white people I'm working with are "the good guys." *The Buffalo Project* [1990] people wouldn't accept cross-burners in their families, except that when the stories came out, there were the little things that resonate in your psyche, like "lock your doors from the horde, from the danger."

PATRAKA: And that fear is irrational, you can hardly control it.

McCAULEY: Now there is a psychological syndrome, fear of young black males. It's become a psychological syndrome disconnected from all the real reasons that anybody should be afraid of danger. Of course, you're stupid to get into a subway car late at night with a bunch of guys who look tough, but it is a syndrome when you see a bunch of young black males and go nuts. That's how those guys got shot by Bernard Goetz, which was why I put him in my performance as a metaphor. It's the white man, the Goetzian type – my father was what the Goetzian white man feared. It's a white syndrome to have that terror of black people that's out of control.

PATRAKA: I remember a moment in *Sally's Rape* where you say to your audience, "Don't worry I'm in control." What are you telling them when you say that?

McCAULEY: I might have felt then as if they're going to think I'm crazy, going to lose control. I don't want them to think that. I want them to know that I'm under control. There's a perception that black people getting too close to rage is dangerous. It's one of the big fears in this country. I think people have been sold the metaphor of how bad black is and that's associated with all those other negative images that are unspeakably dangerous – you know, black is dark, black is violent, black is anger, black is our deepest, darkest.... And I set myself up as the messenger who is black. I'm not neutral and therefore, at that moment, you saw me saying "Don't worry...." Some people may find that patronizing, but I think many need it.

PATRAKA: Let me see if this works with what you're saying. When you perform the part about Sally being raped, there is tremendous anger and pain, and also, visually, the tremendous physical vulnerability of standing there naked on the auction block. Do you think your own physical vulnerability is part of the reason the audience can hear the anger without being so scared that they shut down?

McCAULEY: I did that because I had to. I got an impulse, I dreamed the taking off of the clothes and the feeling, "Do you see this now? Now can you see me, who I really am, and that this is essential to who I am?" I know that here is where the artist and the person meet. I know that it is a strong moment because I'm so vulnerable and in performance vulnerability is strength. And I wanted to find a way to make the point as strongly as possible that the real rape – and this is not to diminish anybody's individual experience of rape – was that we couldn't even begin to have a rape crisis center, "There is no rape crisis center on a plantation." That kind of rape changed who we were as a people and that was not our choice. We didn't choose to make ourselves as a result of that rape, we had to improvise ourselves.

PATRAKA: I was glad to have the opportunity to see the improvised beginnings of the current piece, *Persimmon Peel* [1992], in the 1990 tape of Laurie Carlos and you performing at La Mama. The special rapport and trust between you is both physical and in the improvised dialogue. In a sense you and Laurie are not only performing the "Star Spangled Banner" and trying to reconceive it, to invent new words for new concepts, you are also performing your friendship and intimacy with each other. Is it just the shape of *Teenytown*[2] [1988] and its different purpose that makes that rapport less palpable?

McCAULEY: Yes, you are comparing two different things. The dialogue among the three of us, Jessica Hagedorn, Laurie Carlos, and me, can have the same flavor. What you didn't see is the rapport amongst us performed in other contexts. *Teenytown* was our content piece, *the* show with all the elements in it, and we did it as a theatrical piece, so there was very little organized improvisation in it. In a more recent work called *The Food Show* [1992], our dialogue has that same kind of improvisatory flavor. It's because we know who we are individually that we can have that kind of play between us.

PATRAKA: So it has to do with the quality of an improvised piece as compared to the quality of a piece that's deliberately planned and episodic, made out of various individual pieces you've written and then worked into a structure containing arias, duets, trios.

McCAULEY: Right. *Teenytown* was more structured than any of our other performances together.

PATRAKA: Robert Hurwitt labeled *Teenytown* "in-your-face comedy" [1990]. What is in our faces in *Teenytown*?

McCAULEY: The subject matter. And the subject matter is that there are three different non-white women from three different places – one of us is from a colonized country and the other two from different parts of the US, one South, one North – and the three of us are connected and we state that connection in performance. *Teenytown* is a microcosm of the connection that non-white people today have all over the world. While the separations amongst us are useful to the oppressor, the connections are those that *we* understand and make and can, in that sense, put up in your face.

PATRAKA: And there's a kind of cross-cultural dialogue happening among you.

McCAULEY: We share similar experiences we had in different cultures of US racist oppression – me in the apartheid South, Laurie in the unofficial apartheid North, and Jessica in the colonized Philippines.

PATRAKA: Another element performed in *Teenytown* is how ugly racial, ethnic, and sexual stereotypes are still circulating despite our conscious rejection of them, that they've filtered into our unconscious – especially the ones in those cartoons you show.

McCAULEY: Yes. Stereotypes have a lot of information. They tell a lot about both the perpetrator and the object of the stereotype. For instance, the minstrel comedy shows how easy it is for all of us to laugh at stereotypes of non-white people, how easily disrespect becomes internalized.

PATRAKA: There's a part in *My Father and the Wars* [1985], I think, where your grandfather says that the men in the family respect themselves a lot and because of that they're going to end up on the chain-gang.

McCAULEY: He says, "That's why I'm taking you boys out of the South, because you're strong, mannish boys. Stay down here and you'll end up on the chain-gang." I'm sure that lesson struck deep in them.

PATRAKA: When we talked earlier I mentioned your generosity in the way that you do *Sally's Rape*, and you said I'm not being generous, that's a particular strategy. Maybe we need to mark this strategizing more for this interview.

McCAULEY: Well, in this work I continually explain what I'm doing as part of the form. And I'm not trying to push people away. It's the ritual aspect, the joining that's important. Even though I often exaggerate difference, I make it possible to explore what I'm doing with the audience's participation.

PATRAKA: In one performance tape of *Sally's Rape* you bring on the table/auction block again and Jeannie stands on it this time and you say to her, "Take off your clothes," and she can't do it, or she chooses not to. I've thought a lot about that, it suggests that you can't necessarily inhabit somebody else's history, or that you won't take the same kinds of risks showing it if it's not your history. I try to imagine, if I were a performer, the circumstances under which I would take off my clothes. And the only circumstances I could come up with, where my body would be an instrument for history, is if I were to stand there as a person, as a woman, in the Holocaust. Tied to a situation I claim as my own history, I could do it and I would have to do it.

McCAULEY: That's it. She didn't have to do it. As a performer she could have chosen to do it. Or I could have asked her to do it as the director-creator of the piece, and she would have done it. But we decided in dialogue with some other women artists that it would be stronger to show that she didn't have to do it. I think the point reads better that way.

PATRAKA: She also tells the audience, before you get up there, "Come on, you have to help her" by chanting "Bid 'em in" while you're on the auction block. Does the helping mean participating and so acknowledging complicity or connection to these events?

McCAULEY: It means sharing the ritual. I'm not on exhibition, I'm doing it as part of a ritual and so it's like helping the drummer by dancing. Jeannie is the interlocutor at that moment, so it's up to her to get the people to participate.

PATRAKA: It's a very different kind of collision, having her in front of you leading the audience with you up there, than the first time I saw the piece at our Women and Theatre Program conference [1989, New York University], where there is no Jeannie figure yet.

McCAULEY: That was really hard because I was alone. Dialogue is always better. When I'm touring by myself and do excerpts from *My Father and the Wars*, I make sure I am in dialogue with the audience somehow, at least a kind of social dialogue. And I always have food, use it in *My Father and the Wars* when I'm traveling alone as a way to connect with the audience, so I don't feel so alone up there. But part of it is also that I get hungry during a show, and want to eat, and we were taught that you can't eat in front of anybody without offering.

PATRAKA: When you talk about private schools for black children in *Sally's Rape*, you make very clear that those schools were about reading and writing and knowledge, but that you also learned to walk, keeping your hips in, being slightly provocative. Would you want to change the part of it that relates to how women should behave?

McCAULEY: I have a line in *Sally's Rape* that says, "Sometimes I think we did it for the sake of itself alone." That's about upward mobility, but it's also about survival. This piece is about class, but more about the complicated issue of survival for black people and how it relates to class. I mean, you'd get knocked upside the head if you said or did the wrong thing, because it could be misinterpreted, and then the whole family would be in trouble. That's an irrational, though rational, fear that black people in the South ... if you looked wrong, had the wrong expression on your face. . . .

PATRAKA: It reminds me of how abused children become careful readers of people, responsive to the slightest shift in their behavior and mood, all of which are actually unpredictable. And you're suggesting that the situation of racism is full of unpredictable violence, and one has to make up a code of behavior, of having papers, of giving the right signals to ward off the danger when ultimately. . . .

McCAULEY: . . . there's nothing you can do.

PATRAKA: And when your father responds in the gas station, it's a kind of performance he does based on his personal power that makes the other person participate in a kind of negotiation between them.

McCAULEY: *My Father and the Wars* and *Indian Blood* are about men from a special point of view. I mean, it's from the daughter's perspective. I have no large analysis of what it must feel like for African-American men to be in that struggle all day, every day. But I imagine it's pretty overwhelming, which is why feminism is different for us. In the piece I say, "I know he fought their wars. And they defined manhood for him. And don't anybody tell me you know what it is. I know men tend to go in circles and women can think straight ahead, but I will not let my arrogance about blood and the moon obscure my perceptions of the government."

PATRAKA: C. Carr wrote that *My Father and the Wars* testifies to the everyday wars that don't make the evening news [1986]. What are some of the wars that you include in this piece?

McCAULEY: The survival from moment to moment of the men. The man who is trying to be a man, whatever the value of that is, whatever the value of a man being able to take care of and protect his family. Whatever its value, it becomes a life and death struggle every day that is particular to black men. That's what I saw with my father. He could have been killed at the gas station, all that guy had to do was pick up a phone and signal to somebody. It was literally the strength of my father's bearing that made it come out like that. And my father had trouble all over the place in terms of his inability to maintain his strength and power as time went on.

PATRAKA: In *Indian Blood* and *My Father and the Wars*, you talk about the appeal for black men of the visible symbols of authority, such as the uniform. Also, you talk about their intense patriotism, partly simply as a commitment to the country, but partly as a kind of strategy to create racism as un-American.

McCAULEY: Yes, and for my father and grandfather to use patriotism for survival is understandable. I also want to show that it is *my* story that puts it in perspective. Someone challenged me for telling my grandfather's story through my own contradictions, and I thought, "He doesn't have a story, *I* have a story," And so at the end of the piece I say, "Somebody said, is it fair to stir your fathers in their graves," and I say, "I'm not sure they are resting there," because I think it's up to me to state the contradictions. They were such patriots they couldn't deal with contradictions about, for example, hurting other people of color.

PATRAKA: One of the most powerful lines in *Indian Blood* is "We are exiles and yet we are at home." Is that one of the "resolvable contradictions" you mention in *Teenytown*?

McCAULEY: It's who we are. I mean some people call it schizophrenia or ambivalence, but I think that our ability to live with the history, with both the reality of being in exile and being home, is what makes us strong.

PATRAKA: Africans are the people who didn't immigrate voluntarily, who were dragged to this country and died in the process. What Julie Dash does in *Daughters of the Dust* is reconfigure black people on that island as immigrants coming voluntarily to America. At the same time she includes much on the history of slavery right beside this voluntary journey.

McCAULEY: That's why they had that long leaving. "You can't go nowhere unless you know who you are, girl" – that's what they would tell me. There's the line I have in *Teenytown*, "You tell what we know down here, girl. If you got to go, girl, you tell what we know down here, girl." That means carry it in you. Or, as I say in *Sally's Rape*, "These young ones with the alligators act like they weren't born with no memory." To deny your history is to disconnect yourself from the planet.

PATRAKA: What does it mean to be a witness to that history, because I think that's one of the things that you're performing?

McCAULEY: I'm being a witness by choosing to remember. What's important about the witnessing is that the audience is doing it with me. One of the problems with modern industrial society is the disconnection from that constant witnessing of the past, of where we came from, of being with the stories, and so that's my work.

PATRAKA: And what the audience is witnessing is not simply "your history," it's not about I-came-to-a-performance-to-watch-black-people's-history, but it's their history as well.

McCAULEY: Yes, and it's not folklore, it's not something they're outside of.

PATRAKA: Therefore the performance is a ritual?

McCAULEY: Yes, because it's not like "us and them" or "me and them." I invite them to participate and the ritual happens differently each time. Your part in it may be to listen, but that is certainly a participatory listening that I'm asking you to do because you're in it.

"TELLING IT" AND "GIVING RANGE TO THE TELLER"

Performance Strategies

PATRAKA: When you talk about witnessing, one of the things that interests me is the shift in how video is used from *My Father and the Wars* to *Indian Blood*. In *My Father and the Wars*, when you're speaking on one of the videos, the "live" you may watch it in silence or may speak in unison with what's on in the tape. In *Indian Blood*, you made a decision to shape very definite personae, such as the school teacher, who are clearly different personae from the live one performing onstage. Does this create a kind of multiplicity of witnesses?

McCAULEY: Yes, and it also gives more range to the teller. Part of it is a range of characters and emotions, theatrical elements. But the visual part has to do with the television set as comforting to an audience these days. One person talking, going on and on, can be too much or just tiresome, so in *Indian Blood* the use of various elements helps give variety and texture.

PATRAKA: Tell me about the use of the ladder. It's an important piece of the set in both *My Father and the Wars* and *Indian Blood*.

McCAULEY: Again, it's a way to add texture. Laurie Carlos, who helped stage the first *My Father and the Wars*, saw the ladder as the climbing up, but that climbing up was shaky. She wanted me to be unbalanced on the ladder. This was trying for me.

PATRAKA: And on that ladder, you talk about Medea?

McCAULEY: Yes. I talk about my identification with Medea. Not as a character in Greek literature, but as someone who the Greeks called a Barbarian, but whose father was king. As for the ladder, I always want to carry the image that Laurie gave me. She says it's like climbing up into a loft, and looking down: I sort of have the answers, but it's shaky giving them from up on top. Laurie does not pull any punches.

PATRAKA: Another context for your voice is information, especially as staged through the slides. The slides give perspective, tell us and remind us about history but are finally, in these pieces, still in the service of what your voice and your body are telling us. By contrast, in the earlier piece, *Nicaragua in Perspective* [1984], we can barely see you, and the visual content of the slides is a central text. In *Indian*

Blood and *My Father and the Wars* you are always visible, and there's not the same kind of moment when we only focus on the slides.

McCAULEY: Those earlier pieces were more like lessons. They were not personal stories. It was information that was essential and I was nothing more than the teacher, but not as a character, that's not my persona of the teacher. She appears in *Indian Blood* and *My Father*.

PATRAKA: Tell me more about the early work with the Sedition Ensemble.

McCAULEY: Ed Montgomery and I met in 1979. He saw a piece I did at NYU. He told me he was doing political jazz and we decided to work together. Other people helped both improvise and perform some of the text with us and added their texture to the work – Verna Hampton, April Green, and incredible jazz musicians like Bern Nix, Jay Oliver, and Luci Galliher.

PATRAKA: What's it like to collaborate with someone who is also your mate? Maybe I shouldn't ask that question, but it interests me as much as the race- or gender-related ones.

McCAULEY: [*Laughter*] Yes. The other stuff is easy compared to that. The issues that are in the relationship came up in the work and it was difficult to understand that was happening and work with it. We never found a language for speaking about it, though we tried, and therefore both the work and our relationship were affected. The early working together didn't survive, but our relationship did, even though our working together was the foundation of the relationship. And Ed does compose the music for several of my current pieces and that works well. But I want it all, and I'm not sure you can have it. We want to work together in the future because we both miss it a lot.

PATRAKA: One of the things that you told me was that *Nicaragua in Perspective* served as a transition from the Sedition Ensemble pieces to what you call your "personal biography work." What made you decide to concentrate on personal biography work?

McCAULEY: Well, I think the story gets told better. I was also moved from my ancestors to do that. I was dogging the government so much in my work that I heard my father tell me to tell it. "Well tell it," he said in a dream. And I didn't know what he was talking about until I just started writing. *My Father and the Wars* came out of that message. I do have dreams where my ancestors talk to me. I don't even understand it, but I do accept it, because it happens, but I have no rational discourse about it.

PATRAKA: And part of that is to tell the unofficial history and make it a history that is shared among people.

McCAULEY: When my father said "Tell it," it was the part of him that

Figure 13.1 In *Indian Blood* (The Kitchen, 1987), McCauley speaks about her obsession with connecting with her ancestors, even if it means telling the "untellable stories." (Photos by Vivian Selbo © 1994)

I connected to as a child, the part that was special between me and him, where he knew that I had something to say to the world. He used to tell me to write down things so I wouldn't forget them. So

Figure 13.2 In *Indian Blood* (The Kitchen, 1987), McCauley speaks about her obsession with connecting with her ancestors, even if it means telling the "untellable stories." (Photos by Vivian Selbo © 1994)

I started with notebooks. He was always telling me how to act, was very authoritative in that way, but he and I used to sit up late at night and he would drink his bourbon and I would drink cocoa and eat cheese and sardines and he would always end up telling me, "Well just tell it; if that's what you think, just tell it." And I never remembered that until his voice came to me in the dream and said "Tell it." And I'd been just running around, sprouting all this anti-imperialist text like what was coming out in the Sedition Ensemble work. But my own voice wasn't there, my own story wasn't there. As a performer, I always knew the power of that voice, I just didn't know how to get there and when my father spoke to me, suddenly the connections came. The first image was him dressed as a soldier or sailor: "Seems like my father was always in somebody's army, navy, air force, national guard."

PATRAKA: So telling your story is partly telling his story. You're telling a story of race and gender about the men in your family in these pieces. You say in one of these pieces, in response to people who have told you your rage is at mothers, "No, my rage is at the government."

McCAULEY: I tend not to identify with my mother in my work. I tend to identify with my father and see my mother as a co-conspirator with authoritarian values. But I know better now. And that's what I mean by "My rage is at the government," not at my mother. My mother understood survival.

PATRAKA: And like many women who feel that they don't have very much power, she was often conservative.

McCAULEY: Of course she ends up the most radical as time goes on. I think for women, the survival of their children and themselves is number one. And they're not dumb about their compromising choices for survival. Men can miss a lot of things, because they can leave. Once they get the kids out of the way, if they live long enough, women tend to get more and more radical.

PATRAKA: One of the things Lucy Lippard quotes you as saying in her book *Mixed Blessings: New Art in a Multicultural America* is that "music is the art that has *functioned* for my culture. The music comes out of the pain of being chained to the ship. Amiri Baraka's play *Slave Ship* is the image of everything about our lives in the US symbolized on that ship. Pain, being bound. The one thing that wasn't physically bound was the voice. The scream turned into music. Although I'm not trained as a musician, blues and jazz inform all of my work. The idea that one can hurt and turn it into something beautiful is the way I use the pain" [1990:90]. And so, music is partly about pain, music is about voice.

McCAULEY: Not only the music, but most of the talking in my pieces is orchestrated. This comes out of a long tradition of black perform-ance culture. During the 1960s black poetry – which I ought to name as an influence on my work – was directly connected to jazz. You also see it in the old minstrels, which is what *Teenytown* is based on. There's certain drum beats, certain kinds of takes, and certain kinds of transitional rhythms that come from the old black musical minstrel shows. My mother talked about the black medicine shows that came to towns in the South. It had a horn and a dressed-up woman and it came out to sell snake oil. She started off by saying, "Some folks try to act like they don't remember the medicine show."

"BURNING LIBRARIES" AND "UP-SOUTH"

Memory and Geography

PATRAKA: Let's talk about people in their 40s or so. One of the things that's not true for generations after us is we knew, intimately, lots of people the bulk of whose history was in the first part of the century.

McCAULEY: It's a real difference. And it's a desperate call for those of us who remember. People in Mississippi who were in my mother's generation are now old people. And they say, "the libraries are burning down" – that's what they call themselves – "so you better get it because the libraries are burning down." Their line is "come and talk to us, because we're getting out of here." And part of my work is performing those libraries.

PATRAKA: What does it mean when you label your performance "obsessing in public"?

McCAULEY: My obsession is with connection and continuity. "The confessions are a mourning for the lost connections," the telling of the untellable stories. For instance, my grandfather being up there at the border, standing watch, having to shoot Indians who come across from Canada, was a devastating image to me, and I would rather not know it. But if I connect with my ancestors, I have to tell it.

PATRAKA: Somebody described the purpose of *Indian Blood* as an act of atonement, is that accurate?

McCAULEY: [*Laughter*] You can't escape religion in all this. Atonement, though, sounds like a finish, like you have confessed and been forgiven. My work is more an opening than a closing; more like "if I show you mine, then you can show me yours," and we can move together with our imperfections, with our wounds. In the US we often use folklore, patriotism, and mythology to try to make us all "all right," but art gives us the right to make the wounds part of the beauty.

PATRAKA: And those contradictions are painful.

Figure 13.3 McCauley stands next to her father, Robert McCauley, in this photo taken in Washington, DC, in the 1950s. The photo was used as a slide projection in her play *My Father and the Wars*. (Photo courtesy of Robbie

McCAULEY: Yes.

PATRAKA: People live with them. For me, being a Holocaust scholar, being Jewish, having a certain kind of politics, means my feelings about Israel are going to be a contradiction, incredibly ambivalent, and not politically correct.

McCAULEY: Alisa Solomon said that she was reminded by *Indian Blood* of the Israelis [1987]. And there is a connection because we are survivors. I think that the survivors of the Holocaust have unspeakable stories about it, and those are the kinds of things I wish could come up. In terms of my own work, I call it admitting things that we can choose to tell or not about ourselves. For instance, we say, "Black people are not racists," and it's according to how you define the word. Since white supremacy has become a more accurate term for systematic racism, I prefer it. But I wonder, even in the old definition of racism, if my grandfather was not a racist, because he had the power at that border in his hands.

PATRAKA: Brecht said a guinea pig in a laboratory does not learn, through being experimented on, to become a doctor. Oppression is a stain, it does things to you, and it doesn't necessarily make you good or noble.

McCAULEY: There is something both cynical and genocidal about not having good education for black people, because the more we know, the more able we are to survive what's being put on us. I think *we* need to deal with the fact that we sold slaves. The question of who bought them we deal with very well. It helps to have dialogue about these things. To add to Brecht, to be enslaved and then to be free and watch each other stumble around, that's not enough. We can continue to survive by watching, learning, improvising and making it work. That is what I take from my culture and put into performance art.

PATRAKA: How do you position people to read the body in your performances in a different way than they read it in the everyday?

McCAULEY: One thing is for them to see me entering, and exiting. I mark this with theatrical strategies that employ changes of lights, media, rhythms of speech and movement, and various kinds of music. I want the audience to see whoever I am as the instrument, I want them to see me as the instrument, and that it's a moment in theatre, that's all it is.

PATRAKA: A sense of entrance and exit also operates thematically in your work: on the road, in the car, going to the candy store – shifting spaces is especially dangerous. Shifting into any kind of unknown territory, especially if it's white, is about potential danger.

McCAULEY: I think it's true for us all, but the danger of entering a strange space is intensified because of racism, where you enter a space wherein you must have the right bearing or you die.

PATRAKA: I've noticed you play with notions of geography in performance and how the context for this is the history of racism. Two examples I think of right away are first, the terror of being sold off "way down further South," which you image as a deadly and terrifying journey. But second, there's the other thing you say, "There is no North. North is a state of mind, everything is up-South." So there's down-South and up-South.

McCAULEY: The "so further South" is a contextual image. When I did my piece in Mississippi, I started with "in Georgia, they used to say Mississippi, like something was worse than Georgia." For me and others, the textures are clear in terms of place. Up North during slavery time was free, the up-South image instead of North came later in our culture because we realized racist attitudes were deeply embedded in both places. There's also the geography of the ocean that reflects its history. In *Teenytown*, I have that piece called "Sharks." I actually heard the story that "there is a place in the mid-Atlantic where the sharks still go, still remember the blood where thousands of us were thrown overboard midpassage." And that image helped me understand my overwhelming feelings of fear about the water, to be able to approach the water, because the spirits are there, present and clear.

THE BUFFALO PROJECT

Community Collaborations

PATRAKA: I'm thinking about the notion of the artist as cultural worker, as somebody who goes into a community and tailors work to the needs and histories of specific communities, even though the work that gets done there is part and parcel of a larger history of racism. Could you tell me about *The Buffalo Project*, which is about the Buffalo riots in the 1960s, and how you and the actors gathered material for this piece?

McCAULEY: I conceived of the project right after a trip to Buffalo. I got interested in it because I was thinking of the up-South idea, in a way to find out more about what happened in an industrial town in the North that would prompt a riot in 1967. Interviews with people about the riots became a format for the conception of the project. I used 10 actors of various ages and ethnicities from Buffalo. They researched the incident by getting testimony from witnesses, by collecting stories, and that became the basis of the performance piece. The purpose was not to tell the stories as history, but to use the stories as a basis for the text. The rest of this performance piece was then generated by the dialogue between me and the actors about the stories. So I ended up doing some collecting, writing the material, directing the piece, and playing a kind of interlocutor role, especially in the process of rehearsal.

PATRAKA: There's one actor I noticed, a middle-aged black man with a very powerful voice. There are moments when it seems as if he's telling his own story, like the one where he tries to stop the police.

McCAULEY: Oh, that's LaVern Clay, he's a wonderful actor, and that's the personalization process at work. You make yourself the character, you do not play the character. You involve yourself in the telling and shaping of the material. Also, the characters were close to him and he loved them.

PATRAKA: For the section called "Black Confessions and White Confessions," it's the dialogue among the actors on the material that helped to create it?

McCAULEY: Yes. And my pushing for it.

PATRAKA: The piece is very site-specific. Can it only be performed in Buffalo, or do you think with certain kinds of shapings that give people additional information. . . .

McCAULEY: Absolutely, especially in the context of somewhere else in the US. People from out of town who happened to see the piece said to me, "This is Milwaukee." The dream would be enough money to tour it.

PATRAKA: It sounds like there was pleasure in working on this with other people.

McCAULEY: Yes. The work is difficult, because you are entering into another community, but in my experience that problem is overplayed, perhaps because I used the actors to contact most of the community sources. One often hears that if you go into another place, you will be rejected because you are not of that place. And that's true in many circumstances. What made this particular process so joyous for me was the connection that the actors made to the work and to the process.

PATRAKA: What did you want to convey to audiences about those riots, and the silencing of information and dialogue about those riots?

McCAULEY: Well the fact that they *were* a community story – one of those things that, "everybody knew," but nobody talked about. Since telling their story back to the community was so successful in Buffalo, it became the basis for future community projects. The images that came through most strongly in the piece were white flight and deep racist, stereotypical fears that came out in white people after the riots; the destructiveness of red-lining by banks and the way black people were prevented from getting loans and owning the businesses in their own neighborhoods; and the negative change that happened when more blacks came up from the South, when more blacks came in – more than the few that everybody can get along with. Many people, even black people, said it used to be a wonderful place, until the Southern blacks came up. It's amazing how stereotypes get internalized.

"THE STRUGGLE AS THE AESTHETIC"

Defining the Work

PATRAKA: Let me suggest a way of grouping your work into four categories and see how you like it. I'd put the early work, done with Sedition and so on, and also *Nicaragua*, in one group; I'd put *Sally's Rape*, *Indian Blood*, and *My Father and the Wars* together as a continuing serial performance of family stories; I'd put the collaborations with Thought Music in another and think of them as a kind of continuing performance; and another group would be the site-specific projects that involve community interviews and shaping a piece in response to them. Does that make sense?

McCAULEY: Sure. Everything that's happened in the last almost 15 years has been the cycle that you're talking about, from Sedition through to the community work, the issues are the same: bearing witness to racism, really, that's what I do.

PATRAKA: Let's focus on some of your earliest theatre experience. Which lady did you play in *For Colored Girls* ... [by Ntozake Shange]?

McCAULEY: I played them all. I ended up playing the Lady in Red, but I went on as the understudy on Broadway for all of them. And the Adrienne Kennedy work was very important. I did *A Movie Star Has to Star in Black and White* at the Public. The first professional piece of theatre I did was *Cities in Bezique*. So now when I criticize the lack of vision in theatre, I still want to acknowledge that I got nurtured by the good stuff.

PATRAKA: You've acted the role of Joan Little in Ed Bullins' *Joanne!* and been in his play *The Taking of Miss Janie*. You've been in Joseph Chaikin's *The Winter Project* and a production of Shakespeare's *Coriolanus* at the Public Theatre. The list could go on. How is your acting experience related to your performance work?

McCAULEY: The acting roles and what they were connected to began to open up voices inside me, especially the roles of rebel, intellectual, angry black woman, all of that. The actor has to be connected to the subtext, and the subtext started to emerge, and that stimulated the emergence of my writing. So, my work comes directly from acting in that way.

Back to categories for a moment. They do give some sense of how to look at my work but I'd also like to talk about context itself as category. My work is the work of an actor, whatever I'm doing is connected to playing the actor's thoughts. There are descriptions of the craft of African-American acting. The National Black Theatre, I think, came up with certain personae or attitudes that are affecting our work. There is the militant, the radical, and the Negro or assimilator. What I try to do in my work is to break open even those categories, and out of that comes text and the form of the work. What I'm interested in comes through a system of work that is based in African-American traditions – I don't mean I've learned them systematically – but this is what I call on in myself. The contemporary avant-garde art world has been part of that, but I've found that it calls on the same kinds of things that I call on. For example, there is no collage art without an understanding of jazz, admitted or not. So when I talk about my work, I like to talk about the sources that are African-American, so that it's clear … I'm glad to hear that you teach *Slave Ship* by Amiri Baraka because I think that it is the main source in black culture for all that I'm talking about. His work is based in the idea that the aesthetic *is* the activism itself, the involvement in the struggle. And his work is an ongoing, changing, inspiring presence. When the struggle is the aesthetic, then criticizing particular pieces of work becomes irrelevant. I'm trying to say this simply: I am not struggling to get a piece done, I am struggling to help get us through to a more equitable society.

PATRAKA: And one of the reasons you call your performances "works-in-progress" is because you are constantly shifting the work in response to audiences?

McCAULEY: Yes, but this is also a play on that word "progress." Because it also means a work-in-*progress*, in people moving forward. So the working in progress is also the labor of struggle that shapes the performance.

PATRAKA: I think those groups I came up with were from the point of view of you as a writer: particular kinds of collaboration with jazz musician and writer Ed Montgomery; pieces that were solely written by you; pieces that were conceived in a particular community to be shaped by you; and collaborations with other women of color.

McCAULEY: Just bringing up how to talk about the work is important, because *we* must define our work. Otherwise people will do it for us. Suddenly we start playing out these definitions rather than going back to our own sources. In one way, the point of the kind of work we do is understanding how *we* define it. It's something that has to be understood from a non-white supremacist perspective – that our work is complicated and broad, that it has specific sources and is universal.

PATRAKA: And you're saying that while you do work on an avant-garde performance circuit, that's not what you want to define you. Unlike a postmodern conception, you see yourself as working from a black tradition that you acknowledge and that isn't separated off between modern and post-, but that you are fracturing and expanding in certain ways.

McCAULEY: In my view tradition and ritual are misunderstood. Tradition tends to be thought of as something "back there" that is romantic and has little to do with contemporary politics, and ritual is conceived as closed off and exactly repeatable. Yet in the way I understand it, the way people I work with and the black folks I admire understand it, tradition and ritual are expanding constantly. That's why I think the black classical music and/or jazz metaphor is the right one for black art.

PATRAKA: You've performed at La Mama, at The Kitchen, at Franklin Furnace, at The Painted Bride, at many major performance venues. How did you get there?

McCAULEY: Well, the performance art world in New York had been closed to people of color except for tokens. When I got in, I was surprised to find so few of us there, so what I like that has happened once one of us does perform is that we open the doors for more of us.

We turn each other on, we write a grant. The whole grant world was unconsciously white, though they wanted to do the right thing. But in the performance world they thought they *were* doing the right thing, and they suddenly looked around and went, "Oh! Look at us!" So, how did I get there? Lucy Lippard.

PATRAKA: She is an amazing figure, isn't she?

McCAULEY: Who has done a great deal in terms of making our work known on a broader scale. Lucy Lippard, who I didn't know at the time, was one of only two people in the audience with three of us onstage deciding to do the show anyway. It was the first time we did a collage of elements from *My Father and the Wars* and *Indian Blood*. We did the whole thing – me, Ed Montgomery, and Bob Carroll (who died a few years ago, and was an important source for me in performance). In fact there were four of us, because I had my daughter Jessie in my arms, onstage with me. It was 1981 because Jessie was just born, and she was great, she just went on through it. And Lucy asked me if I'd heard of Franklin Furnace. And I hadn't. And she told me how to write a grant for them, and I did, and that's the first place I did *My Father and the Wars*.

PATRAKA: The story has a certain power to it about what people can do when they take responsibility. In "Variations on Negation and the Heresy of Black Feminist Creativity," Michele Wallace writes that "in more politically articulate fields, such as film, theatre and TV news commentary, black feminist creativity is routinely gagged and 'disappeared'" [1989:69]. How do you combat this?

McCAULEY: You keep doing the work. I mean, like my story about Lucy, we could have gone home that night instead of performing. Use as much energy as you can to keep going as long as you can. You can use a little bit of that old work-ethic stuff but *for yourself*. And what we do as black women is to support each other. I have nurturance from women, especially black women. We call on each other. We don't disappear from each other, we cannot disappear to each other. When you feel like you're being disappeared, the thing is not to dwell on it. What you must dwell on is keeping your nurturance, your sources. You die out there by yourself.

PATRAKA: I'm interested in those moments of refuge in *Indian Blood* and *My Father and the Wars* where you perform the ritual of going to the garden. That's interesting in the context of Alice Walker's essay, "In Search of Our Mothers' Gardens," because although in some ways in your work you don't spend much time in your mother's garden, you are saying that in the present other black women are that kind of source of creativity, a kind of contemporary garden.

McCAULEY: That garden is not necessarily a garden of plants. For me that garden is my aloneness, and it's very private, and always been an important place for me. I mean I make it up. I think it came from a story of my mother's though. My mother didn't want to stay in Columbus, in Georgia, with her sisters, she wanted to get away. I was the one who got away from my own family, while my mother became a very traditional wife. But she told me that when she was a little girl she went to visit an aunt in Macon, Georgia, who the family wasn't even that close to. But every once in a while the children could just go off for a visit because the house was full of kids, and she volunteered to go. And the way she told it was in a voice of wonder and delight. "And she had a garden, and there were little rocks in the garden, and I just played all day in that garden by myself." And when my mother told me that story I realized that it was a part of me that was connected to my mother, though as her daughter it was always a problem for me because she had such a privacy about her. But when she told me that story I realized that she and I both had that same need for privacy.

"WRITING ON MY FEET"

Performing the Body, Constructing the Audience

PATRAKA: How do you go about writing one of your performance pieces?

McCAULEY: What I want to write about comes first. I write on my feet. I dance and move around, I sit down and I talk to myself, do scenes. I do it until I feel like writing. I become the audience, I become the story, I ask myself what happens next? That opens up a process. My pieces often come out of mournings I have within me and I know for a long time I'm going to write about them.

PATRAKA: What you're telling me especially makes sense for a performance artist: first, that the writing comes out of experiences that are inscribed in your body, through your own past. And second, that you're moving through them physically, and making performance through that moving. So there isn't a space where you have a script, words, separate from your body, the body and the words you perform come together.

McCAULEY: Yes. And that is the reason I have a hard time talking about it; I want it to sound rational because it is perfectly rational. And when I do work in other communities, for me even the taped interviews have a physicality to them. And some of my dialogues are snips of conversation, since so much of my writing is based in live sources. I think most writers have these thoughts that come through the body.

PATRAKA: Part of what you've just described are pieces that follow your own personal history. What comes out of the body is only viewed as irrational when you don't consider the social construction of the body and the way in which the body is mapped by history.

McCAULEY: It's getting harder for me to keep the memories of the process of how a piece came to me in my body. I used to be able to do that really easily, work out of it in performance, but everything is getting slower with age. So I'm trying to find other ways of writing than that process, while keeping that source.

PATRAKA: I'm thinking about the topic of nudity in performance and women. Karen Finley's nudity has become a kind of signature, and one expects her to be nude at some point in her work. One does not expect that in yours; there is only one piece in which you disrobe. One woman I talked with after seeing Finley's *We Keep Our Victims Ready* [1992] in Ann Arbor was unhappy about Finley's nudity, because she hated to see a woman's body displayed in front of men and wanted an all-female audience instead. I tried to think about that, and about the way in which a performer's body is her instrument in a way that it isn't, for example, when an actress is nude as part of someone else's script. The control is yours when you're performing as Robbie McCauley and not as an actress. Even if you are enacting objectifica-tion, that's precisely the point, and the power of that body belongs to you when you enact it. Because saying the female body can never be shown is almost acceding to a sense of powerlessness. There's a kind of ownership of that body in performance that's made very clear in your work.

McCAULEY: Right. And Karen Finley is on the list of people who have affected my work – for her boldness, which is one way we make our point. The idea for *Sally's Rape* came years ago, but I'm not sure I would have been able to do it without Karen opening up that area to make women comfortable with using our bodies for our own point within our own context. She's bold, she's satirical, and she's made an opening for me to step in there and do that strong moment in *Sally's Rape*.

PATRAKA: I want to congratulate you on winning the Obie in 1992 for the best new American play for *Sally's Rape*.

McCAULEY: It was especially important and exiting that the award was for being a writer. In a sense, I still feel like "a performer on paper." But it's great to have that recognition from people that my work is a play or has the same stature as one.

PATRAKA: There are moments when your voice is soft, and moments when it's loud and intense. When do you raise your voice in performance?

McCAULEY: It has to do with rage. In *Sally's Rape* I try to pull my voice back in, I personalize that moment. It is about the rage that I have embraced, that is necessary, that is healing, and I release it out of a personal need to do so, but I don't want it to push people away, so I find out in the process of making a performance where it comes, and then I plan the places for its release.

PATRAKA: When I saw Finley's *We Keep Our Victims Ready*, people almost felt Finley wasn't angry enough and they were hostile to the idea that she was attempting to create community with her audience. It's as if we have a kind of resistance to the 1960s, whether we lived through them or not, that translates into a kind of resentment that someone may want to create community.

McCAULEY: What you just described is part of our conditioning to resist communion. What I've been trying to do is pay attention to that resistance, to feel audiences pushing themselves away and find ways to connect. What some performers are doing when they attack the audience is keeping the audience alienated, which isn't my major strategy. And some people don't want to be brought in. It's like going to church, when you come for one thing and get another. And if you're not open to it, you resist it. I mean, the relationship between theatre and the church is direct in terms of community. You come and engage in a ritual and either it's very stoic and rigid, or it's very inclusive, and you either give yourself to the ritual or not.

PATRAKA: I'm always curious about the kind of audience who prides itself on a certain knowledgeability and resistance to being moved. You know, they understand the "trick" of it, they understand the strategies of it, almost past the point where it can be effective.

McCAULEY: For those reasons, I think the most challenging audiences are in New York. And yet I learn from that to try to get through to them and learn from their looking for the seduction, looking for those things that I'm using to involve them. To me that's a challenge, not an insoluble problem.

PATRAKA: Would you like to have the opportunity to perform for more black audiences?

McCAULEY: The best performance of *Sally's Rape* Jeannie and I did was at Crossroads Theater, a black theatre in New Jersey. The audience really enacted the role of group number three, whose function was to comment. They also did the slave ritual, the auction block ritual, with relish. They knew what playing an auctioneer meant. This was part of the Crossroads Genesis project, and at the panel afterward we were told, "Thank you for bringing us into the dialogue, we really appreciated it." That certainly disproved the idea that black audiences don't want performance, are not ready for it, want something safe and familiar. The problem is that the business of theatre, *because* it is business, is conservative. And so black theatres have had to be conservative. Now black performers are beginning to be more innovative in performance, such as at Crossroads where people like Sydnay Mahone, who does so many wonderful things there, is responding to this fact. Black theatres need to keep doing that.

THE MISSISSIPPI PROJECT

Community Collaborations

PATRAKA: Tell me about the current projects in Mississippi.

McCAULEY: *The Mississippi Project* [1992] is part of a three-project series being produced by the Arts Company, by Marie Cieri. What I'm doing in Mississippi is part of a larger project of interviewing people in various places about historical events related to civil rights. The first part, in Mississippi, is mainly about voting rights. The second part takes place in Boston and will be about the 1970s busing in Boston, and the third project will be about police brutality. We're considering Watts, Los Angeles, and Chicago as the city.

Part of *The Mississippi Project* is called *Mississippi Freedom*, named for the Mississippi Freedom Democratic party that Fanny Lou Hamer was connected to. I knew Fanny Lou Hamer's story because at the time it was unfolding I watched it with my head pasted to the TV. I wanted to explore the voting rights struggle and the personal stories about it, and, among the actors, dialogue about the voting rights struggle now. The process was the same as *The Buffalo Project*; I found a good group of actors in Jackson, Mississippi, both black and white, who traveled throughout the state, collecting the witnesses and their texts. There's a theatre company in Mississippi called Potpourri, led by a woman named Sameerah Muhammad. She was instrumental in helping me find the actors.

The other project was done at the Rural Organizing and Cultural Center in Lexington, Mississippi. I taught and directed teenagers in a storytelling piece that came out of the stories on civil rights they had already collected. In the process of making it, adults came and sat in – the aim was to make it an intergenerational story group. The teenagers performed it at Tougaloo College and a busload of community people came to see it. What we did was to revitalize the telling aspect of the culture, and help make that happen again – not the telling of the old stories but the work with dialogue about them in the present.

PATRAKA: I'm going to ask you a very unpleasant question, that I don't necessarily agree with, but I'll ask nonetheless. I heard someone saying that the audience for theatre and performance, especially political theatre, never really expands, and so what you are really doing. . . .

McCAULEY: . . . is preaching to the converted. I think that criticism is a cop-out. First of all, how much do the converted know? And things resonate, ripple out. This is not to say that you do not work constantly for audience development; we need to grapple with finding ways to expand audiences. But we don't need to put that problem in the way of doing the work, making our work clear and beautiful for our audiences. The whole issue is just a block.

PATRAKA: Do you think that it's also a way of underestimating our own potential power and effect, the way the Right never underestimates it?

McCAULEY: That's what I mean. The oppressor is smarter than we think about our power. It's debilitating to have them with the power to develop audiences, and not us, but I think to understand our possibilities now is essential.

"LIVING IN AMERICA"

Final Questions

PATRAKA: Is there anything else that I haven't asked you that I should have? In this hour number six? [*Laughter*]

McCAULEY: Oh, sure, there's four more hours. [*Laughter*] Did I mention Marxism? Marxism informs my sense of history, which is probably the least original statement I could make. I worried about using it until I realized it was the rigidity in Marxism that always bothered me. Russia is, of course, a horrible example of communism – for me, one of the repeating images of Russia is of those *same men* you see in all of Western culture, that same bunch of big, well-endowed, powerful-looking white men. This was not the picture of studying Marx and his explanation of history I had imagined. I'm interested in the way that using Marxism explains materially why things have happened and in using it creatively.

PATRAKA: One thing you're trying to do, then, is portray a range of the factors that relate to oppression at once – class, gender, and race.

McCAULEY: Yes and the specific ways that they're related. When we are not given the time and space in which to understand how these connect, and how it's possible to change, it's useful for the systematic oppressors. It's useful that we work too hard. A line in my song "Nuclear Meltdown" goes: "Living in America is so hard, you get so tired, it's too hard to change." And it's useful for them that we're fatalistic and stuck, for us to think "that's the way white people are, that's the way black people are, that's the way men and women are, you can't change it."

PATRAKA: So the dialogues you create demystify things. And show the relations and connections between them.

McCAULEY: Yes, that racism is not natural or innate, or genetic . . . I'm thinking about race being at the bottom of it all. And that racism is also material. Even now, thinking about art, we feel that even if we are given the credit as sources, what happens to us materially? In the music world, it's admitted that the Beatles wouldn't be the Beatles without the blues singers who ended up with a few cents in their pockets. The admittance of that brings up some overwhelming changes that white people would have to go through in order to make things right.

PATRAKA: Instead, there are silences about situations that get worse and worse.

McCAULEY: And so we are in this spiral that is worsening. I think the feelings of our own past mistakes, past misunderstandings, are so scary that we keep the denial and reaction going on. My feeling is that denial is the worst response possible and that we have internalized it. Under that is the material reality, the question "How do we get out of here?" Instead of facing it, we get the idea of black people in particular as "the bad guy" in order to lock this denial (and us) up – that's what's going on in this country now.

Performance Production History

Robbie McCauley

The production history below cites some of the major venues at which a work written by McCauley was performed, including the site where a performance piece received its major reviews. Most work by McCauley travels extensively, so this is not an exhaustive listing. I have grouped McCauley's works in four categories based on their mode of composition and performance. It should be noted that the borders between perform-ance pieces are permeable and parts of one piece are sometimes recycled into another. This differs somewhat from multiple uses by McCauley of a family story where that story is revisioned and recontextu-alized for each piece. Many of the pieces, especially those in the Family Story and Thought Music groupings, are envisioned as works-in-progress rather than as completely set texts and continue to evolve in response to new ideas and local performance conditions. Several of the works have a strong improvised component to them, especially in the earlier stages of performance. Many of McCauley's pieces include slides and live music; some of them (e.g., *My Father and the Wars*, *Indian Blood*, and *Teenytown*) include video or film.

The Family Stories: A Continuing Serial Performance
These first three pieces listed are sometimes grouped as a trilogy entitled *Confessions of a Working-Class Black Woman*.

1983   *San Juan Hill*
        Brecht Auditorium, New York, NY
1985   *My Father and the Wars*
        The Franklin Furnace, New York, NY
1987   *Indian Blood*
        The Kitchen, New York, NY, and Painted Bride, Philadelphia, PA
1991   *Sally's Rape* (sometimes subtitled *The Whole Story*)
        Directed by McCauley and performed by McCauley with Jean-nie Hutchins at The Kitchen, New York, NY. Earlier versions of the piece were performed in New York at Lincoln Center (1990); P.S.122 and the Studio Museum of Harlem (1989); and a very early version was performed solely by McCauley for The Women & Theatre Program Conference, New York University (1989)

Site-Specific Pieces Involving Community Collaboration
For these pieces, McCauley shapes and directs the work of local theatre workers – who also perform the pieces – based upon their dialogue with each other in response to stories collected from witnesses and including these stories themselves.

1990   *The Buffalo Project*
        About the 1967 Buffalo riots. Performed in Buffalo, NY, at three sites: the Hallwalls Contemporary Art Center, the Langston Hughes Institute, and the Polish Community Center

1992   *The Mississippi Project*
        Includes two projects: *Mississippi Freedom*, about the voting rights struggle, performed at the Smith Robertson Museum, Jackson, MS, and another project on the civil rights struggle, performed at the Rural Organizing & Cultural Center, Lexington, MS, and at Tougaloo College

1993   *The Boston Project*
        Tentatively titled *Turf*. A work-in-progress about busing planned for 1993

Collaborations with Thought Music
Thought Music includes writer/performers Laurie Carlos, Jessica Hagedorn, and Robbie McCauley, and visual artist John Woo.

1988   *Part Two: Thinking Out Loud*
        Written and performed at the Danspace Project, St. Marks Church, New York, NY, by Carlos, Hagedorn, and McCauley

1988   *Teenytown* (sometimes subtitled *The Too Little Too Late Show*)
        Written by Carlos, Hagedorn, and McCauley and performed by all three at Franklin Furnace, at the Whitney Museum, and at the Schomburg Center for Research in Black Culture, New York, NY

1988   *Heat*
        Developed and performed at The Kitchen, New York, NY, by the dance theatre company Urban Bush Women, and Thought Music (Carlos, Hagedorn, and McCauley)

1992   *Persimmon Peel*
        Written and performed at The Working Theatre, New York, NY, by Carlos and McCauley. An earlier version of the piece was done at La Mama in 1990

1992   *The Food Show*
        Written and performed at Nuyorican Poet's Cafe, New York, NY, by Carlos, Hagedorn, and McCauley

Sedition Ensemble Pieces
Co-written by Robbie McCauley and Ed Montgomery

1980   *The History of the Universe According To Those Who've Had To Live It*
        La Mama Etc., New York, NY

1983   *Calling Out!*
        La Mama Etc., New York, NY

1983   *Loisaida War Party*
        Charas, New York, NY

1984   *Nicaragua in Perspective*
        Off Center Theatre and Taller Latino Americano, New York, NY

1988   *Congo New York*
        New Museum of Contemporary Art, New York, NY, and Great Woods, RI (currently being developed as a jazz opera by Ed Montgomery)

PATRAKA: What do you mean "as the bad guy"?

McCAULEY: As the welfare mother, the young black male, the intellectual who keeps on speaking about this stuff, rather than just assimilate on in, who can then be dismissed.

PATRAKA: As opposed to say, the older woman who takes care of your house, and loves your children, and gives you her caring?

McCAULEY: She's considered human. What I feel hopeful about in all of this is the ability to keep trying to understand it and work on it.

PATRAKA: If for some terrible reason, and I'm not even sure I want to pose this kind of question, you were to wink out tomorrow, what would you most want to be remembered for in terms of your performance work?

McCAULEY: I can never answer that in the moment, it's too hard ... I want people to have their own memories, that's what I want. If I can inspire people to connect with and value, use their own memories, that would mean something important.

NOTES

1. I wish to thank Mary Callahan Boone, my research assistant, for her valuable help in preparing this interview. Her labor was funded by a Graduate Research Assistant Award from Bowling Green State University, 1992.
2. See *Out from Under: Texts by Women Performance Artists*, edited by Lenora Champagne, 89–117. New York: Theatre Communications Group, 1990, for a printed text of *Teenytown*.

REFERENCES

Carr, C. (1986) "The Unofficial Story." *Village Voice*, 18 November: 93.

Hurwitt, Robert (1990) "*Teenytown*: In-Your-Face Comedy." *San Francisco Examiner*, 12 October.

Kennedy, Lisa (1990) "Cameos." *Village Voice*, 30 January:100.

Lippard, Lucy R. (1990) *Mixed Blessings: New Art in a Multicultural America*. New York: Pantheon.

McCauley, Robbie, Laurie Carlos, and Jessica Hagedorn (1990) *Teenytown*. In *Out from Under: Texts by Women Performance Artists*, edited by Lenora Champagne, 89–117. New York: Theatre Communications Group.

Solomon, Alisa (1987) "True Confessions." *Village Voice*, 8 December:115.

Wallace, Michele (1989) "Variations on Negation and the Heresy of Black Feminist Creativity." *Heresies* 6, no. 4 (#24):69–75.

14

HOLLY HUGHES

Polymorphous Perversity and the Lesbian Scientist

An Interview by Rebecca Schneider

Dress Suits to Hire won Holly Hughes the distinction of having authored her own genre. When the play opened in May 1987 at P.S. 122 in New York City, C. Carr of the *Village Voice* heralded Hughes as queen of her own "Dyke Noir Theatre" and broadcast her reputation as bad girl of the bad girls. "She's hell on heels, a twisted sister – a character from the timeless, tasteless world of dyke noir as imagined by Holly Hughes." Where is Hughes' dyke noir since *Dress Suits*? If Carr is right, "Wherever she goes it's the wrong side of town" (1987:32).

I found Hughes close to midnight in the East Village. She was popping out of a glaring pink, plaster-of-paris pig at performance space P.S. 122. It was 16 September 1988, the beginning of *World Without End*, Hughes' latest work-in-progress. The pig bore the name "Trojan Pig" because, Hughes told me, she wanted to appear as "some kind of Sappho reincarnate." Hughes stood with her naked back to the audience as four lovely negligee-clad attendants helped her don a pinkish bra to complete her garish girdle outfit. The beauties guided her to a pink scallop-backed chair center stage where, for the rest of the night, like some kind of Venus on her shell, Hughes told it all – from her own version of Genesis in which Eve and Adam ride the IRT subway, to the particularly smutty Gospel According to Mona, Hughes' mother. In the course of her raunchy tales, spicy asides, and sometimes painful personal sagas, Hughes, with a winsome smile, proclaimed herself the "preeminent lesbian playwright of my generation."

The campy butch–femme role playing of Hughes' early *Well of Horniness* evolved through *Lady Dick* and *Dress Suits* to receive quite a bit of critical attention, especially from those interested in ways lesbian theatre disrupts traditional constellations of gender and power on stage (see Davy 1986; Dolan 1988). Hughes' latest "dyke noir" appears in new garb as the sinuous and long-winded monolog *World Without End*, a piece which pays a surprising amount of attention to the specifics of Adam's anatomy:

This is the start of history,
starting with my hand wet, on your wet dick.
Which is wetter: Adam or Eve?
Which is closer to the sea?
And then Adam says:
"I dunno about you, but let's just take it up against the wall."
And that hero spreads Eve's legs like, um, like um, nothing else
     could,
be cause, *recuerda*, remember:
This is the beginning
Beginning with Mr. Adam sliding in that cock kinda slow kinda real
     slow a bit too slow for our heroine,
So we have to give our hero a little credit here! Maybe Mr. Adam is
     no dumbo afterall!
He knows that shame didn't just ram its way into the newborn human
     mind!
Tragedy takes time!
More time and care than the 16 thrusts average for average coitus.
O la la.
Eve is happy, Adam is happy too there's sheetrock surrounding her
Garden of Eden. And Mr. Adam is happy too cause he's all the way
inside her and he feels her feel him hit –
paydirt.
When alla sudden Eve's gotta say: "Do you have any idea who you're
     porking?
I'm the preeminent lesbian playwright of my generation!"

(Hughes 1988)

It may be that this dyke-noir-in-progress is in some ways flavored
by the recent appearances of lesbian theatre before more diverse
audiences. When *Dress Suits* moved from downtown P.S. 122 to
midtown Women's Interart in 1987 to a 1988 guest appearance at the
University of Michigan, its steamy scenes between lesbian lovers were
suddenly playing for the "general" public. Questions as to the reception
of that sexual dynamic took on a certain urgency within the lesbian
theatrical community: Outside of the framework of "women for
women," will lesbians displaying sexuality automatically read as
women displayed for men? In *World Without End*, Hughes puts herself
on display and seems to invite some of those questions. Her sultry
theatrics are an elaborately devised tease: "Do you love me? Are you
faithful? I'm faithful to you," Hughes says to her audience. But who
is this "you"? To whom is she faithful? And who is being teased –
the performer or the spectator?

Packaged in her stiffly gartered get-up, Hughes is both pushing and resisting an easy reading. The sexual testimony dripping off her tongue is consistently qualified by her commanding image as sexually autonomous – her bevy of beauties, we suspect, are dutifully waiting in the wings. Autonomy and the expression of sexual desire are an unusual mix for a woman to so adroitly control onstage, especially one as slight and spritelike as Hughes, but in *World Without End* Hughes attempts to twist the gaze of the spectator through the tangle of her tease, playing for control of the pink bon-bon body she wields onstage.

In the following interview Hughes talks about her evolution as a playwright and addresses some of the issues facing lesbian theatre. Though she says she doesn't write with a particular audience in mind, she's found a way to negotiate her position in the gaze wars. "I'm a lesbian scientist," she says, experimenting with something she fondly calls "polymorphous perversity."

SCHNEIDER: Talk a little bit about how you became involved with WOW Cafe.

HUGHES: I came to New York and I was a painter – I was going to be a big feminist painter and I was going to build giant vulvas that were going to topple the corporate structure and I wanted to work with a community of women. I found a community of women who were making giant vulvas – they were also bashing each other's heads in with words like "sisterhood" and "trust." They weren't able to find a language to deal with things like competition and other things that women aren't supposed to have – balls – you know, things that are phallic values that of course we're trying to lop off.

I stopped painting after a while and was just a waitress living in Queens. Things looked pretty bleak. One day I was walking down E. 11th Street and bumped into WOW. I came in to WOW when it was at 330 E. 11th Street and started volunteering there. I had gone to a few WOW events before that. They were having double-XX-rated Christmas parties at Club 57 [the original "East Village Club" on St. Mark's Place, see *TDR* 29, no. 1 – it was just a whole different kind of approach to feminist performance than I had ever seen before.

SCHNEIDER: As opposed to sisterhood?

HUGHES: Yes. Sisterhood. . . . We had women like Diane Torr trouncing around in negligees and kissing booths and lingerie shows. It was *for* women. People would come in there and strip off their clothes and put on lingerie. It had a lot of the drag theatre flavor and permission. And everybody became a performer – it was so *avant*. And it was a great time. So I started serving coffee there as a volunteer and within two weeks – two months – I had seized the reins of power because everyone else had left to go on tour to Europe and I was the only one left with the keys. So I didn't know jack shit about performance or

Figure 14.1 Holly Hughes in *World Without End*, September 1988 at P.S. 122 in New York City. (© Dona Ann McAdams)

about running even a tiny theatre space, I didn't even know how to turn the lights on, but we just booked Jane Doe Feminist to come in with her rocks and crystals and abortion stories – like, "Hey, you can have a show here!" Then it began to evolve into a repertory theatre company.

SCHNEIDER: In and around performers Peggy Shaw and Lois Weaver?

HUGHES: Peggy and Lois were . . . how should I say it? They were role models in a sense in the beginning because they'd been doing this work a lot longer than anyone else and at that point they had more recognition. They encouraged people like Carmelita Tropicana and Alice Forester and myself.

SCHNEIDER: There were a lot of dress-up parties, right? Military drag and medical drag parties?

HUGHES: Yeah and "I Paid the Rent in my Maidenform Bra" parties. They usually revolved around taking clothes off.

SCHNEIDER: How does *Dress Suits to Hire* respond to that? There's all those clothes back in the closets and lots of dressing up and stripping down.

HUGHES: I think girls just like to dress up and take it off. *Dress Suits* actually came into being because after I'd done *Lady Dick* – which Peggy had been in and Lois had been real supportive of – they asked me to write something for them. They had the idea that it would be in a tuxedo rental shop and based on some rumors surrounding an actual rental shop on Second Avenue. And the idea evolved that there would be these two sisters in there – I use the word "sisters" euphemistically – I mean like two lesbians living together presenting the fact that they were sisters to the rest of the world, but also in that way that lovers become sisters, that they become a family.

SCHNEIDER: The energy between Shaw and Weaver is very highly charged and sexual, but there's also a real claustrophobia of the space – a very small shop crammed with lots of things, yapping Linda [the mechanical dog] –

HUGHES: – It's a microcosm of the whole lesbian situation!

SCHNEIDER: You answered my question.

HUGHES: It's about relationships in general, in the way that you form a binary unit. It becomes a little world unto itself. I think that two people always have some kind of a baby. The relationship is the baby.

It becomes a whole world, a whole system of reality between themselves.

SCHNEIDER: A lot of crying in the night, a lot of shit to clean up?

HUGHES: A lot of shit to clean up. And stories of the past. Stories about how you met start out as the actual fact, then become a story, then become a ritual – in the way that you repeat the stories of Exodus to reinforce a sense of identity.

SCHNEIDER: Michigan and Deeluxe's hula hoop ritual in the gas station scene, for instance?

HUGHES: In the gas station scene.

SCHNEIDER: Time here is irrelevant. Past and present slide in and out of each other in your narratives. In this intimate space that the characters say they're trying to leave, but never do, the present is almost entirely spent maintaining these ritualized memories of the past.

HUGHES: Yes, I thought about how older people, or people who are really isolated, think. Past and present – there's not really a distinction, time is not always moving forward. My grandmother had Alzheimer's and would slip into her childhood and be experiencing things the way she did as a young girl.

SCHNEIDER: But what's interesting about this is that two people are consciously performing the act together. Michigan will get out the boots and she'll get out the hat and they know what's coming. One of the most erotic points is when Shaw just grabs Weaver and kisses her in the middle of this gas station ritual. They know the road and they've been there before – it's mapped out on a geographic space. A geography which turns out to be Weaver's body. Weaver says, "You're gonna see California but you're not leaving this gas station."

HUGHES: Yeah, it's real elaborate foreplay. But it's also about lesbian relationships, about the desire to make a lesbian culture, to try and isolate it from mainstream culture. But there's problems in isolation – you are still part of the culture. There's Little Peter cropping up in all of us. [Little Peter is Deeluxe's errant hand that speaks like a pimp and is referred to as "he."]

SCHNEIDER: I want to get to Little Peter later, but before we go on, can you briefly say how *Dress Suits* moved from WOW to P.S. 122 to Women's Interart uptown?

HUGHES: Well we did a reading of the script in February of 1987 at

WOW and it was in a real raw state. C. Carr of the *Village Voice* came and was *real* supportive. Then I did extensive revisions in the text and we did it in May 1987 at P.S. 122 at the Veselka Performance Festival. And in December 1987 it went uptown to Women's Interart and ran through February 1988.

SCHNEIDER: *Dress Suits* was your first piece written with the awareness that a general audience would see it – written to be performed at P.S. 122. It was an attempt to bring lesbian theatre to a broader audience, right? How did that affect the collaboration? Were you and Peggy and Lois expecting a potentially different reception when putting the piece together?

HUGHES: I would have written the same play if I thought only women were going to see it. I absolutely didn't alter it, I just planned to have it be in a different venue. I feel strongly about putting lesbian work out. I want to make it as kinky, dirty, specifically women-oriented – as true to myself as I can make it. But I really feel like I don't want to preach to the converted. I really feel that it's very important for women's work to be seen in a more general context. It's scary.

SCHNEIDER: Yes, it's scary. When *Dress Suits* was at Michigan University in Ann Arbor, there was a discussion afterward in which Sue-Ellen Case made the point that perhaps the piece would be better served performed exclusively for women. The argument was that the context of academia – in the lap, so to speak, of dominant ideology – undermined the radical content of the play. And that for straight audiences it became ... entertainment; that straight audiences and specifically males in that context couldn't somehow "read" the piece correctly.[1] What do you think?

HUGHES: Well, first of all, I don't feel like there is a correct reading. I really don't. If I felt that there was a correct reading for something I'd be Jesse Jackson. Jackson is great, but the kind of writing he does is rhetoric and it's political, didactic writing. This is not that. People will approach my work in different ways. People have thought that *Dress Suits* is about incest because of the mention of sisters. People have thought all sorts of things. And those things could be there! I really believe in art and I believe in allowing the audience to have their own personal subjective view. I give the audience a lot of credit – I think people are really bored with a straight white male perspective in theatre and can relate to the story in a lot of ways. A lot of people have experienced being an outsider. Everybody feels queer in some sense of the word. I think that there are various windows into an experience

... all of a sudden they're inside of an experience that's formed by a lesbian.

SCHNEIDER: Some say that art, or representation, is always political and that lesbian theatre has a chance to really provide a way out of the mainstream economy of male desire which appropriates the female image for its own. Case, for instance, has written that butch–femme roles are the answer for feminist theatre. For her, butch–femme couples onstage – and on the street – defy the patriarchal gender-biased power structure by creating and outwardly symbolizing a woman-controlled economy of desire (1987). Jill Dolan, after Luce Irigaray, writes of lesbian theatre as the goods getting together and redefining the market. I guess my question is: What happens when lesbian theatre enters the mainstream theatrical market? After all, when Michigan gives a "peepshow" for Deeluxe, she's also giving one for the audience. Considering Case's butch–femme argument, and given the fact that the Michigan University issues were such a problem for some people, what does it mean that this lesbian play has two femmes on display, or –

HUGHES: I don't think Michigan and Deeluxe are two femmes. I think it's really about role playing on all the different levels. Look at Peggy Shaw! She's wearing a dress but look at her body, man! She's like drop dead Martina! It's a comment on drag performance –

SCHNEIDER: Oh no, that's true. By "femme" I meant that for the most part it's a female iconography they're playing around with – the negligees, the gown, the boa. . . .

HUGHES: Yeah they are playing with it. So you're saying that what's difficult about it is that it's not using the traditional understanding of butch–femme?

SCHNEIDER: I don't know. I'm trying to get at the problem of reception, to find out what was difficult about the show in terms of its reception for a heterosexual audience. Why the question of keeping *Dress Suits* a women-only show would come up? We would like to believe that desire, in the hands and eyes of women, fully resists traditional reading. But in *Dress Suits* it's almost as if you're saying that the hands of women are complicated – look at Little Peter. What is it about the piece that makes it uncomfortable for some or too easily appropriated in a straight context?

HUGHES: I don't know why they have a problem. I think it really comes down to the fact that I really feel that I am a theatre artist first and a lesbian second. And that to grow as a theatre artist I have to put my work in challenging venues. It has to stand up as art and I don't believe that it's something so fragile that people will – I mean, it's not going to be performed in the middle of Independence Plaza – but I feel like ... I don't know that there is a straight male audience. I think that you can be noticed by the mainstream and not coopted. Irene Fornes – she's absolutely her own person and she's gotten attention. I mean she's not a household word like Sam Shepard, she's really remained true to her vision, and her work comes from a very female-identified place. But she's putting it out there. And the whole butch–femme thing – I don't think anything is that black and white.

I think the problem these chicks are having with the show is that I'm just refusing to make this lesbian-feminist fairy tale that only affirms what women want to know about themselves and that we're better than everyone else and that we're this and that and that lesbian relationships are perfect. Are they really any better than any other relationships? They're just as twisted. And they're twisted in specific ways that have to do with homophobia and sexism in the culture and the desire to create something new and the frustration of not really being able to construct something new. I want to explore things that are actual as opposed to posing some sort of utopian solution. I don't think that it's all so beautiful and that women's desire is so completely different from men's desire. There's desire to possess and voyeurism and objectification. Hopefully, the object becomes a subject in women's desire, but it's not all clean-cut and whole wheat berries. I hate that stuff. Where are they hanging out that they get these ideas? Its like creating a lesbian utopia, a lesbian Disneyland.

SCHNEIDER: I think that part of all the energy put into the various forms of feminist theatre is just to open up the boundaries of women's expression and open the lens on its reception. Kate Davy writes in her article on *Dress Suits* [Chapter 10 of this volume] that there's an infinite flexibility suggested in the role-playing – in the scarves and the boots and the different things that they put on, like the frames of past and present they slip in and out of. There's no one essential, riveting identity or role at all. But it's not merely a happy playful arena. There's also a sense of frustration with the games and with the rituals. And so there's a tension, an ambiguity in the fun of the masquerade.

Still, despite the flexibility of the roles, there is a significant difference between Deeluxe and Michigan and its far more evident on the stage than in the text. It has to do with two things, I think. One, with Shaw's history playing butch roles in WOW, a reputation that travels with her that the audience really responds to. The other thing is that Shaw is the one who gets to lose the feminine iconography in the show – she goes back to what she does best, with the cowboy hat and the toothpick between her teeth. Weaver is at home with the "feminine wiles," whereas, in that hilarious song number with the fan, Shaw is awkward and definitely in drag. As Deeluxe, Shaw is putting on the costume. But for Michigan the femme seems more than a costume. Michigan is a "state" after all – maybe a state of being. And Deeluxe is spectacle, as Davy writes. Could you speak about that difference a little bit?

HUGHES: Deeluxe is a stripper who performs for an audience of maybe two, if you count the dog. There is this cat and mouse game. Michigan is the desirous one and Deeluxe is the love object. It's some sort of a role reversal because she [Michigan] is a femme, but of course she's not really femme. If you think of butch in terms of looks then she's femme, but if you think of the roles in the way they conduct their lives – being sexually aggressive and stuff like that – she's definitely butch.

SCHNEIDER: What I was getting at in terms of Michigan and the state is the sense of "stuckness," of restless unhappiness with the "state" of her desire. She's the female body as landscape, the terrain, the "state" of California and the site of desire. She's "Marineland." Deeluxe is the one that gets to go there, to take a ride. Michigan performs the "peep-show" with the flashlight/spotlight shining on her body. But at the end, Michigan sadly talks of the repressed she-monster, of women's voracious desires and the insatiable toothy vagina. She, the femme, kind of pathetically asks the butch in drag, "Do you really want to be like me?" It seems that little is "liberated" or "satisfied" for Michigan. Why is that?

HUGHES: Well I think that's really about terror. Right now – being out there performing and being sexual in my new piece *World Without End* – I'm experiencing that there's an absolute terror in this culture of women's sexuality. It's absolutely frightening. And I don't think it's any less frightening for women than it is for men. But it's like, yeah, women are multiorgasmic, they're insatiable. There have been so many constraints put on our sexuality and so many blinders by every possible institution in the culture that we're just beginning to notice that there's this volcano beneath the surface. I'm not a sociologist; I'm just a "mere artist." All I can say is that I sense this absolute terror – a terror that comes up in women when they realize that they're sexual. So many women are so castrated. I think it's interesting that castration is a fear of men, but when you think of the ability to pursue desire to satisfaction, castration is a fact of life for women – they're not allowed to be empowered sexually. And I don't understand why the most insulting thing a man can say to a woman is probably to call her a cock-sucker, when it's probably the thing that he wants the most. It has to do with becoming the receptacle of his filth, you know –

SCHNEIDER: A man's bad self-image?

HUGHES: Yes, and she becomes the screen that he projects that on. But women do that too, I mean we internalize that idea.

SCHNEIDER: That's another thing I could bring up at this point. We talk about men's self-image and women as the receptacle. One of the things feminists have reacted against has been the constant representation of woman equaling sexuality and the body of woman signifying sexuality. And yet, in the theatre, that's your terrain.

HUGHES: It doesn't mean that there aren't other things to talk about. I just can't get out of bed in terms of my writing. The worst thing in our life is that our life ends. We're given two things to deal with that fact: one is creative work and the other is love, specifically sexual love. It's like one of those little sets of elephants that you keep pulling smaller and smaller elephants out of, or something that has endless layers you keep peeling back. It's something that you could endlessly observe, like Cézanne realizing that apples could be a fine subject to paint for the rest of his life, that even the space between apples is endlessly significant. There are other things to talk about, but I think that sex is so much the kernel of your self-esteem and your sense of empowerment. It's no accident that I use male terms like "impotence" and "flaccid" because there aren't any female terms. There's no positive terms for a strong, sexual woman. "Whore" or "slut" do not equal "stud."

SCHNEIDER: Whenever Michigan and Deeluxe come close against that really hot, or strong desire, either Little Peter comes in or Michigan will start talking about poison and she-wolfness and then put herself down.

HUGHES: It's very much the position that I see women in. We're just beginning to see that we have this desire, but it's terrifying to us. We back down from it all the time. There's just something monstrous about it, it's so unnameable and unknowable and you know you're going to go off the main drag if you pursue this –

SCHNEIDER: – Or get derailed by the larger culture.

HUGHES: Right.

SCHNEIDER: Talk a little bit about why you use camp in your productions as a theatrical strategy.

HUGHES: Camp is a style of humor that seems dated in a way. It seems TV-oriented. It's a post-World War II kind of thing and/or it has a gay sensibility. It's about a love/hate relationship with popular culture. I like the artifice of theatre a lot. Naturalistic theatre really bores me. The reason I use camp is sheer pleasure, it's like a spice. Stuff that's completely camp, and there are few really good camp performers, is a style that gets really wearing, like eating nothing but hot fudge. I tend to use camp in my work as a spice, except for the *Well of Horniness* which is nothing but campy and trashy. Also, camp is an outsider sensibility, kind of commenting and exaggerating and ironic.

SCHNEIDER: What about Little Peter?

HUGHES: This play is really not about men at all except in the fact that a lesbian relationship exists in a larger culture. The whole inside–outside kind of tension that exists in the play – are they going to go outside; the windows keep blowing open; they never leave the space – we're not completely free of a culture that has a bias. Little Peter is a lot of different things. I always liked the goofy hand-choking-your-throat kind of convention. I mean what is that? That some part of yourself would turn against the rest of your body. And I'm also inspired by *Dr. Jekyll and Mr. Hyde*. There's an unknowable part of yourself that – call it dark, evil, whatever – is something we're not comfortable with. In Dr. Jekyll's desire to get rid of that he actually allows that part of himself to take over. There's some part of Deeluxe, whether it's her masculine side in a Jungian sense, or whether it's a certain part of herself that's aggressive or dark, there's a part of herself that she has not accepted. She obviously associates that part with male values. It's a lot about what we've internalized from the culture.

SCHNEIDER: I'd like to talk about your new piece, *World Without End*. There's a great deal of time devoted to penises, among other things. I'm interested in this because penises are, as you say in the piece, an interesting subject for the "preeminent lesbian playwright of our day." We were discussing before whether a woman looking at another woman, full of desire, as Michigan looks at Deeluxe, disrupts traditional female passivity, traditional one-way objectification. But what happens when a woman looks at a man? That's where we get sluts, *femmes fatales*, she-monsters, whores, and the "vagina dentina" you're so fond of. Some feminists say that women looking at men with desire cannot "disarm male desire because the erect male penis is still a powerful image". When Deeluxe strangles Little Peter –

HUGHES: – Well, Little Peter may be a dick but he's not a penis.

SCHNEIDER: OK, but in *World Without End* a great deal of juicy description is devoted to the penis and heterosexual sex. Are you moving onto a new frontier? Are you trying to manipulate penises to be less of a power-filled image – to rewrite the penis? Basically, what is this penis stuff?

HUGHES: What *is* the penis all about?! Well, the work's real personal, real autobiographical and it's about at some point coming to terms with, for lack of a better word, the fact that I was bisexual. I was trying to figure out some things about that. I'd like to think of it not so much as bisexuality that I'm exploring as polymorphous perversity.

SCHNEIDER: And bringing it to the stage –

HUGHES: I have a piece that I didn't include where I said that I have a lot of rules in my life and having a lot of rules convinces me that I'm still a lesbian even though I might fuck a guy. In fact, I'm a lesbian scientist and I'm just going through this stagnant glass-bottom boat, gazing and going "Uh-huh, Uh-huh."

First of all I feel like women should be really free to explore their sexuality in whatever form it expresses itself. And it may change and permutate in their lifetime. I'm really anti anyone other than individuals defining their own sexuality. I don't have any conclusions about what to say about being a powerful woman sexually vis-à-vis men. It's absolutely terrifying to men. Absolutely terrifying. They like it, but it's absolutely terrifying. But it's interesting – it's material for my plays.

SCHNEIDER: You mention Karen Finley in *World Without End*, alluding to the fact that your work is similar.[2]

HUGHES: I like Karen Finley a lot. She's exploring from a female perspective what Burroughs and Henry Miller and those people talked about from a male perspective. She's really going into the dark part of sanity and the wackier side of sexuality. She's like some sort of theatrical proctologist – she's pokin' around in there. I think she's amazing in a lot of ways in that there's this absolute meshing of presentation and text, like I can't imagine Meryl Streep doing one of her monologs. It comes out of this sort of Cassandra wail, in a very primeval way. One of the differences in our writing is that I find that in a lot of women's art that deals with sexuality – and I'm thinking of Karen Finley and Kathy Acker and others – I tend to find that the dominant mode of sexual expression, sexual relationship, is rape and violation. I know that exists. I am interested in talking about sexual pleasure and what it could mean for women. I'm also not interested in exploring sex as a form of alienation. There's a whole East Village literature – gay, straight, whatever – that has a kind of mindless fucking, where you feel like fucking is just the manner in which our alienation and dehumanization is revealed. I'm interested in talking about sexuality as a return, and a way of re-creating your life as a powerful thing, as a positive force. I'm interested in trying to invent new images for women sexually.

You know, someone interviewed me and asked why there wasn't more lesbian theatre. And I said, there's not very much theatre produced by women. Seven percent, less than seven percent, of all "legitimate" theatre productions in the last year were women's productions. And of that, well . . . what percentage will be lesbian?

SCHNEIDER: What do you see in terms of the future of WOW?

HUGHES: WOW is just growing by leaps and bounds. Five years ago there were about four of us. Now there's tons of people there that I don't know. Last year we did 18 original shows. This year I have no idea how many shows but there's more than that. WOW is basically a developmental theatre, both in the sense of developing new women theatre artists and in the sense of people who have more experience using it as a place to develop new work. It's really an incubator. It's just not set up to take things to full bloom.

SCHNEIDER: Because of the space?

HUGHES: The space and the fact that it's a cooperative.

SCHNEIDER: What about funding?

HUGHES: There's no funding. There's no funding.

SCHNEIDER: Why is that?

HUGHES: Some people have gotten individual grants. I got a Franklin Furnace grant this year. But there aren't very many funding organizations that are set up to fund something developmental. It's not systematized enough in terms of lengthy résumés and stuff. People, women, can come to WOW and work for a year on other people's shows and then do their own show – they don't have to have any credentials. I think that's really important. You don't have to prove anything other than your willingness to work.

NOTES

1. I was not in Ann Arbor to hear the postperformance discussion of *Dress Suits to Hire*. I formulated my questions from the description of the event in Kate Davy's article in this issue.
2. See *TDR* 32, no. 1 (T117) for Karen Finley's script *Constant State of Desire* and interview with Richard Schechner (293–302 and 254–263 respectively in this sourcebook). See also Elinor Fuchs' "Staging the Obscene Body" on Finley in *TDR* 33, no. 1 (T121).

REFERENCES

Carr, C. (1987) "The Lady is a Dick: The Dyke Noir Theatre of Holly Hughes." *Village Voice*, 19 May:32–34.

Case, Sue-Ellen (1987) "Toward a Butch–Femme Aesthetic." Women in Theatre Conference, keynote address, 2 August: Chicago, IL.

Davy, Kate (1986) "Constructing the Spectator." *Performing Arts Journal* 10, no. 2 (PAJ29):43–52.

Dolan, Jill (1988) *The Feminist Spectator as Critic*. Ann Arbor: UMI Research Press.

KAREN FINLEY

A Constant State of Becoming

An Interview by Richard Schechner

SCHECHNER: You say bookers are canceling *The Constant State of Desire* and your other pieces. What's going on?

FINLEY: People are scared of my information. They really don't know what I'm going to do, they don't like me dealing with sexual issues or political issues.

SCHECHNER: Or the combination.

FINLEY: Yes, the combination.

SCHECHNER: You're a woman in control of yourself. It's not the sexual material in itself. You can go anywhere in this country and rent videos of hardcore porn.

FINLEY: If I was doing porn they'd be very happy. When they book me they think they're going to get some kinky chick from New York going out there shoving my tits in their face. When they find out I'm more than that – well, in London I was canceled out this summer, I was banned by the Westminster Council and Scotland Yard.

SCHECHNER: Did they send you a letter or anything?

FINLEY: I don't have a letter, I can't really prove it, but sponsors are really scared that their funding is going to be taken away from them. The first place [in London] I was asked to stop was at the ICA [Institute of Contemporary Art] and next was AIR [Artists in Residence], a gallery. People say, "Oh, we can't really put you on here, but maybe we could set something up in a loft, not announce it publicly." I could go on performing underground, but I don't want that. I don't do anything that's illegal.

SCHECHNER: Has the same thing happened in the USA?

FINLEY: Yes. At Scream, a club in Los Angeles, they canceled me a week before I was to go on in August. Lydia Lunch performed there, and they were scared of what I was going to do. They told me the vice squad threatened to take their license if they put on someone like me. I lost out at Club New in Miami where they told me I would upset their yuppie clientele. And in Atlanta the owners of a club there all of a sudden chickened out.

SCHECHNER: What scares people so much?

FINLEY: I've gotten letters from institutions – whose names I won't mention – telling me that I just could not perform there, that their city is just not ready for me. In Philadelphia I really want to perform at Painted Bride, but I was told they said, "Oh, Karen Finley, there's no way that she's going to perform here."

SCHECHNER: It reminds me of the 1969 Midwest tour of *Dionysus in 69*. Members of The Performance Group were arrested in Ann Arbor at the University of Michigan, there was a near riot in Colorado Springs at Colorado College, and in Minneapolis we weren't allowed to perform on the University of Minnesota campus although we were booked. The Firehouse Theatre gave us a space downtown. It was a tumultuous time. We were using nakedness and the play combined sex and politics. But a whole lot has happened in 20 years – what is it in your situation that arouses such fear?

FINLEY: I think I stir people to be responsible for what's going on in their own personal lives, in their one-to-one relationships, inter-weaving this into the whole society's corruption. That's very disturb-ing. I destroy the games people live on, a very yuppie world where security is having a $40,000 a year job, or $120,000. People really don't want that questioned. What happened to the motivations of 20 years ago of having a much more socialist-humanist society? We're supposed to have more time on our hands because of technology. But I don't see it going towards culture or helping people.

SCHECHNER: What do you see?

FINLEY: I see people with a lot of anger towards anyone who can't make it, anger towards the homeless, or if you're 18 years old and can't afford to go to college, well it's your own problem. No one wants to help anyone at all. You can see how our social programs are deteriorating. That attitude goes on even in the arts.

SCHECHNER: But how does this relate to, say, in *The Constant State of Desire*, turning men's balls into candy.

FINLEY: I'm talking about abuse. I talk about how old people are disregarded – that if they've only got 10 bucks to their name they're lucky to have 10. Also we're really scared of our own sexuality which is no longer a sexuality of love but a sexuality of violence.

SCHECHNER: It's not only the ideas behind what you're saying, but the very words themselves that scare people – because "sexual women" are often constructed by males as being visible, physical, and literally dumb, without words. Men, and many women too, obviously continue to see women as objects. Women are subjects only in selected fields where they must act according to definite rules that have been set down by men: women are corporate executives, police "men," politicians, etc. But what you are presenting is a woman who is a subject expressing the sexual violence and humor that women are still supposed to be the objects of, or ignorant of, or excluded from. You don't just show it, you talk about it – the shock is in the words you use, more than the gestures.

FINLEY: I think my gestures too. Because if you're not a mother and you're not a whore in this society you're considered unproductive. Woman's value is still based on her biology. If a woman becomes a bank president she still conforms to a male image of what that is. Women executives have not been able to establish their own imagery. The only two things that a woman does that is not compared to a man is giving birth and spreading her legs. I bring that to light, and that's very threatening. Female oppression is everyday, it's the anchor I have to society. If I would choose to have a child right now there are basically no childcare facilities – it's a Catch-22 situation. They want us to do our biology's job, but at the same time they really want to put that down. That's what *The Constant State of Desire*'s about, womb envy. Not penis envy, but womb envy.

SCHECHNER: Go into that a little more.

FINLEY: The reason why the feminine way or the maternal way has been oppressed is because the male energy is so scared of it. And so the only way males can deal with it is to knock it down, to not allow it to come up. In *The Constant State of Desire* I wanted to show vignettes of capitalist, consumer society where people go far out, stretch the boundaries – but still they never can be satisfied. So they take things into themselves, and this is what incest or abuse are about.

SCHECHNER: What about the style of your performances? You're not like Spalding Gray – I also admire him very much – who's laid-back, cool, a person who only occasionally shows how much he's involved in the autobiographical stories he tells. Your stuff is obviously about you but not literally true, a kind of surrealistic, automatic talking. And the way you present yourself is to very often go into a trancelike state, a blank look on your face, a sing-song delivery of lines.

FINLEY: Umm-hmm.

SCHECHNER: How did that style come about, and now, at this moment, could you reflect on that state of being?

FINLEY: That state of being is very natural, so I'm surprised when

Figure 15.1 Karen Finley tossing candies at the audience in *The Constant State of Desire* at P.S. 122, New York City, March 1987. (© Dona Ann McAdams)

people call it a trance state. It's something really lacking in our culture – any kind of religion, or any kind of spiritual mask, or any way of breaking the usual routine of day-to-day acting. When one is emotional, when an event takes someone by surprise, whether it's a death, a birth, or anything, it breaks that nine-to-five type of behavior. That's what I want to be showing. I do go into somewhat of a trance because when I perform I want it to be different than acting. I hope this doesn't sound too dorky or trite – I'm really interested in being a medium, and I have done a lot of psychic type of work. I put myself into a state, for some reason it's important, so that things come in and out of me, I'm almost like a vehicle. And so when I'm talking it's just coming through me. And it's very exhausting. After I perform I have to vomit, my whole body shakes, I have to be picked up and sat down. It takes me about an hour before I stop shaking. When performing I pick up the energies from the people, I got to completely psych into them because I want them to feel that I am really feeling it. Maybe not even my words, but just that energy. I'm giving everything I have to make it an experience. You can't pick that up on film or on disks. It's the live experience, and that's really important.

SCHECHNER: How do you get yourself into that?

FINLEY: Usually a few days before – if I'm working or something – I'm not really there, I'm always thinking what's happening at this moment, so all the information of this moment, any experience that happens to me, I really believe this experience is important to me, everything is a story, everything that I come on is cause and effect. I look on everyone who comes to me as being precious about three days before. I have to be alone; I go into a room and do associative writing. I just open up and start writing. Like I don't rewrite any performances, they're like trance writing, like lots of times I just wake up and it just comes to me. And sometimes I really believe I have other voices coming to me. So I open up to the voices.

SCHECHNER: So this would be a couple of days before?

FINLEY: Yeah. And then the day of it I do not eat from the night before. And what makes the strongest performance is if I completely seclude myself, fast, and not take baths and stay in this certain state I get myself into.

SCHECHNER: And then just before, when the audience is assembling and you're off stage?

FINLEY: I get such horrible stage fright. The day of it I can't remember anything at all. I jitter, horrible smells come out of me, I smoke and

I usually don't. And I never see the audience, I never know if they're there. I never perform for the audience – I mean, sometimes I do, sometimes I break it, sometimes it's too much so I break it – but usually I stay within this energy. I can have things happen to me up there, like pain. You see I never rehearse a performance, that's the scariest thing – that I'm going to go out there and I don't know what I'm doing. That to me is the performance part.

SCHECHNER: But you do the same thing night after night.

FINLEY: Well I have to do that for runs. But I don't consider that performance then. I consider *The Constant State of Desire* a "performance procedure" because I change it, I change the act – but it's getting to be experimental theatre.

SCHECHNER: So *The Constant State of Desire* is a theatre piece not a performance piece?

FINLEY: Yeah. I just did something recently at the Cat Club [New York] that's a performance; it's site-specific.

SCHECHNER: A one-time-only thing.

FINLEY: I can start doing it again, but once you start preparing it and doing it, it changes. I mean I still go into the trance –

SCHECHNER: But then it's something you enter that's familiar to you, rather than something you're hoping will come to you.

FINLEY: Yeah. So that's why I still like to perform in clubs because art spaces – at least in New York, except for Franklin Furnace – have completely removed themselves from spectacle or happenings or any kind of performance event. Nowadays, you have to know, you have to have a proposal. That's really completely destroyed the whole idea of ritual. Ritual is not celebrated at any performance spaces except Franklin Furnace and maybe some other little spaces. I think ritual's something that needs to be celebrated in our culture. You see, I went to school in the late 1960s and 1970s so –

SCHECHNER: Where?

FINLEY: The San Francisco Art Institute. We established the idea of community there. That's also why I like New York a lot, there's a community of artists. I don't think that what I do is anything strange or bizarre. It peeves me off when people act like, "Oh, wow, this is something new," but it's not new at all.

SCHECHNER: Each piece may be new but it's also always in a tradition. Art is like great cooking – food is never new, it's the way things are recombined and displayed.

FINLEY: I feel I'm part of a tradition.

SCHECHNER: Who do you admire in your tradition?

FINLEY: Actually I like writers a lot, and musicians: Truman Capote, Tennessee Williams, Gene Ammons, and Ornette Coleman.

SCHECHNER: You're kind of old-fashioned.

FINLEY: I like old-fashioned stuff, I like Uta Hagen a lot.

SCHECHNER: You don't like punk and new wave or whatever's trendy now?

FINLEY: Yeah, I love the Butthole Surfers, and I like Frank Moore's work a lot, and Survival Research Laboratory.

SCHECHNER: Where is Survival Research?

FINLEY: In San Francisco. And I like Johanna Went. I like people who perform one night and that's it. I like people who take risks.

SCHECHNER: What does it mean to you then that *The Constant State of Desire*'s getting printed in *TDR* with this interview and your photograph?

FINLEY: Well I'm just really, really happy about it because I got some horrible reviews on the piece, and I felt extremely depressed. I felt completely misunderstood, that I had no place to take my work. I wanted to get a legitimacy so I could be doing runs somewhere. I hope that a lot of people who have theatre spaces or who are in organizations that sponsor theatre will say, "Oh, wow, it's in *TDR*, maybe it is OK."

SCHECHNER: You want it to be rebellious, subversive, and OK.

FINLEY: I don't think I ever wanted it to be rebellious.

SCHECHNER: : Really?

FINLEY: I wanted to destroy certain people, but I thought that was part of my tradition. I consider good art that which destroys the last generation's hopes.

SCHECHNER: You just wrote *The Constant State of Desire* straight out?

FINLEY: I didn't do a lot of rewrites. It took a lot of time, I write little sections, and then I sort of associate to them, and it just comes. A lot of the writing happens after I speak it, and then it's written.

SCHECHNER: Is it you – ? Your dreams, your fantasies, or what? Who do these words belong to?

FINLEY: When I write, a lot of it I have actually seen. And a lot of it is from me. They are my words. But I don't write the way some people do – they go out, they look, and they write from a situation. I write more from me.

SCHECHNER: Are you the characters then?

FINLEY: No, no. It's not – no. It's really larger. They're transparent, they're pale pink, and pale blue, and silver –

SCHECHNER: Who are "they" – ?

FINLEY: And a lot of chiffon. I feel they come from here [*gestures to her chest and stomach*]. It is me, but when you do automatic writing, it's a different way of writing. I just go and sit down and I say, "Now is the time," and I start doing it. I have lots of notes, I have eight or 10 boxes, and I do a lot of writing, and I keep notebooks. I write down sentences like all of a sudden I'll write down, "She should not be made to feel ashamed." And I'll go off on that, feel ashamed, or I might know of people's lives that have been shattered, and that it's important for something of their lives to come out. I don't like the writing to sound too calculated. I don't want my pieces to sound like theatre. The chanting, I don't know where that came from.

SCHECHNER: Where did some of the imagery come from? Breaking the eggs in a plastic bag and then rubbing yourself with it?

FINLEY: I wanted to do a celebration and it came to me in 30 seconds.

SCHECHNER: That whole image?

FINLEY: Yeah.

SCHECHNER: It fits so well: womb envy, eggs and women, and the violence against women, the breaking of all those eggs.

FINLEY: At the same time it was beautiful, and afterwards it was a celebration. We don't seem to party with naiveté anymore. Except when I'm playing before people who just don't have any idea about performance art. This past weekend I played in a Chicago club, Metro, and my brothers were in the audience saying, "Wow, this isn't bad, this performance art stuff is pretty good!" They allow themselves to enjoy. Whenever I go to a performance I stand at the back so I can walk out. I always expect the worst. Whenever somebody starts doing really well, people put them down.

SCHECHNER: How old are you? And where have you performed?

FINLEY: Thirty-one. I've played in Chicago, where I was brought up, and San Francisco, and New York. I went to school in San Francisco from 1978 to 1981, then I went back to Chicago. And I came to New York in 1984.

SCHECHNER: Anything else biographical I should know?

FINLEY: One thing that's come up in a lot of articles is that my father committed suicide. That put an effect on me that reality is stronger than art. And it makes me interested in real time. When I'm performing, real time is stronger for me than theatre pretend-time, or the-show-must-go-on attitude. I really don't like that attitude.

SCHECHNER: How old were you when your father killed himself?

FINLEY: I was 21, I was just starting to perform. I was home on Christmas break. I didn't expect him to do it. He went into the garage and shot himself.

SCHECHNER: It was very violent.

FINLEY: Yeah, it was a violent – but I think that – right, it was a violent act.

SCHECHNER: Every suicide is violent, but sleeping pills are a different kind of violence.

FINLEY: In terms of statistics men usually use guns, women use pills.

SCHECHNER: Talk a little more about how this affected you.

FINLEY: Nothing else matters. When something like that happens it doesn't make any difference if at that day I had a million dollars or if I had – or if I had anything materially or careerwise, anything, it would not have made any difference in terms of that act happening. That really put me in such a reality state, of realizing that nothing really ever matters. In some ways, it actually freed me: whatever you have won't matter. Somehow that energy I really put into and show in my work. So even in terms of my content, still even if I'm up here, if five minutes beforehand something happens that's always going to take –, is much more important. Someone suffering is always more important than this work.

SCHECHNER: Does that mean if something were to happen you would stop your work and attend to the person in pain?

FINLEY: Definitely.

SCHECHNER: That puts your work in question, makes it fragile, however strong you may seem, however assured and safe in that trance. Your work is a kind of shimmering that may at any moment get blown away by something that is solid and destructive. The art which you said is destructive is itself susceptible to being destroyed.

FINLEY: My generation, except now with AIDS, has never before had any similar situation – it's always had a sense of immortality.

SCHECHNER: Right. Even nuclear obliteration feels far away, not personal. AIDS is imminent: "Is this person I'm kissing killing me?"

FINLEY: For me it's: "Am I going to see this person in two years? Will this person be gone?" I think it's good to question your mortality. That sense of preciousness is a good respect to have.

PART IV Texts

16

DRESS SUITS TO HIRE

Written by Holly Hughes

(Co-created with Lois Weaver and Peggy Shaw)

(DEELUXE and MICHIGAN are seated as the lights come up. DEE-LUXE's chair faces upstage, MICHIGAN's downstage. They are facing each other as DEELUXE begins to sing.* Gradually, DEELUXE's attention becomes focused on dressing herself, specifically on putting on nylon stockings as she sings. MICHIGAN faces upstage, mouthing the words silently.)

DEELUXE: Gonna fill my mouth with red wine
Gonna fill my head with cement
Gonna fill my ears with cotton wool
Gonna fill my nose with cocaine
Gonna buy myself a diamond ring
Gonna get me on a fast train
Gonna pack my soul in a handkerchief
But will you be there when I come back again?

I will go where you will never find me
I will change so you won't recognize me
Everything I know I'll leave behind me
A distant memory of all the things there used to be
When there was only you and me
I'm gonna run run run
Catch me if you can
I'm gonna run run run
Catch me if you can
I'm gonna run run run so far away
But will you be there when I come back again?

*"Run Run Run" by Peggy Shaw.

You're gonna sit down in your easy chair
You're gonna look out of your window
You're gonna fill your lungs with nicotine
You're gonna bite your nails down to the bone
You're gonna buy yourself a diamond ring
You're gonna get you on a fast train
You're gonna pack your soul in a handkerchief
But will I be there when you come back again. . . .

(DEELUXE's right hand starts to chock her neck until she falls to the floor, apparently lifeless. In fact she is dead for the rest of the play. It seems rigor mortis has set in rather early. MICHIGAN is facing upstage. In her lap a small white dog of a mechanical species – LINDA – begins barking. MICHIGAN turns around to see what LINDA's barking at and discovers DEELUXE.)

MICHIGAN: *(Addressing the right hand of DEELUXE.)* I suppose you know what this will mean. There will be no show. She will be unable to do the show. You're not going to like this. *(MICHIGAN begins searching through the suit coats. She pulls out a phone receiver. Pink, plastic, sans cord – it should be as phony as possible.)* Hello? Ninth precinct? Yes, I'll hold. *(To DEELUXE's hand.)* You're asking for this. *(To phone.)* There's a man in here. I can't say if he's dangerous or not. I don't know any other men so I can't compare. Through the door! He lives with us. More with her than with me. Me, this man, and the body. Yes there certainly is a body. Did I discover it? Many years ago. I first discovered the body in the Hotel Universal in Salamanca. A single light bulb. The light came in through the window. The streets were lit by little oranges. The oranges were perfect and bitter. In this light I lay down on the bed and discovered the body. Especially the legs. She's part palomino. In the legs, pure palomino. Do you know what a palomino is? A race horse covered with Parmesan cheese, yes. That's her. And after that first time I would discover the body again and again. And even when I hate her, I love the body. Who does the body belong to? Partly to me. It belongs to her. I usually say she's my sister and most of the time we are sisters. Sometimes we're even worse. I don't know the address. I don't go out much. I don't go out at all, so I don't need an address. I could describe the place. We live in a town. I've forgotten the name. In the bad part of town. We live in a rental clothing store. It doesn't look like much from the outside. But we have too many clothes for our own good. Is that enough of an address? Could you find us based on what I've just said? You're not there anymore, are you? She's not there anymore either. She's dead.

Do you understand? Never mind, I understand. She probably won't be able to perform anymore. And I will never again lie down in the afternoon and discover the body. (*MICHIGAN replaces the phone in the suit coat. She begins speaking to LINDA.*) Is it cold in here or is it me? (*To DEELUXE.*) Oh, it's you. You should relax. You know there are worse things in New York than being killed by someone who loves you. Like trying to cash a check! Are you mad at me because I said your body belongs to me? (*MICHIGAN kneels down and opens DEELUXE's robe.*) Remember the night we became sisters? I looked out and there were no more stars. The sky was full of teeth. Blue and sharp and they were falling towards us. We were already in the wolf's mouth and it was closing in around us. Our only chance was to become twins. To be swallowed whole. But being twins slowed us down. People don't rent dress suits from twins. But then there was always the body to come back to. I'm not going to look at you any longer. I got to look where I'm going. I never thought I would have to go anywhere.

(*MICHIGAN crosses to the stereo and puts on a scratchy version of Frank Sinatra singing: "A Lover is Blue." While the record plays, MICHIGAN paces, drains her drink and, looking at DEELUXE, polishes off hers as well. The stereo cuts off abruptly. MICHIGAN starts. A small wall sconce comes on. When MICHIGAN turns around to look at it, the light cuts off. The stereo comes on suddenly, it's the beginning bars of "Temptation" by Perry Como. MICHIGAN backs away from it. DEE-LUXE's dress falls off its hook. MICHIGAN stands still, afraid. Lights slowly crossfade up – it's morning. MICHIGAN begins talking to LINDA again.*)

MICHIGAN: Born in that cold snap spring won't come time of year. Under the sign of Go Fish. My Venus was stuck in the mud. Mud a' the Bad River, she's acting up again. Outgrowing her banks. Slipping through locked doors, spitting up coffins and dead Chevrolets. Leaving turds in the hope chest. Stores running outta Birdeye's Frozen Vegetables and everything plaid. People getting nervous they'd have to eat fresh food and wear solid colors. Thought the end of the world had come to Michigan. Nobody's hair would hold a set. Forsythia blooms so hard and sudden she cracks the plate glass windows and then freezes all the way back to the ground. And they blamed my mother. She was full of too much bad river water. The end of the world, not spring, was coming to Michigan. And I was the first robin of disaster. When I started breathing on my own the doctor went and beat me anyway and Momma she's screaming, "What is it? Is it a girl?" And the doctor's screaming, "She's an animal!" Animal, doc, you said it! I do the Rin-Tin-Tin, I get down on all fours. Being a girl is just a phase I'm going through. I feel my own ass up and it's ticking like a time bomb. I am the end of the world after. Tick tock through the teacher's lounge where Mr. Science pins you against the wall in the name of higher. I like being pinned down, an' what do you think of that? An' he says, "I bet you wish you hadda father," an' I say, "Nope, I wish I had his clothes though," and I play with his tie and he's screaming to stop it o please stop it but we don't stop it we both want it till his tie is exploding in my hand like a trick cigar and he slaps me hard and says: "You're an animal!" Bomb on outta there. By now I'm sweating hard and I break out in titties. See the girls in the hall and my milk drops down. I got what they want, and I wanna give it to them and I do. Right on the pink plastic floor. Ever seen a bunch a lamprey eels up close? Well they're everywhere in Michigan now and there're these girls too, their mouths are little oohs. Just made to suck. Go on, suck the life outta me, I wanna feel my life in somebody else's mouth. Makes me know what Jesus feels. At communion. He feels good. We take communion to make Jesus feel better. Jesus feels like a big rare roast beef on a platter squirting blood and fat on a platter and lifting his hips to heaven beggin' for it! "O God, yes! Yes, I need it, this is my body, hurry up and take it! Take me! Ketchup, Mustard, and the Holy Ghost are with me! Please god, o my god, O my god EAT ME!" Then the girls get what they want, what we both want and they stop being eels and go back to being girls again and I'm just barely ticking when they slap me hard an' say: "You're an animal!" I don't want nobody anymore. I wanna be myself, just me and moon. I feel her before I see her. The moon pulls something tight in me. I get that ocean feeling. Ol' Michigan she was an ocean before she was anything else. A blue-green bottomless pit, that's what's in me. The moon she could be anything she wants. She's a bigger prize than you can win bowling, she's that white bread women keep between their legs. She's a mirror, I'm not afraid to look. Oh, yoo hoo! Mrs. Moon? (*Piano music up – "Amato Mio." French windows swing open.*) You're so smart and Italian. Tell me what I am.

(*DEELUXE begins to sit, opening a giant fan as she does. She's singing "Amato Mio" à la Bela Lugosi, i.e., lots of rolling eyebrows. At the end of every phrase DEELUXE strikes another pose against the fan. She looks like a singing Art Deco vase. MICHIGAN strikes poses of terror in unison with DEELUXE. At the song's end, DEELUXE picks up the illuminated tulips and offers them to the horrified MICHIGAN.*)

MICHIGAN: Why did you come back?

DEELUXE: The car.

MICHIGAN: The car?

DEELUXE: The keys!

MICHIGAN: They won't let you. Expired!

DEELUXE: Why? My license is good!

MICHIGAN: Not your license! You're no good. You're expired! They won't let a dead woman run around in a Chevrolet!

DEELUXE: I'm taking the Cadillac! Kiss me and say you're sorry.

MICHIGAN: You'll make me sick! Your kisses are more ice water down my neck.

DEELUXE: You're my sister. I got rights.

MICHIGAN: I'm not your sister. I'm a White Christmas. I'm the wrong age for you. The age when you can't be sick. The Ice Age! (*Pause.*) Close the window. (*DEELUXE crosses and closes the window. She remains facing upstage, her back to MICHIGAN.*) We need more sherry.

DEELUXE: I've had all I want.

MICHIGAN: We've exhausted the reserves.

DEELUXE: I'm sick of sherry.

MICHIGAN: There's money in the pocket.

DEELUXE: Is that a threat?

MICHIGAN: Get enough.

DEELUXE: I've had enough.

MICHIGAN: We need more.

DEELUXE: (*Turning around to face MICHIGAN.*) We? You! You need more. More of what?

MICHIGAN: You know.

DEELUXE: More of the same. More of the same conversations. More of the same air. Well not me. I want.

MICHIGAN: What?

DEELUXE: I don't know. But it's not in this shop. It may not even be on this block. I may have to cross Second Avenue to get it. I know I don't want the same thing because day after day I have the same thing and at the end of the day I still want.

MICHIGAN: Hurry.

DEELUXE: You can't tell me what to do anymore. Well, I'm going. And I'm taking the money. (*DEELUXE removes a piggy bank from a suit coat pocket.*) Not for sherry. I'm getting what I want. (*She moves toward the exit.*) And if I come back and I'm not saying that I will, I'm not telling you a thing. I need a secret. Well, my mind's made up. Nothing you can do or say can stop me. (*Pause.*) Well, this time I'm really going. Don't try to get in my way. Goodbye.

MICHIGAN: Go on.

DEELUXE: (*Turning around and recrossing the room.*) I'm doing what I want and I want to stay. (*DEELUXE hunts through the boxes to find her clothes. She begins dressing. MICHIGAN and LINDA observe.*) They said a lot of things about us. 'Cause of where we lived. You know that swamp. Used to be a river running through there but the river got lost and turned belly up. Went dark and stinky and we called it "home." Said we must be a lot like that lost river. Backed-up. Scum. Living there in that place mutts went to die. Most people don't like mud. That's 'cause they don't know anything about it. And they said we went to the Dairy Queen any chance we got. Just climbed outta the mud and went down and grabbed a Mr. Softee. But not them. Dairy Queen wasn't good enough for the McDonald's crowd. And that was just another reason for them to hate us. Us. Me and my mother, talk of the town. And my talk stank worse than their mud. About my mother they said she wasn't a full-time woman. That other times she was a mud puppy and a river pussy. That we lived in quicksand and ate outta cans. That she had every single Petula Clark record and had to play them up full every night before she could get to sleep. That she looked right into men's crotches and if she didn't like what she saw she gave them a faceful of her muddy spit. Nasty talk about my mother. But it didn't hurt me none. Because it was all true. Every stinky last word of it, true. And the truth can't hurt you. Not if you're a young girl with mud on the brain. And everywhere this young girl went the talk went too. Most of it about me and the new one. Me, you know my story by looking at me once. And her, that two-bit, small-town Pekinese. About her and me being lesbians. And that talk didn't hurt either. I coulda laughed. Lesbians. If it was that simple, that easy. Muff-divers. They didn't know the half of it. (*DEELUXE is fully* *dressed in her satin strapless gown. LINDA begins barking in MICHIGAN's lap.*)

MICHIGAN: (*Placing LINDA on the floor.*) What is it, Linda? You want to go out? You don't want to go out. I went out once. Five years ago. There's nothing out there. What do you smell? Pussy! No, Linda, no! No more pussy for us. That's just Little Peter. You know him, Little Peter from across the street. He had a nice thing going till he got his hands on that wildcat. No man can handle a wildcat. Nothing cuts as deep as mean pussy.

LITTLE PETER: (*Spoken by DEELUXE. LITTLE PETER occasionally possesses DEELUXE's right hand.*) That's it. We're closed! Scram! Everybody but you sweetheart. (*To DEELUXE.*) Let me see your face. Hmmm. I like the eyes. Let's see the teeth. Nice. I like the face. But I don't like your song.

DEELUXE: Nobody likes it, that's why it's so good.

LITTLE PETER: Ooooh, honey, you're what's good.

DEELUXE: Deeluxe.

LITTLE PETER: (*Slaps DEELUXE.*) Guess again, sweetheart, you don't got a name. You don't need a name. You work for me now. Only name you got to remember is Little Peter. All you got to do is let him, love him. Let him touch your hair. How you make your hair do that? The way it comes out of your head like your brain's on fire. (*LITTLE PETER's hand reaches for DEELUXE, who flinches.*) What started that fire in you? You can tell Little Peter.

MICHIGAN: That tiger was getting the best of Little Peter and he didn't even know it. We just called her a tiger 'cause there weren't words for what she was. Half woman, half something weird. French, maybe. All cat.

LITTLE PETER: You think I want to hurt you? I want to be nice to you. It's you that makes me hurt you. You hurt yourself. Look at me. Not the eyes. At the hands. Don't the hands tell the truth? They want to be nice to you. Think of them as your own hands. Think of me as a part of you. Hmm, there. What's your name now?

DEELUXE: Deeluxe.

LITTLE PETER: Forget it! That part is over. Got it? Put some clothes on. Some, but not too many. And honey. I don't like girls who cry about their mother. Don't sing that song again.

MICHIGAN: Maybe I was as big a sucker as him. Even a dog's got sense to be afraid of cats. One look at her pelt and I went stupid. Maybe I was as big a sucker as him. I knew what a 150 pounds of killer pussy'd do to a man. What I didn't know is what it could do to a woman. (*MICHIGAN crosses to DEELUXE. The spirit of LITTLE PETER seems to have left her, but DEELUXE is wary of MICHIGAN.*) We need more sherry to tide us over.

DEELUXE: You can see into the future, can't you?

MICHIGAN: (*Reaching for the LITTLE PETER hand.*) Give me your hand.

DEELUXE: You know how it ends, don't you?

MICHIGAN: I need your hand.

DEELUXE: Why this hand?

MICHIGAN: That one you were born with and this the one you made for yourself. Give.

DEELUXE: It's not mine to give.

MICHIGAN: What?

DEELUXE: It's not MY hand!

MICHIGAN: What could it be then?

DEELUXE: It could be anything. It works against me. I have no feeling in it. And it's not an "it." It's a he. He does what he wants and when he wants. He's an underground river that empties into my heart. I know what my heart is. It's a red whirlpool and I got to watch so I don't fall in. And this hard is proof. Proof I was hit. Heat lightning. My own fault. Storks like trailer parks. I could never stay but when the pressure drops.

MICHIGAN: You look fine. (*Still trying to get the hand.*)

DEELUXE: I'm far from fine. I'm a tree and I been hit bad. Still look like a tree on the outside but on the inside there's just animals and disease and no tree left. (*MICHIGAN is finally able to get DEELUXE's hand.*) What's he say?

MICHIGAN: He says your head line and your heart line split early on. He says you have a long life.

DEELUXE: How does it end?

MICHIGAN: It doesn't end really. Your life line runs into your veins.

DEELUXE: It's not forever I want!

MICHIGAN: OK. It ends with you getting sherry.

DEELUXE: That's not how it ends. It ends with me leaving and never coming back! And then my life will start. You can't stop me!

(DEELUXE crosses to the rack of tuxedos and begins rifling through them as though she were going to get dressed and leave. MICHIGAN watches without concern. DEELUXE pulls an innocent-looking scarf out of a suit pocket but the scarf is a huge backdrop of a desert scene. At this point, real time stops. That is, time stops moving only forward. The following scene works in two ways: as a flashback – à la Billy Pilgrim in Slaughterhouse Five, the characters become unstuck in time – and also as a ritualistic reenactment of a past event. MICHIGAN begins to loosen her robe, and DEELUXE pins up the scarf-backdrop like a sheet hung out to dry.)

DEELUXE: *(Without conviction, as MICHIGAN throws over her robe.)* I'm going anyway.

(In unison, the two begin to dress for the ritual. MICHIGAN holds up a pair of pink high-heeled cowboy boots as DEELUXE removes a pair of rhinestone earrings with fetishistic attentiveness. DEELUXE picks up a toothpick while MICHIGAN sticks a wad of bubble gum in her mouth. They reach behind the hanging suits to pull out a pair of day-glo hula hoops. As MICHIGAN begins to cross downstage center, DEELUXE puts on a cowboy hat.)

MICHIGAN: *(Addressing the audience and slinging her hoop.)* Thirteen years old. Mama called me a woman and slapped me hard and gave me a silver dollar with a Bible verse. "Ask and you shall receive." I put my Bible verse into the candy machine, pull hard, nada. Being good don't buy you sweet things anymore I'm thinking when the foreign car pulls up and snake pops out. A real señor monsieur type a snake: cologne, real leather shoes coiling down the sidewalk. No offer a candy just gives me one hard bite and he's off. Greases back his hair with mother's milk and takes off with those other too-handsome kinda guys. Nothing showed on the outside but I was bleeding bad on the inside. Skin goes the color of flophouse sheets. Poison's working on me and all I wanted was some more poison. Mama taught us to feed a fever and I got a hot python squeezing that little girl's heart. All that sugar and spice running down my legs and staining up those spanky pants. My heart was sweating and contagious with that secret dirt and I ripped those panties off and went without underwear. Hoping for an accident and soon. Poison's gotta work itself outta you and the only way outta you is into somebody else. Felt like touching my new wound, but didn't dare. Knew somebody would lose a finger in there and it wasn't gonna be me. Disguised myself with a cross around my neck and a kilt on too. Let that skirt ride up and my bare ass rose like a wet moon over the candy store. Snake on down to the mall. Coiling and uncoiling in the dust. Looking for somebody to infect. Poison's gotta work itself out. Staring at all those girls that never got bit. The blonde that would bring out the blonde in me. Take my sweet meat out behind the cheap shoe stores and lay her down in the astroturf and make her mine. Carve my initials on the insides a her thigh with my tongue. Gonna give her a little scar to remember me by, gonna match mine. I'm shaking, I'm rattling, baby needs a new way to sing the blues, come on, come on, let's go, snake eyes.

(*MICHIGAN drops her hoop. Music up, it's the instrumental theme from "A Man and a Woman." DEELUXE crosses to center stage moving as much like a cowboy as you can in a strapless gown and heels. DEELUXE snaps her hula hoop over to MICHIGAN so that it rolls past her, then boomerangs back. MICHIGAN catches it. Music fades out as they begin to speak.*)

MICHIGAN: Filler up?

DEELUXE: Just five dollars, thanks.

MICHIGAN: Oil OK? Water? Small engine.

DEELUXE: Checked it this morning in Tulsa.

MICHIGAN: Oh, the big city, huh? And they didn't tell you about me in Tulsa? They didn't tell you this was your last chance?

DEELUXE: Every place on this road says that.

MICHIGAN: Well I am flattered. You know what they say about imitation! Everyone wanting a piece of my action. Maybe they can sucker a few but they can't improve on reality. Believe me, I've tried. I'm the only real thing for 50 miles around, I'm it. I'm the end of the line.

DEELUXE: OK, keep the change, just give me the keys.

MICHIGAN: Just where you think you going in such an all-fired hurry? California?

DEELUXE: So what?

MICHIGAN: California! Whatcha gonna do in Cala . . . ha, ha, fornia?

DEELUXE: Look around.

MICHIGAN: Oh, there's a lot to see out there in California, all right. Man-size mice dancing with movie stars with missile-sized tits. Or is it tit-sized missiles? Two-stepping through the mud slides. No, you sure don't want to miss that. You'll never make it.

DEELUXE: I'm gonna see California.

MICHIGAN: You're gonna see California but you're not leaving this station. 'Cause I already seen California and I'm gonna show you my shots. I got all the best places. (*MICHIGAN begins to display her tattoos as though they were souvenirs.*)

DEELUXE: Disneyland? Knott's Berry Farm? Universal Studios? Marineland? (*DEELUXE's hand is resting on MICHIGAN's crotch.*)

MICHIGAN: Sorry about Marineland. Dropped my camera into the killer-whale tank. Didn't dare go in after it. Sharks are terrified of me. Are you ready to see California? (*"A Man and a Woman" theme music up, DEELUXE takes out her toothpick as MICHIGAN spits her gum out into her hand. They kiss. After the kiss, they replace the toothpick and gum. Music fades as they begin to speak.*)

DEELUXE: So that's California, huh?

MICHIGAN: Yeah.

DEELUXE: So we should do something.

MICHIGAN: So.

DEELUXE: Why stay here?

MICHIGAN: So what and just because.

DEELUXE: That's what I thought.

MICHIGAN: So what if I got no friends and no money. There's no snakes here. I could go someplace and get friends and money but then I might get snakes. Besides, my nothing is better than your something.

DEELUXE: Well, I was just thinking. . . .

MICHIGAN: Don't start. Just shut up and be happy. (*She picks up her hula hoop and begins to rattle it.*)

DEELUXE: What's that?

MICHIGAN: A snake.

DEELUXE: You promised no snakes! (*MICHIGAN slips the hoop over
DEELUXE's head.*)

MICHIGAN: Quick!

Figure 16.1 "Marineland?" (© Dona Ann McAdams)

DEELUXE: What?

MICHIGAN: Here!

DEELUXE: How?

MICHIGAN: Suck! (*They kiss. The hoop drops.*) I'm beginning to like this desert air. So refreshing. (*Pause.*) You spit it out didn't you?

DEELUXE: What?

MICHIGAN: The poison.

DEELUXE: What poison?

MICHIGAN: My poison. You spit it out?

DEELUXE: I swallowed it. (*MICHIGAN crosses upstage and begins folding up the backdrop. DEELUXE faces the audience.*)

DEELUXE: She's got a bad heart. The kind you die from. Runs in the family. I gotta bad heart too. Just not the kind you die from. The kind that makes you wear too much eye makeup. She's my cousin, come up from one of those sweaty states. She wouldn't sweat in a forest fire. Ice wouldn't melt in her mouth. I make a little bet with myself. I can make her sweat. The first time I know for sure I got heart problems is when my cousin came to visit. Heat spell. Bad heart and bad heat spell couldn't keep my cousin from pitching pop-ups in the garden. Takes everything she has and makes it into a ball. Something in me follows that ball up, and it hangs in the air a moment seems like forever then into the dirt. I can't throw, can't make a fist. She can throw and stay cool. She's a little bit Catholic. So yellow her hair it hurts my teeth. I sneak her weenies on Friday and I don't tell on her forbidden patent leathers hoping they'll reflect up to that place she's got muscles girls don't, got heart places boys don't. Don't want to do nothing about it yet, still that bad heart of mine wanna bite. She's still not sweating but I get to sleep with her because there's not enough beds. I iron my father's shorts and bleach his stains to send her roses. Downstairs with her, the fake wood, the pump straining to keep us from going under. The earth sweating through the fake wood. Lip syncing to 45s I got the aspirins she got the cokes waiting for it to happen. And the sweat is all over us now, hers and mine together tasting like a memory of a place I never been. Waiting for it to happen, for one heart to give out, for the rattler to strike. (*LITTLE PETER begins to invade DEELUXE. Her hand begins twitching and finally, singing.*)

LITTLE PETER: She may be weary,
Women do get weary,
Wearing the same shabby dress.
And when she's weary,
Try a little tenderness.

(*To DEELUXE.*) Yeah, go on and try it sucker, see what it'll get you.

DEELUXE: I can do it.

LITTLE PETER: We aren't talking about an "it" here to do. We are talking skirt, a woman, a Jane.

DEELUXE: So?

LITTLE PETER: So you don't do a woman. You handle her.

DEELUXE: Like you used to handle me, huh.

LITTLE PETER: Correction, carrot brain, like I did, do, and will handle you.

DEELUXE: Stay outta this.

LITTLE PETER: I'll sit out this fox trot, but I'll be around. (*DEELUXE crosses to MICHIGAN and takes off her hat.*)

DEELUXE: I'm back. I'm sorry.

MICHIGAN: No you're not.

DEELUXE: I know you said you wanted to be alone.

MICHIGAN: Did I?

DEELUXE: You said I shouldn't see you again. (*MICHIGAN starts laughing.*) What's so funny?

MICHIGAN: You should laugh. Be happy. I thought tall people laughed a lot.

DEELUXE: What about?

MICHIGAN: About me being such a liar. I didn't want to be alone. Did you want me to be alone?

DEELUXE: No.

MICHIGAN: And wouldcha leave me alone?

DEELUXE: No.

MICHIGAN: Until?

DEELUXE: No until. I won't leave.

MICHIGAN: Period?

DEELUXE: Period.

MICHIGAN: Wouldcha leave if I asked you to go?

DEELUXE: I would try.

MICHIGAN: You would.

DEELUXE: If you asked.

MICHIGAN: Oh.

DEELUXE: But I couldn't leave.

MICHIGAN: Well if you can't leave then I guess you can stay. (*MICHIGAN starts laughing.*)

DEELUXE: This time it's really not funny.

MICHIGAN: Show me. Make me stop laughing if you don't like it.

DEELUXE: (*Addressing her LITTLE PETER hand.*) Help me. I don't know what to do.

MICHIGAN: (*Singing.*) You won't regret it,
> Women don't forget it,
> Love is their whole happiness.

Aren't you glad I stuck around? OK, now let's try a little tenderness. (*DEELUXE displays an invisible key to MICHIGAN. Then she mimes locking the door with it and swallowing the key. It's as though her entire body has been taken over by LITTLE PETER.*) Did you see what I did with that key?

MICHIGAN: So what?

LITTLE PETER: That's what I'm going to do to you.

MICHIGAN: Huh.

LITTLE PETER: I'm gonna swallow you whole. There's a part of you nobody sees. A part I know is there. Like I know that white stuff is in the middle of those black cookies. But you gotta twist open the whole rotten thing to get to it. (*He/she begins caressing MICHIGAN more fiercely than tenderly.*) That's what I'm gonna do to you. It's your secret now but I'm going to know it too. Make your cream the glue between us. No matter what it costs me. Or you. (*He/she yanks MICHIGAN to her feet. LITTLE PETER addresses DEELUXE.*)

MICHIGAN: Aren't you afraid?

DEELUXE: No.

MICHIGAN: You should be. You're lucky you're so dumb.

DEELUXE: You're afraid.

MICHIGAN: Of what? I'm the scariest thing going.

DEELUXE: There's something even worse.

MICHIGAN: Yeah?

DEELUXE: The cold.

MICHIGAN: What's that? I ain't been cold a day in my life. You afraid?

DEELUXE: Yes I got no feeling anywhere.

MICHIGAN: So?

DEELUXE: So I could die and not even notice it. (*French windows blow open. Howling wind is heard.*)

MICHIGAN: Shut it!

DEELUXE: You shut it!

MICHIGAN: You're closer.

DEELUXE: Closer to what?

MICHIGAN: The window.

DEELUXE: I wasn't talking about the window! (*MICHIGAN closes the window. Howling stops.*) I thought you were hot enough for both of us. I guess I was wrong.

MICHIGAN: I got the heat sweetheart, I just don't give it away. (*MICHIGAN pulls a long black flashlight out of a suit coat pocket.*)

DEELUXE: What's that for?

MICHIGAN: Stars.

DEELUXE: It's aimed down at the street. That's a funny place to look for stars. There's no stars on this part of Second Avenue. Just three bums pissing on a futon. Hey! You can see right into my bedroom! You been looking at me!

MICHIGAN: No.

DEELUXE: Yes you have. This is proof.

MICHIGAN: I been more than looking. I been watching. That's looking with a reason.

DEELUXE: What's the reason?

MICHIGAN: 'Cause you're my kind of star.

DEELUXE: What's that?

MICHIGAN: A falling star. Wanna see one? It's a nice night for viewing. Rare to see so many binaries.

DEELUXE: Binaries?

MICHIGAN: Doubles. A pair of stars so close they cannot escape each other.

DEELUXE: Close as sisters?

MICHIGAN: Closer. Like twins.

DEELUXE: How come they stay together?

MICHIGAN: Gravity.

DEELUXE: I don't see anything like that.

MICHIGAN: And the closer they get the worse it gets.

DEELUXE: What?

MICHIGAN: The pull, and then it's . . . kaboom. But there's that moment right before the end when they're the brightest thing on Second Avenue. Just a big red nova.

DEELUXE: I hadda one of those once. Not fancy but a good car.

MICHIGAN: 'Course even the brightest star can get stuck with a black hole.

DEELUXE: What's that?

MICHIGAN: Something so dense you can't imagine it. You wait and wait and the bang you counted on never comes.

DEELUXE: Is that what makes a star fall?

MICHIGAN: Almost anything can make a star fall. Here's one now, about to fall. (*MICHIGAN directs DEELUXE's flashlight so it shines on herself. Throughout the following monolog. MICHIGAN strikes different peepshow poses while DEELUXE observes her as attentively but asexually as a nerd looking at an ant farm.*)

DEELUXE: I see it. Looks familiar. Looks like me. That was the year I was living alone in Bad Axe. Just wouldn't move in with him. "What's the difference?" he'd say. Then he'd go off and leave me trying whether to decide whether to be a lesbian today or put it off till tomorrow. And then I'd put on plastic nurse's shoes. Wait on tables. Getting tips in Bible verses. People with one eye ate at this place a lot. I guess it was just about the favorite place of one-eyed people to eat. Down at the mall. Not even a real mall, fucking shopping center. One day I get up with him and alla sudden I'm falling. And I tried to break my fall by reaching out for him. But it didn't come out that way. I socked him once, twice in the jaw and kept falling. Falling into the Chevy with the bad plates with a cat and a raincoat. I don't know what started it and what I'm falling into.

MICHIGAN: (*Directing flashlight so it falls on her breasts.*) Probably the moon.

DEELUXE: I dunno. Is the moon that strong?

MICHIGAN: Take a look and see.

DEELUXE: Wow. Get a load of that moon. She's so full. There's two moons and they're both full.

MICHIGAN: Don't tell me she's not strong enough to pull you off course. (*MICHIGAN takes the flashlight out of DEELUXE's hands.*)

DEELUXE: What's going on here?

MICHIGAN: I got nothing to hide. (*MICHIGAN grabs DEELUXE's bodice.*) What about you?

DEELUXE: Don't get me naked. I get so Italian when I'm naked.

MICHIGAN: Thought you wanted that secret. Wanna touch it? Touch me the way you touch him.

DEELUXE: I don't!

MICHIGAN: Don't lie. Just tell me you love me.

DEELUXE: I can't say that.

MICHIGAN: (*MICHIGAN wraps DEELUXE in the strand of pearls.*) There, does that make it any easier? (*The two are bound together and begin a slow circle dance.*) Soon as they start to shine they start to change. The center contracts. Pressure at the center rises. And the center can't hold up. (*DEELUXE backs away. The pearls break. DEELUXE and MICHIGAN face each other for a long beat. Then*

DEELUXE turns away. MICHIGAN sinks to the floor and begins picking up the pearls.) You take care of something, it grows. You can see I got the knack. Too big? Is there such a thing as "too big"? Besides it's just the way I am. Too damned juicy for my own good. With you around gets wicked. One look at you and my pink pulp starts pounding. (*DEELUXE begins to unzip her gown.*) Wanna know something? They're gonna get bigger. That pink is gonna go all the way into red. Then you watch out. My sap's running from the heat of your eyes. That special blue heat outta the eyes gets the pink ocean stirred up. That's when you squeeze them. Put the muscle on those peaches till my bucks are bucking like I'm riding an invisible palomino. (*DEELUXE is in her underwear, black tap pants and a corset. She reaches out for MICHIGAN. Pause.*) Well, I dunno, I might let you. These peaches getting mighty tight. But I gotta decide. What you ever done for me except make me cry? Right now I'm sobbing bad. Just look, I'm crying for you. You look hungry. Come on get it, squeeze it outta me, suck it outta me. I wanna be totally Spain when you're done with me. (*MICHIGAN begins to put on a filmy peignoir as she sings the following song. Her actions are as flirtatious as if she were stripping. MICHIGAN sings.*)

> Bugs are bitin'
> Fish are jumpin'
> When my baby starts a humpin' me
> Hot cross buns
> Always beg for jam
> Every beaver
> Needs a beaver dam
> Taste of fish
> Taste of chicken
> Don't taste like the girl I'm lickin'
> She puts the cunt back in country
> Pulls the rug out from under me
> In case you are wondering
> She can put what she wants in me.
> Hot sweet cream
> Dripping from my pet
> How I scream
> When she gets me wet
> With her finger
> On my sugar plum
> There she lingers
> Till I start to cum

'Cause she puts the cunt back in country
Pulls the rug out from under me
In case you are wondering
She can put what she wants in me.

(DEELUXE is tired of the tease. She dons a black tuxedo jacket. Its a magician's jacket: there are scarves, paper flowers, etc., in the pockets. During the following monolog, DEELUXE fumbles with the jacket and the objects seem to fly from her pockets. DEELUXE is facing the audience.)

DEELUXE: Alotta people ask me: What about Ohio? And I have to tell them what I know. Because I'm part buckeye. Not that you would know. That's why I never take all my clothes off all at the same time so you can never see the Ohio in me. But I haven't forgotten about Toledo and I won't. The very mention of the word "Toledo" makes me wanna puke. Toledo used to belong to us. We went to war to save it. People always ask: "Why'd you bother to have a war in Toledo? Aren't the winters there war enough?" Things got pretty bad between me and Toledo and a pig was killed. The government came in like they always do but the fighting went on when no one was looking. They took away Toledo. Gave us this little chunk of perpetual January that used to belong to Minnesota. Don't even get me started about Minnesota. When everybody else is dead I'm going to get a nice slab of Ohio. Right now it's my Uncle Bert's asparagus patch. I hate asparagus. I'm afraid of it. Especially at night when the stalks look like dead people from Toledo giving you the finger. We'd take these trips to visit the land. Going as fast as we could, pretending to be going someplace else. I guess that's the only way to live through a trip to Ohio: pretend to be going someplace else. And keep the window rolled up tight. Ohio air can make you dizzy if you're not used to it. Remember: in the winters here they set the rivers on fire. We get to the land and they break out the asparagus and put on the ham. Aunt Helen is fat and she waits on the skinny people. We do things that way in Ohio: the fat people wait on the skinny ones. 'Course everyone in my family is fat. Except for Bert. But then he's not one of us. The only reason they let him stay in Ohio is he porked Aunt Helen back in that freak thaw last leap year. After dinner Bert helps Helen up the stairs. I do the dishes and they do it. When a 350-pound woman has sex in a wood-frame house in Ohio, you know about it. Bert liked to get her right after the ham when she still had mayonnaise on her arms. Helen died before Bert learned what to do about asparagus. He just went out back and lay down in the mud. Face down. We left him that way. Very polite. And then I read in this magazine about this man that loves mud.

Loves it better than he loves his dead wife. "Mud is better than any woman. You don't have to wait till after dinner. And it's romantic. After a rain. During a sunset. You just find a place and stick it in." And the letter was signed. Bert from Ohio. And that's Ohio.

(MICHIGAN crosses to the stereo and puts on a record – "Temptation." They do a tango which ends with MICHIGAN dipping DEELUXE. Suddenly, LITTLE PETER appears and begins talking to DEELUXE. MICHIGAN watches the dialog like someone watches a seizure or a crazy on the IRT.)

LITTLE PETER: We gotta talk.

DEELUXE: Leave me alone.

LITTLE PETER: Alone, who's alone? You're not alone. You probably couldn't ever spell it. Always had me on your side. Don't sleep alone. Don't take a shit alone. Little Peter holds your hand. I seen alone and it's not for you. Maybe I know the wrong kind of alone. You wanna be alone all right, alone with her.

DEELUXE: *(To MICHIGAN.)* Would you like some more sherry? *(MICHIGAN shakes her head no.)*

LITTLE PETER: Why don't you ask her if she wants to be alone with you? Maybe she'd like a chaperon. Go ahead, ask her.

DEELUXE: I'm not going to ask her.

LITTLE PETER: Maybe she'd like me better, huh?

DEELUXE: She won't like you. She can't see you.

LITTLE PETER: She can see me. You're the one who can't see me.

DEELUXE: We're over. I'm not talking to you anymore.

LITTLE PETER: What?

DEELUXE: I said I'm not talking to you anymore. You're not real.

LITTLE PETER: You're doing it sister. Not real. What kinda thing is that to say to a friend? Hey, if I'm not real what does that make you?

DEELUXE: Keep your hands off me.

LITTLE PETER: Deeluxe, please!

DEELUXE: One minute. Just one. But don't go touching me. *(To MICHIGAN.)* There's this guy I know, um – outside. He's outside. That's why you can't see him. I gotta go give him some money. I'll be right back. (*DEELUXE crosses to the stage right window and pulls down the shade. The area is backlit so her shadow appears. The LITTLE PETER hand comes out from behind the shade. DEELUXE's hand follows, grabs LITTLE PETER and "strangles" him. After the LITTLE PETER hand is limp, DEELUXE crosses to MICHIGAN.*) You got to show them. They never believe you till you show them.

MICHIGAN: Is he gone?

DEELUXE: He's gone. Don't think about him. (*Pause.*) What you looking at?

MICHIGAN: You.

DEELUXE: Quit it.

MICHIGAN: You quit it.

DEELUXE: Me? What am I doing? It's not coming from me. I heard about you. What you do to women, what you make other women do. I'm not going to let you do that to me. I'm going to open the window and cry for help. I'm going to get the National Guard, the Marines, the *New York Times*, the Weight Watchers. I'm going to tell the world that evil is alive and well and living on Second Avenue. I'm going to –

(*French windows blow open. Sound of howling wind. MICHIGAN stands up and crosses stage left. She puts on a fox fur stole. It's a larger, more gory version of the type with the head clipping onto the tail.*)

MICHIGAN: Tell me again. What are you going to do? That's what I thought you were going to do. Nothing! And what did you say you thought I was? Tell me.

DEELUXE: You. You're an animal.

MICHIGAN: And what do you think you are? A fucking zucchini?

DEELUXE: Stop. Why don't you stop?

MICHIGAN: Because you don't want me to stop.

DEELUXE: I could make you.

MICHIGAN: Go ahead. Make me.

DEELUXE: Cross this line.

MICHIGAN: I already crossed that line a long time ago. And this line. Go on honey. Do it to me. Do it to me before I cross this line too.

DEELUXE: That's enough.

MICHIGAN: Sure it is. When you're really good you don't have to touch. She walks in the room and you don't touch. You don't even talk. But you feel her on every inch of your body like a suit of clothes you put on and can't take off. Feels like silk. But tight. Like a silk straitjacket. You're in deep and getting deeper. It's like being buried alive. And you like it.

DEELUXE: I won't.... (*DEELUXE attempts to exit, but MICHIGAN grabs her breast.*)

MICHIGAN: There's nothing you won't do. This is what you wanted all along and no one has to know. It'll be our secret.

DEELUXE: What will?

MICHIGAN: Our secret will be what makes you tick. (*DEELUXE's bodice rips. Pearls and magic flowers explode out of it as she breaks away from MICHIGAN.*)

DEELUXE:　　I was never right
　　　　　　Look into my eyes
　　　　　　See the trouble
　　　　　　See the fire under water
　　　　　　See my brain's too big
　　　　　　See my heart's too small
　　　　　　I gotta pump it
　　　　　　That's why I gotta pump it.
　　　　　　I tried to make my heart move another way
　　　　　　But the blood's too thin
　　　　　　Like the see-thru blouse
　　　　　　Momma puts on when Daddy leaves the house.
　　　　　　My body's too fat like Crisco in the pan
　　　　　　It smokes it steams it cries out for meat.
　　　　　　There's no other way your ham sure hits my spot
　　　　　　And if that don't grease the clock
　　　　　　You gotta pump it.
　　　　　　I call my private Jesus on the pay telephone
　　　　　　Down on my knees in a booth filled with piss
　　　　　　Asking the King O'Love won'tcha please
　　　　　　Strike me dead.
　　　　　　I can't live a life with a head too big
　　　　　　I can't get a laugh with a shrunken love pump
　　　　　　My too big head's filled with a too bad thought
　　　　　　It stinks it bites it goes straight to the brain
　　　　　　Till I pump it.

It's not just bad
It's more than bad it's wrong
In the wrong place
My heart got stuck between my legs
You wouldn't think I wouldn't think
Such a tiny thing could put the muzzle on the brain
On those full moon nights the way it beats so bad
No Top 40 drum machine
More a solo with a shake
I gotta bad heart but I'm a nice girl, girl.
I'm not a girl at all, I'm more like a car.
A nice new car, why don't you thumb me down.
I'll let you take the wheel
A woman with a bad heart gets lonely when she drives
    herself insane
Take the wheel and I'll let you bite my ham.
Turn the key over quick, put your boot to the floor
If you don't get the power first
Gotta pump it.

MICHIGAN: I'm getting out of here!

DEELUXE: I'm dying, you can't do that! Rip somebody's heart out and leave them to die!

MICHIGAN: I do it all the time.

DEELUXE: Then it's true!

MICHIGAN: Yes, it's true, let me go!

DEELUXE: If you go I'll die.

MICHIGAN: If I stay you'll be worse than dead. You'll be like me.

DEELUXE: What are you? (*DEELUXE collapses.*)

MICHIGAN: There's a word for it in Michigan. From the early days of Michigan. Before Michigan was Motown, or Ford four-doors, or Gerald Ford and Chevy hatchbacks, and before the soybeans, sweet cherries, and mint fields went in. Before they started burning the sugar beets and soaking the kirbies in barrels of brine. Before they opened the Keewanah for copper pennies. Before all that when all Michigan was cold. Mooneye, steelhead, alewife, all of that. A coupla shriveled spits of land shivering in glacial puddles that'd lost their salt, that's what Michigan was. All she grew was protection from the cold. Beaver protection, and weasel, fisher, marten, mink, red fox, gray fox, catamount, muskrat, lynx, and bobcat too. Fur. Pelts. And all of a sudden, Michigan was full of Frenchmen. They set their trap lines out on the ice. Along the Manistee, the Ausable. But the animals they caught didn't die right away they lay out on the ice freezing and snarling and bleeding until the stars, most of them, fled to Canada. And Orion bent down out the January sky and put a silver bullet in their brain. Silver on the brain, they changed. Became monsters out on that ice. Until the Frenchmen came back and the monsters became hats. Fancy hats and pocketbooks. But there was something else out there. Another sort of animal. Or a woman. They always called her a "she." She came along the trap lines before the Frenchmen. She ripped open the steel and tossed it into the Tittabawassee. She set free the monsters. Whatever she was, she had a mean head on her shoulders shaped like a wedge of Pinconning extra sharp Cheddar cheese gone bad and a fat ass. She was always about 56 years old. And the monsters crashed through the split-level prefab houses of the French-men and fucked their wives and got them full of baby monsters. They don't say this anymore in Michigan. No one knows what happened to the woman who set the monsters free. The woman who was an animal. Loup Garou. They said that women were monsters. Because they had teeth in their parts. And now they say we're not like that. We're not dangerous anymore. But it's a lie. We are monsters. We got teeth in our parts and we're so hungry. If you stay here, I'll eat you alive. Do you understand? Do you still want to be like me? (*MICHIGAN turns upstage and crosses to hang up the fur. While she is still turned upstage, DEELUXE slowly sits up.*) Why did you come back?

DEELUXE: I live here.

MICHIGAN: Lived here. I liked it when you were dead because I got to do all the things I always wanted to but you kept me from doing.

DEELUXE: Like what?

MICHIGAN: Redecorate.

DEELUXE: It's the same.

MICHIGAN: It's not the same. (*DEELUXE moves toward MICHIGAN who is seated.*) This is my chair.

DEELUXE: (*Sitting down in her chair.*) I only been gone five minutes. (*A blue airmail letter falls out of the skylight. MICHIGAN rushes to pick it up, then hands it to DEELUXE.*)

MICHIGAN: It's for you.

DEELUXE: (*Reading the letter.*)

"Dear Deeluxe,
You asked about the future. Here's the deal: it's gonna be just like the past. In the past the heart of the world was filled with carbon and water and that is why we had life on earth. When everything got heavier the world started collapsing in on itself, an old heart in a fat body. Aunt Helen collapsing in Cleveland. After the baby was born. The one who couldn't talk. Or get up to go to the bathroom by herself. The one who's being born killed Helen's only daughter. And Aunt Helen, she just collapsed. Carbon and water into diamonds. And in the future, women will replace the world. In a woman's heart there is rice and water and that is why there is life on earth. But in the future, women will start collapsing the world thick with babies who can't talk and only daughters who live alone on Oreos. And rice and water will be crushed into tears. But no one will cry. The tears will stay inside. They will be the hardest things known to man. Women's tears will be used. In the future, women's tears will put a man on the moon. And in the future, all the men who kill for a living will wear pinky rings with women's tears.
Love always,
Little Peter."
(*Pause.*) So that's the future, huh?

MICHIGAN: (*Pouring sherry for a toast.*) Don't worry. We'll never see it.

(*MICHIGAN starts to raise her glass to DEELUXE's, but the upstage window shade flies up. There is a hand at the window with a pinky ring. DEELUXE and MICHIGAN continue staring at the hand as the lights fade down and out.*)

17

THE CONSTANT STATE OF DESIRE

A Text by Karen Finley

Editor's note: The Constant State of Desire *was first performed at The Kitchen in New York City, December 1986. The following text was altered somewhat in every performance.*

ACT I

(Enter in yellow dress. Hair in chignon. Monolog from overstuffed chair.)

Baby Bird

She dreams. She dreams of strangling baby birds. Bluebirds, wrens, and robins. With her thumb she pushes back on their beak, against their soft small neck till it snaps like a breaking twig.

She dreams. She dreams of being locked in a cage and singing loudly and off key with her loved ones standing behind her whispering very loudly. "She has an ugly voice. Doesn't she? She has an ugly voice." Oh, leave it to the loved ones. To judge us like they do. It's always the loved ones who always interfere with our dreams.

She dreams. She dreams of falling out of a fifth-story window. But she catches her fall by holding onto the window ledge. It's January and the ledge is made of stone and icy cold. The stone, the ice, the cold cuts through her flesh, her fingers, her bone. It doesn't matter though, for she has ugly fingers. And she sees the blood gush out of her limbs, the harder she holds onto the ledge. She can hear her own death. And her husband walks below as she hangs out of the building. But her husband hadn't memorized her shadow and she didn't know how to wear perfume. She wasn't that kind of a girl. So she calls out for help. Help. Heelp. Heellllp. But the wind was in a mean mood and took her cries halfway round the world to a child's crib, so its mother could hear her own child's cries.

This dream was considered very important to the doctors. For in the past she had dreams of tortures, rapes, and beatings where no sounds would come out of her mouth at all. She'd open up her mouth and move her lips but no sounds would come out at all.

But she knew that these doctors were wrong. For these were the same doctors who anesthetized her during the birth of her children. These were the same doctors that called her animal as she nursed. These were the same doctors that gave her episiotomies. No more sexual feelings for her during and after childbirth.

But she knew that it really wasn't the doctors' fault. That the problem really was in the way she projected her femininity. And if she wasn't passive, well she just didn't feel desirable. And if she wasn't desirable, she didn't feel female. And if she wasn't female, well, the whole world would cave in.

Like when Martin died. Like when Desi Arnez, Liberace, Danny Kaye died. What is happening to my heros? They are all dying on me. And Desi will never get back with Lucy. All of my boys are dying on me. All of my babies are dying on me. Oh, I wish I could relieve you of your pain. I wish I could relieve you of your suffering.

Like when my father finally told me he loved me after 40 years then went into the bathroom, locked the door, put up pictures of children from the Sears catalog, arranged mirrors, black stockings and garters to look at while he masturbated as he hung from the shower stall. Whatever turns you on, girl. It's that ultimate erection. It's that ultimate orgasm. Whatever turns you on. Whatever, whatever turns you on.

And when he died – volcanoes erupted, cyclones appeared, coyotes came out of their caves, old people were struck by lightning. Don't you know that I don't want any more deaths on my conscience?

For I already have an abortion on my conscience from when a member of my own family raped me. Don't worry, I won't mention your name. Don't worry, I won't mention you name. And the reason why my father committed suicide is that he no longer found me attractive.

And by now you can tell that I prefer talking about the fear of living as opposed to the fear of dying.

ACT II

(Easter baskets and stuffed animals sit on table. Take off clothes. Put colored unboiled eggs from basket and animals in one large clear-plastic bag. Smash contents till contents are yellow. Put mixture on body using soaked animals as applicators. Sprinkle glitter and confetti on body and wrap self in paper garlands as boas.)

Scene 1
Hate Yellow

I hate yellow. I hate yellow so much. And I see you walking down my neighborhood with your new teeth and solid pastel colored shirts. Yuk.

Don't you know that I'm only happy when I'm depressed? Don't you know I'm only happy when I'm wearing black? That I'm only happy at night. Yes, I'm a creature at night.

Nothing Happened

So I put my head in the oven and nothing happened.

So I fucked you all night long and nothing happened.

So I went on a diet and nothing happened.

So I became macrobiotic and nothing happened.

So I went to the Palladium, the Tunnel, and nothing happened.

So I went down to SoHo and checked out the art scene and nothing happened.

So I quit drugs and nothing happened.

So I worked for ERA, voted for Jesse Jackson and nothing happened.

So I put out roach motels and nothing happened.

So I petitioned, rioted, terrorized, and organized and something is going to happen. Something is going to happen 'cause I'm not going to let you gang rape me anymore walking down my streets that I built with my soul, my creativity, my spit. And you just look at all of my art, Mr. Yuppie, as just another investment, another deal. My sweat, my music, my fashion is just another money-making scheme for you. You are the reason, Mr. Entrepreneur, why David's Cookie McDonald's is the symbol of my culture.

You are the reason why fast food is the only growth industry of this country.

Tie You Up and Steal Your BMW

So I take you Mr. Entrepreneur, Mr. Yuppie, Mr. Yesman and tie you up in all of your Adidas, your Calvin Klein, your Ralph Lauren, your Anne Klein too, your Macy's, your Bloomingdale's. I tie you up in all of your fashion, your pastel cotton shirts of mint green and lilac and you know what? You like it. You like it.

So I open up those designer jeans of yours. Open up your ass and stick up there sushi, nouvelle cuisine. I stick up your ass Cuisinarts, white wine, and raquetball, your cordless phone and Walkman up your ass. And you look up at me worried and ask "but where's the graffiti art" and I say "up your ass." And you smile 'cause you work all day and you want some of the artistic experience, the artistic lifestyle for yourself after work and on weekends.

So I take your yuppie body and let you lick the piss and shit off me on Avenue B. Just let your tongue lick the artistic experience, the attitude off of that street. Then I make you lick the tires of your BMW. Then I leave you on the street and I steal your BMW 'cause I know nothing is going to happen.

So I drive the BMW down the street at full speed. Scaring to death anyone who looks like they hold a political office, anyone who looks like they own private property (I'll show you the burden of private property), anyone who wears a suit. 'Cause you know according to Mr. Andy Somma suits and rock 'n' roll don't mix.

Cut Off Balls

I drive down to Wall Street and break into the Exchange. I go up to all the traders and cut off their balls. They don't bleed, only dollar signs come out. They don't miss their balls 'cause they're too busy fucking you with everything else they've got.

So I gather all their balls, scrotum, testicles and stick 'em in my mouth. I roll 'em around my mouth and I feel like a squirrel in heat. I love the sound of scrotum. I take the balls home and boil them. 'Cause they're small balls and need to be plumped up. After I boil the balls I roll them in my own dung, my manure. 'Cause I'm the Queen of the Dung Dynasty. Then I roll the Dung eggs in melted Hershey's Kisses. Then I roll the scrotum, manure, chocolate-coated balls into fancy foiled papers from found Eurotrash cigarette boxes. Now I've got gourmet Easter egg candy to sell. I sell these Easter eggs to gourmet chocolate shops. And I love to see 9-year-old boys who only communicate with their computers eat their daddies' balls. I love to watch all of you Park Avenue, Madison Avenue know-it-alls eating your own chocolate-covered balls for $25 a pound.

I get my revenge. Oh, I get my sweet revenge.

Lord, why don't you appear to me now?!

Is it because you're a man?

Whatever happened to the Tooth Fairy? Whatever happened to the Easter Bunny? Whatever happened to Andy Warhol?

Dead, girl. Dead.

I know I live in a dead-end time. A dead culture, a dead-end world. I know I've got a dead-end job. Got dead-end housing and a dead-end future for my kids. I know it's a long, long dead-end road. A long, long dead-end road.

Ruenne. Ruenne sleeps with a gun under her pillow. For every time she has intercourse with her husband he defecates uncontrollably as he has orgasm. And the shit is running loose and splatters. Even though she puts down Hefty trash bags over the carpeting and walls, lets the crap dry before pulling it off the plastic, she found the gun to do a better job. She puts that gun in her husband's asshole everytime he is about to cum. The gun up his ass gives her such a sense of power. And for a few fleeting moments the tables are turned for her as she forgets the time when at gunpoint she was forced to perform fellatio in front of her children and pets in her own garage.

And father when I said goodbye to you before I went off to war, you were too busy with your head in the toilet to reply. I just wanted that fatherly hug to a son turning to a man. No, you had to puke your gin, rye, and whiskey in the toilet bowl. And I never forgave you for that. And they sent me to Vietnam on Christmas Day to eat a meal of gray. To clean a dead man's gun, to sleep with an old wound for a blanket. And every man, child, and woman I killed was my father's face in that toilet. And I prayed I'd die at war so my father would learn guilt. I told myself it would be different when I had children. We'd share our experiences and feelings together. We'd be so close. But I'm just like my father, a drunken slob. And the only feelings I share are no feelings at all. Just no feelings at all. The only feelings I share are no feelings at all.

Scene 2
(Return to chair in same costume as Act I.)

Freud
It was really Freud's problem to begin with.

Really. You don't say.

Yes, rumor has it Freud had been sleeping with his daughter and sister-in-law on repeated numerous occasions.

I knew it. That beard and that book on cocaine.

What I wanted to bring up today though is that all fetuses are innately female for the first six weeks.

Is that so. Then that means that perhaps the penis and scrotum are merely an exaggerated clitoris and labia?

Perhaps.

Well, I hope you aren't going to tell me the theory that woman was man's first possession?

Oh, no. I wouldn't dream of saying that. I merely wanted to suggest that it wasn't love that motivated man but the need to possess and master!

Isn't that a little harsh?

The truth is harsh. What are you making for dinner tonight?

Richard's favorite, Hungarian goulash.

Don't you enjoy women's studies' classes?

I certainly do. All of the books. All of the subjects. But if it ever got in the way of me being a proper hostess for Richard's business I'd give it up in a minute. I'd sacrifice anything for my family. To the point of being a boring and phobic person.

Is that why you get headaches?

I'm sick and tired of your asking me about my headaches, my ways, my life. Don't you know that my illness is all I have? That my headaches are my only form of nurturing? My disease is my life, my health. Sure, I take valium. But how can I look at my daughters and sons and try to dispel the myths that have been a tradition for centuries? To just say, "Sure, we're all created equal." I've never been treated equally my entire life. That I'm supposed to be excited that Mary Boone Gallery signed up two women. Wow. Yeah, big fucking deal. Like I'm supposed to be *so* thankful 'cause a chick is on the Supreme Court. You can read your fucking books. But nothing's changed. Nothing has changed.

So let me continue. The one thing then that man could not destroy was woman's ability to produce children that loved her unquestioningly. And even though the man was stronger than the woman slave he could not destroy the bond between the mother and her children. And the father learned that he must earn his child's love.

So maybe it's womb envy instead of penis envy?

Perhaps.

This must've made the father very jealous indeed. Especially when he discovered the woman's ability to produce multiple orgasms. OK. I know some of you guys think you can fuck a couple of times in a row. Big fucking deal. We never have to wait to refuel. Just keep on going.

Perhaps that is a way of looking at it.

So actually man put woman into a position of passivity when it is really the woman who is sexually superior.

Perhaps. But don't ever let them know it!

Paranoia

LET ME TELL YOU ABOUT PARANOIA. Sixty percent of the world's commercial fish stocks are in danger.

Let me tell you about obsession. Grown men force-feeding young boys to produce the perfect shit. The perfect size shit. The perfect smell shit. The perfect color, size shit. In the toilet he slowly drops the turd out of his big pink butt. Let it drop, drop, drop and suck the turd up. Let it drop. Then suck it up!

Let me tell you about POWER. Being gang raped by a group of youths at the age of 15 in the subway. Until they discover my secret of being born without a vagina. They throw me onto the train tracks with their embarrassment and the train rolls over me. And all my mother could say was "See, the reason why God didn't give you a vagina is so that you wouldn't be violated in this way." So I knew I couldn't be a mother or whore so the only occupation left was religion. Until I discovered that God is a man. So I spend my life thinking of a time when virgins had babies and miracles happened to the meek.

And we all discussed our psychological disorders. Gary had overdosed, fell into a coma, and imagined tigers and angels dancing on his neck. Rachel imagined she had cancer and all of her organs were infected. Rita washed her hands all night long till her hands were chapped raw and bleeding. Jeffrey heard voices. One told him to marry Manson. Two told him to kidnap Mrs. Stern and impregnate her, and three to become Jodie Foster's bicycle seat.

ACT III

First Sexual Experience, Laundromat

My first sexual experience was at the time of my birth, passing through the vaginal canal. That red pulsing tunnel, that alley of love. I'm nothing but a human penis. And at the time of my birth I had an erection. I'm fucking my own mama at my birth. It's the smell, it's the sight of my mama that keeps me going. Keeps me kicking.

So I spend my life looking for hot mamas with hot titties in hot laundromats. I go out in my real car. The symbol of my masculinity, cruising for mothers. I love to find a hot, young mama with a young, bald baby. A brunette, a page boy. And she wears a pink gingham dress, the symbol of her martyrdom. I love the smell of the dryer, the sound of a spin cycle, the sight of a woman working a machine. Oh, it gets me going, seeing a woman's body against a vibrating machine. I just take that mama and push her against that washer. And I take her baby, a bald-headed baby, and put Downy fabric softener on baby's head. Then I strap that baby around my waist till it's a baby dildo. Then I take that baby, that dildo, and fuck its own mama. 'Cause I'm nothing but a motherfucker. I'm nothing but a motherfucker. Just puttin' that baby back where it belongs. Back to its old room, the womb. Back to its old room the womb. And then I take out those titties. Hope the bitch is still nursing. But she's a dried old cow, a dried old sow. A DRIED OLD SOW!!

AND THEN I BLACK OUT.

AND IT'S 20 YEARS LATER.

AND I'm in my mama's house.

And my mama is still watching the stories. The stories are still on. Oprah is on with a story on incest. *Dallas*, *Dynasty*, *The World Turns* too.

She's sprawled out on the avocado-green shag carpeting wearing her washed-out plaid housecoat. Safety pins pinned all together. I never knew why she wore all those pins. Like rubber bands round a door knob. Ooh, those pins excite me. 'Specially pins near sagging old flesh. And she smokes her Pall Malls, her Camels, her Pall Malls. Flick THAT ASH MAMA! FLICK THAT ASH! Look at me! Look at me! You never looked at me. No, you didn't. I'm nothing to you.

And there's tomato soup on the stove, macaroni and cheese on the fire, fish sticks in the oven. All that good white trash eats. Let me make your stick into a fish stick. The tartar sauce is free. No diaphragm cream needed here. So I'll roll on mama's belly onto the shag carpeting. She still not looking at me as I roll up her dress to the small of her back. She still not looking at me. She still watching that show on incest. And I look at her fat thighs and ass. Like uncooked bacon. My hands soothe her rumpled dimpled flesh. My mama! My mama, sweet mama. And I pull down her cotton Carters all pee-stained. Elastic gone. Then I mount my own mama in the ass. That's right. I fuck my own mama in the ass. 'Cause I'd never fuck my own mama in her snatch. She's my mama.

I cum real quick. Cuz I'm a quick workingman. Work real fast. After I cum, I come outta my mama. She don't look at me. Just suckin' her Pall Mall. So I go down on my mama and suck my own cum outta my own mama's ass, outta her butthole. Her coconut Hershey juice. Suck it out. Suck it. Pucker. Pucker.

When I got my mouthful of the stuff, after I felch her good, I move my hands to my mama's face. I touch her red and white temples. Her potato face. I can see the raspberry lipstick leak into the wrinkles of her skin. That space between her lips and her nose. What's that space called? And I gently take the cigarette out of my mama's mouth. 'Cause if I got it wet she'd BEAT THE HELL OUTTA ME. She'd beat the hell out of me. I press my lips to my mother's mouth. And from the corner I spit back my cum into her mouth. Like pearls from an oyster into the sea at last. She just swallows the cum quickly, just keeps on staring at the incest show. Takes a drag out of Pall Mall and says, "Boy, you got lazy ass cum. Your cum ain't salty. You can cum on my pancakes anytime."

Refrigerator

And the first memory, memory I have, I have of my father, is he putting me into the refrigerator. He'd take off all my clothes and put my 5-year-old bare bottom onto the silver rack of the icebox. My feet and hands would get into the piccalilli, the catsup, the mustard and mayonnaise. My arms held on to my Barbi, Ken, Aunt Jemima, and GI Joe. All my dollies would protect me. All my prophets, princesses, and kings would stay with me. My Winnie-the-Pooh. You wonder why I throw up all of my food, whenever I see any condiments I gotta puke. Gotta upchuck all over the house.

Then my daddy is laughin'. Then my daddy is playing. Then my daddy gigglin' and smiling. Don't you know I hate smiles and laughter. Don't you know I hate good feelings! 'Cause the only feelings I show are NO feelings at all, girl. Just no feelings at all.

So my daddy plays behind the icebox door. Then he opens up the vegetable bin and takes out the carrots, the celery, the zucchini, and cucumbers. Then he starts working on my little hole. Starts working my little hole. "Showing me what it's like to be a mama," he days. "Showing me what it's like to be a woman. To be loved. That's a daddy's job," he tells me.

Next thing I know I'm in bed, crying. I got my dollies and animals with me. And I've got Band-Aids between their legs. They couldn't protect me but I'll protect them.

Then I hear my mama come home. And she starts yelling at the top of her lungs. "Whatever happened to tonight's dinner? Whatever happened to the vegetables for the dinner for tonight? You been playing with your food, girl? I wanted to make your daddy's favorite."

And I just cry to myself.

"Oh, mama open up those eyes. Don't you know that I'm daddy's favorite."

Is this what it's like to be a mama? Is this what it's like to be a daddy? No, this is what it is like to be part of the whole human race. And I'm your eldest son. I'm your middle, your youngest, your only son. I'm your son. Named after you. Your name.

When I told you that after all of my years of searching that I finally fell in love with another man. I fell in love with Louis, with Charles. You didn't believe me 'cause you never were in love before. Love didn't make the world go 'round for you. Prestige did. What others thought did.

I hadn't seen you for years. You had disowned me for my honesty of my sexual preference. You call yourself a doctor, a man of compassion. And when I told you I had the disease that mostly afflicts homosexuals, women, and children too, I know you no longer considered me your son, a man, so I went to you as a human being. And all you could say was, "I told you to stay away from those faggots, those fairies, those queers, those queens, those people with the lisps. I told you to get out of San Francisco."

Oh, father, father. You wonder why I send you a crate of shit every day. You call yourself a doctor who relieves pain. Man, you've been giving me nothing but pain since the day I was conceived. You call yourself a father, provider, the punisher, the moneyman. Baby, you sure been punishing me.

And when I died – you wouldn't even announce my death. Oh, no – you just called it accidental, cause unknown, uncertain. How could you announce my death when you never announced my life? Your fucking reputation. Your fucking reputation. Not even a proper burial. Not even a mourning for those who loved me. Oh father, father.

Call him the punisher, the provider, the moneyman.

I'm going to curse you father till the day you die. Going to curse you from the grave. Blame you and God too. You might take my body away but you can't take my soul, my spirit, my mind.

It's the father in all of us that gives us the Berlin Wall, saves the whales, makes treaties, makes decisions and reasons, bridges and tunnels, cures diseases, ways and means. Politics and social disorders. It's the father, it's the father, it's the father in all of us.

And I pray to you father in the sky every night. "Father, make me feel wanted. Oh, make me gain that unrequited love." Oh, it's the father. It's the father in all of us.

Fist Fuck

And after I fist fucked you with my handful of sapphires, emeralds, garnets, and opals. Aquamarines, gold, silver, and platinum. I was fucking you with my will, my property, my esteem, and my values. I was fucking you with pearls and diamonds. Just filling your hole with everything I got. I was fucking you with my talent. That's all I got left. My rings just cutting you. And you just lie there bleeding. Your snatch on liquid fire. I just look down on you. You look up at me with your blue eyes and say, "It's better to feel abuse than to feel nothing at all. It's better to feel abuse than to feel nothing at all."

Vomit Belly

And I just collapsed on your pregnant belly and vomited, for I saw Mr. Reagan on the TV. There is a TV camera up his butthole looking up his asshole for polyps, for his colon cancer. He is so obsessed with what not to put up the butthole. So obsessed with what not to go up, up the ol' shithole. Had to sit with Rather/Jennings talk about yo' old polyps every day. Boy, I call your disease a metaphor. I call your disease your personal metaphor of being a fuckin' pain in the butt. I'm puking, man, on your liberty, your state of the union.

And I had to go out and get some air. I walked on the street and I saw you lying there on the sidewalk crusted in filth and neglect. I walked right over your baked body in the cement. My heel caught the needle in your arm, and tore your flesh with my walk. I knew you once. I knew you when you were to do great things for us. But now you are worthless. 'Cause I know it's every man for himself in this town, it's such a small city. Such a busy busy town. Just keep on walking, keep your head high. Just walk right over 'em.

Ankles

And I just remembered the custom of our nation during war – of tying pregnant women's ankles while they are giving birth. Such a civilized culture. Such a great great land. Such kind peoples.

And after a few minutes there was quiet on the battlefield.

And we all exchanged names of our cats and dogs, memories and smells were evoked like our mothers used to show us when we weren't supposed to cry.

Let me tell you how I like brocades in woolen coats, the sweet scent of magnolia on your breath, the soft spot behind your ears. Let me tell you how I look at young men in blood-soaked costumes. Let me tell you how I look at young women undressing behind closed doors.

Let me tell you how I look at children dancing in their parents' blood.

I'm your voyeur. I'm your exhibitionist. I'm your pervert, your fool, your martyr and fool. I'm your Donald Trump, your Baby M. I'm your real estate, your profits, your greed.

But something's gotta give.

Something's gotta give.

Something's gonna happen.

INDEX